THE TOP GUN PROSECUTOR

Bringing Justice for the Victims

Ronald E Bowers

Former Senior Prosecutor

Los Angeles County District Attorney's Office

Some names and locations have been changed to protect the privacy of individuals connected with this story. Certain events and statements have been inferred from the facts of these cases and public articles about these cases.

Ronald E. Bowers, Publisher
losangelestruecrime@aol.com

ISBN 978-1-7325281-7-8

INTRODUCTION

This is the second book of the ***DA Delta Force*** series, which is about the Los Angeles County District Attorney's Office and their illustrious **Major Crimes Division**. This Division is made up of exceptional attorneys who are entrusted with some of the most difficult cases as well as the high-profile trials that percolated up through the Criminal Justice System. I, the author, worked for that DA's Office for 43 years, and during my long career I spent ten years working **with** the prosecutors in this elite **Major Crimes Division**. Although I was never assigned as a litigator to that Division, one of my duties was to assist its attorneys in their trial preparation and presentation of their legendary trials.

In other words, I had the opportunity to work with the Major Crimes deputies throughout the years, and learned first-hand how they manage to handle such thorny high profile cases. Since I had to personally work with all of its attorneys, I developed a working rapport with them. As a result, I was able to see up close all the challenges they had to deal with and how they maneuvered around all those obstacles inherent in prominent cases.

That was when I noticed a similarity between the members of the DA **Major Crimes Division** and other elite groups we have heard about throughout our lifetime. During the Vietnam era, the **Green Berets** were held in high esteem for their remarkable accomplishments on their tough missions. More recently, the public has been fascinated by the US Navy **Seal Team 6** for their successful mission to eliminate Osama Bin Laden. Everyone wanted to learn more about this special elite team. How did it operate and what were the team's members like? What made them so unique to be able to accomplish such incredible feats? However, the public is more familiar with the Army's Special Forces group called the **Delta Force**, which epitomizes what an elite group can achieve with incredibly well-trained and highly motivated members.

Hence, the public recognizes that the term **Delta Force** means a truly exclusive group that seems to achieve the impossible. That is why I named my new series the ***DA Delta Force***. I think that well describes the distinctive function and operation of the DA's **Major Crimes Division**, which is made up of highly skilled prosecutors whose mission is to take on the toughest cases and litigate them through the complex Criminal Justice System.

After I retired from the DA's Office, I began to write True Crime books about cases that I worked on. For years readers have asked me to tell them about what went on behind the scenes in the high-publicity trials. Readers would ask me, "What was the most interesting case you ever worked on?" The other question was, "Who do you believe to be the greatest attorney you saw in court?" I find it impossible to answer either of those questions by trying to identify just **one case** or **one attorney** as being the best. Then I realized that the readers really meant to ask me, "What cases and attorneys **stand out** in your mind of all the cases and myriad of prosecutors you have come in contact with?"

Since I have handled thousands of cases and worked with hundreds of prosecutors, I needed to narrow down the so-called **stand-out** cases. That was when I decided to concentrate on the trials handled by the **Major Crimes Division**. As a result, I decided to shine the spotlight on the cases handled by that Division as well as the members who work there.

My first book of the ***DA Delta Force*** series was titled ***Prosecutrix—Fight for Justice***, which highlighted the career and cases of **Eleanor Hunter**, who might be described as one of the most tenacious female prosecutors of all times. However, this present book is titled ***The Top Gun Prosecutor*** and highlights one of the most seasoned veterans of the Major Crimes Division. That would be none other than **John Monaghan**, who is one of the most remarkable prosecutors who ever walked into a Los Angeles courtroom. He exhibited a wide range of talent, which permitted him to successfully prosecute some of the toughest cases that fell below the news media's radar.

Hopefully, if God is willing, I will continue to write more books for this new series ***DA Delta Force***, highlighting the incredible talent of the prosecutors who have left their mark on the exclusive **Major Crimes Division.** You, the reader, will have the opportunity to learn about the special cases entrusted to this Division, as well as the attorneys who make up this select unit. You will see firsthand how these special attorneys approach their cases and how they are able to bear the intense pressure of prosecuting such high-publicity cases, which may require them to spend months in trial.

I reviewed the myriad of cases handled by **John Monaghan** while he was assigned to the **Major Crimes Division** and selected seven cases he prosecuted to illustrate why he was considered The Top Gun Prosecutor. You the reader will get the opportunity to see up close how he possesses a sixth sense in knowing what the jurors need to hear and see in order to convict. In the process, you will be exposed to some fascinating cases that few people have ever heard about. John Monaghan quietly took on some extremely problematic cases and without any fanfare made sure that justice was done. The cases we will review are as follows:

People vs. Aswad Pops & Byron Wilson—This case was similar to the infamous Valentine's Day Massacre that occurred in Chicago; however, this time it happened in a Compton car wash garage. Four men were shot dead in their tracks on Super Bowl Sunday. Was it a drug deal gone bad or an attempt to collect on a gambling debt? How do car tire rims solve this case? You will see how the tiny pieces of circumstantial evidence are weaved together to create a tapestry showing the defendants' guilt.

People vs. Chhuon Run and Samreth Pan—These defendants preyed on poor and struggling immigrants who were only trying to make a modest living. These defendants were a pair of robbers who crisscrossed the west coast leaving a path of terror littered with dead bodies. The only hope of stopping this wave of violence was to use ballistic evidence to prove they were involved in so many shootings. The prosecutor had to convince the jurors that microscopic marks on the expended shell cases were like cookie crumbs leading to the defendants.

People vs. Anh The Duong—This case involved a handsome gentleman who was anything but a gentle man. His idea of settling a minor dispute was blasting away at the victim. However, what made this dangerous was the fact he ended up killing three other innocent people who were seated nearby. He was the leader of a robbery crew who operated throughout the State of California. One of the challenges of this case was that the prosecutor had to deal with a number of witnesses who were deathly afraid of the defendant. The prosecutor had to convince the witnesses to cooperate in order to end Duong's reign of terror.

People vs. David Rademaker—So many young women come to Hollywood to be discovered. Unfortunately, there are hundreds of applicants for every modeling or acting job. Young women learn that they have to take chances in order to be noticed. At times they go on auditions or photo shoots where they are vulnerable. This case involved such a sad story of a vivacious beautiful woman going on a photo shoot in the mountains and never coming home. Since there were no witnesses, this case eventually found its way into the Cold Cases files. The detectives and prosecutor took another look at this case and figured out how they could obtain a Pretext statement from the suspect that would break the case wide open.

People vs. Ivan Hill—This case is included in this book to illustrate how difficult certain cases are to solve. The news media likes to complain that the police and DA don't take seriously the serial killing of prostitutes. The real reason is the fact that these killings take place in isolated places where there are no witnesses. The advent of DNA has helped to some extent, but to obtain a conviction the prosecutor still has to find some form of corroboration. In this particular Cold Case, the prosecutor came up with a unique way of supplying the necessary corroboration.

People vs. James Dixon—This case involved a brutal murder in which a college co-ed had her throat slashed from ear to ear. As time went by there was no suspect arrested. Everyone on Cal Poly University campus began suspecting other students, college staff, and even the professors. This prosecutor started working with the Sheriff detectives in hopes of cracking this case. The years went by and finally an old rape case unconnected to the homicide case was solved by DNA. Remarkably, the DNA on a cigarette butt in the homicide led to solving the heinous murder of the co-ed.

People vs Juan Manuel Alvarez—This case was better known as the Glendale Metrolink case. Needless to say, this was an extremely complex case to prosecute, since it involved the crashing of three trains resulting in the death of 11 passengers.

The prosecution was caught in a situation in which the assigned prosecutors were tied up in a retrial and unable to handle this case when it came up for trial. The defendant had a right to a Speedy Trial and refused to continue the case to a date when the prosecutors would be available. Therefore, the DA's Office had to find another prosecutor who could immediately try this Metrolink case. You will see the behind-the-scenes scrambling that had to be done in order for a new prosecutor to stand up in court and announce, "Ready for the People." This was an emergency situation in which the prosecutors did a remarkable job under the worst conditions.

People vs. Stanley "Tookie" Williams—The DA's Office was asked to handle a Clemency Hearing that was set to be presented to the Governor regarding the execution of Tookie Williams. Since the DA's Office doesn't handle such hearings, the prosecutors had to scramble to figure out what needed to be done. What was significant was that the prosecutor came up with a strategy that turned out to be highly effective and resulted in the execution of a violent murderer.

All of these cases are discussed in this book and were all cases assigned to the **Major Crimes Division** and handled by **John Monaghan.** (In the Tookie Williams case it was the Clemency Hearing that was handled by the Division) These cases will give you, the reader, a chance to see firsthand what a resolute and highly dedicated prosecutor Mr. Monaghan is. He has an incredible grasp of the LAW while possessing remarkable LITIGATION SKILLS. But most of all he has GREAT INSTINCTS in preparing and presenting his cases. His common sense approach is a winning formula with all types of jurors and that is what makes him **THE TOP GUN PROSECUTOR.**

CONTENTS

CHAPTER 1 POPS—SHOOTOUT

On Sunday, January 25, 1998, in the City of Compton, California, the police department received a telephone in the morning reporting trouble and shots fired at a car wash and auto detailing business called 'Wheels N Stuff.' One of the Compton police units responded to the location, which consisted of two rundown buildings – a small office structure and an open garage surrounded by a chain-link fence topped with barbed wire. The best way to describe the area would be that it was located on a dusty industrial street close to the Los Angeles River. The only way to find the place was to see a hand-painted sign with the name Wheel's N Stuff advertising car washes at $8 and $10 and full detailing at $40.

The officer eventually was able to maneuver his way inside the garage area where several automobiles were ready to be worked on. Since the business was partly a car wash, the officer got a whiff of soapsuds and the smell of dirty rags as he walked into the office. All that could be heard was a deadly silence. All of a sudden, the officer was surprised when an air compressor in the garage area automatically went on. As the officer's eyes darted around the room, he wondered what this radio call was all about. Was this a burglary situation? But burglaries generally don't involve 'shots fired.'

The Compton police officers knew that the real business activity occurring at Wheel's N Stuff was 'dope and betting.' If one wanted any type of drugs and narcotics, the place to go to was "Wheel's N Stuff." Another specialty was bookmaking on the horses as well as for the sports teams. Because of all the drug and gambling activity at the site, everyone knew that there was a lot of cash that flowed through its doors. Since it was still early Sunday morning, the usual crowd of dealers and bookies had not yet congregated at the business.

The officers preconceived belief was that the 'shots fired' must have somehow involved a robbery. Nothing in the office suggested a robbery, so the officer proceeded into the garage area. His nose immediately recognized the smell of cleaning solvent. To his right was a Chevy that was in the process of being detailed. As the officer advanced further into the enclosed auto shop area, his eyes caught the sight of a body lying on the concrete floor, which startled him and he jerked back. He couldn't believe his eyes as he stared at the motionless body.

The officer's hand gripped his gun tighter, as though his firearm was going to protect him. What an eerie feeling he was getting as he took two more steps toward the body. Abruptly, he looked further inside the garage and noticed shoes on the concrete. His eyes followed the shoes to the pants and then to a body wearing a red and blue sports jersey with a human head lying in a pool of blood. As the officer leaned over to get a better view his eyes were trying to absorb the sight of two dead bodies lying parallel on the garage floor.

He moved slowly to the other side of the garage, and as he rounded one of the parked vehicles, he swiftly stopped before stumbling over another dead body. A stream of blood was oozing along the cracks in the concrete floor. By this time, the officer had seen enough and wanted to return to the safety of his police unit. As he walked toward the side door to get out of the garage, he had to squeeze by some of the tool chests next to the wall. He quickly caught his footing before stepping on another dead body partially lying against the wall. By now the officer thought to himself, "How do I get out of here?"

As the officer swiftly returned to his police unit, he reflected on how he should describe this crime scene to the dispatcher. To him, this looked like a possible gangster shoot-out. Discovering four victims who had been gunned down in a garage conjured up the image of the infamous **Chicago St. Valentine's Massacre** in 1929, which occurred in a garage. In that case, seven men were gun down as part of an old-time mobster's execution. However, this shoot-out in a Compton garage only involved four dead bodies. This Compton shooting occurred on January 25, 1998, which was SUPER BOWL Sunday; therefore, this one could possibly be described as the COMPTON SUPER BOWL SUNDAY MASSACRE.

This was Super Bowl XXXII, and the teams were the Denver Broncos quarterbacked by John Elway against Green Bay Packers led by Brett Favre, played at Qualcomm Stadium in San Diego. If your memory isn't as good as it used to be, I'll let you know the score was: Broncos 31 and Cheeseheads only 24. What a great game!

The Compton officer went back to his radio car and called the dispatcher to notify the homicide detectives they were needed at Wheel's N Stuff. Many people have heard about the City of Compton because of the movie ***Straight Outta Compton*** released in 2015, which told the history of the musical group NWA (Niggaz Wit Attitude).The group consisted of Eazy-E, a drug dealer, Dr. Dre, an aspiring disc jockey, and Ice Cube, a rapper. Their first musical album in 1988 was titled *Straight Outta Compton.* One of the songs on the album was ***Fuck tha Police***, which was obviously controversial since it encouraged violence against law enforcement.

Much of the entertainment world likes to praise and promote gangsta rap. Unfortunately, there is a downside to it all since the young people look upon the gangsters as their mentors and they begin to act out what is suggested in this song. Back in 1988, I was the supervisor for the DA's branch offices in South LA County, and Compton DA's Office was one of my branch offices. As much as some want to glorify the violence in Compton, I can say from a firsthand experience that it was hell having to work in such a violent community. I remember coming to work on Monday mornings and invariably I would receive a phone call from my Compton office telling me how many windows of our office had been shot out during the weekend. It was a dangerous problem for my staff, and I agreed to install bulletproof windows to provide a better work environment.

It was very difficult for me to find staff who were willing to work at the Compton DA's Office. We had to set up a guarded parking area for the employees, and the staff was instructed to drive a specific route to safely get to the Compton Courthouse. Many people who have to work or live in Compton have a hard time understanding why the music and film industry like to glorify violent behavior, because in reality it isn't a pretty picture if you have to be there. The fact that the movie and the MWA album ***Straight Outta Compton*** have received so many awards makes one wonder what are our true values in society.

Since it was Super Bowl Sunday, the detectives' first reaction was that Wheel's N Stuff would be the perfect place to rob since it would have accumulated a large amount of cash as a result of the gambling on the big game. Also, there would plenty of people spending their hard-earned cash to purchase dope so they could fully enjoy all the Super Bowl parties. The detectives came to the conclusion that the motive for the shooting was an old-fashioned robbery.

It was not clear if the shooters were looking for just money or if they were also looking for dope they could use for themselves. It was ironic that one of the cars in the shop had a bumper sticker for S.A.N.E. (Substance Abuse of Narcotics Education) which was one of the anti-drug programs in Los Angeles at the time. This sticker on the car didn't seem to impede the drug dealing business at the location.

The detectives were able to identify the victims from their identification in their wallets and the help of others. The victims were Charles (33), the owner of the business and his three coworkers Michael (41), Shawn (20), and Jessie (36). All of them had been shot in the head at least once if not several times. At this point, the detectives started looking for any form of Forensic evidence that would be useful to determine who the shooters were. The main items collected were four .40 caliber bullets and eight .40 caliber casings. Also, there was found one 9mm live round and five 9mm casings. All of that would be useful if they were able to recover the firearms involved in the shooting. The dusting for prints was of limited value since there were hundreds of latent prints that came from all of the people who patronized the business.

When the CSI technician was scouring the crime scene for any clue, he discovered several shoe prints on the concrete floor near one of the pools of blood. One of them was well defined. The technician leaned over and carefully photographed this perfect shoe print outlined in blood. Later at the crime lab it was determined to be from a SWISS athletic shoe. Granted, this is not as distinctive as a fingerprint, but it at least provided a picture that one of the robbers wore SWISS shoes. Also, the likelihood of useful DNA evidence was remote since so many people passed through the premises every day. The detectives soon realized that this case was NOT going to be solved with the usual forensic evidence.

The detectives were in hopes that someone in the community would come forth with information about seeing someone in the area possibly before or after the shootings. These were seasoned detectives, and they were realistic enough to know that gangster mentality would prevent witnesses from coming forth to cooperate with the police. However, it might have been the sheer number of murder victims or the innocent nature of the victims that for some reason prompted three people to come forward to give the detectives some insight as to what happened and who was involved.

One was named Chris, and he said he was over by the Wheel's N Stuff and saw two men in a dark Honda parked on the side of the building. He didn't think much about these guys until he heard a number of gunshots. Another person by the name Anthony told police he saw one of the men exit the car wash holding a TEC-9 that he was fumbling with since it was jammed and shortly, he returned inside. Moments later he observed the other man drive an El Camino from the rear of the car wash and as he pulled out of the fenced yard, he struck the front gate. When he reached the street, the vehicle sped away.

The detectives were appreciative of these persons coming forward but didn't know what to make of it. He said he didn't know who these guys were but he might be able to identify them. The following day the detectives meet with another man named Randy, who said he was at the car wash when two guys confronted him. These guys were in a dark Honda parked to the side of the building of the car wash near the payphones. He could see clearly that the driver had a Glock 9 and the passenger had a TEC-9. He heard the guys yell at some of the people in the car wash, "Where's the money? Where is the shit?"

This case would be solved because of IROC rims. To most of you, your first question would be, 'What are IROC rims?' One of the benefits of being a prosecutor is that it gives you an opportunity to learn what criminals really value. Most people would go to great lengths to distance themselves from anything that would connect them to any type of illegal activity. However, criminals will commit a serious crime such as murder, and as they are leaving the crime scene they will steal certain property that was possessed by the person who they just killed. Their thinking may be that the dead victim didn't need the item anymore so why not take it.

One would think that it is so obvious that if you commit a crime you wouldn't want to touch anything or take anything that could be traced back to you. But criminals use a different thought process. Their brain doesn't always operate in a logical manner. They might want to take something from the crime scene as a souvenir to remind them of what they had successfully accomplished without getting caught. Or maybe it is greed that compels them to take things from crime scenes. Whatever their reasoning, the act of taking something from the victim is just a dumb idea.

As the detectives checked out the location, it was learned that the owner's pickup truck was missing. It was a classic El Camino that the owner had restored with many hours of bodywork to return it to its original splendor. In order to get it in mint condition, he gave it a custom paint job in a pale-yellow color. This El Camino was the owner's pride and joy. He thoroughly enjoyed cruising around town in his classic pickup as spectators nodded their approval.

To put it over the top, the owner went all out and had installed the fanciest rims available, which made this pickup the talk of the town. These rims are expensive and quite distinctive. In the automobile world, they are known as 'IROC' rims and are much in demand by car buffs. The owner was so proud of the addition of the rims that he had photos taken of the pickup shortly before the robbery. The photo clearly showed the owner's El Camino with the shiny IROC rims on it.

Are car rims so valuable that people would kill for them? This is a question that the police had to ask themselves. It is unusual for thieves to steal an entire vehicle just to obtain the rims on the vehicle. One of the reasons is that rims are so easy to remove from a car and they can't be easily traced back to the original owner. In Los Angeles, there have been numerous homicides where the owner resists the carjacker's demands and unfortunately the car owner ended up dead over some stylish rims. It's hard to believe that anyone would kill someone over car rims. It's even harder to believe that anyone would intentionally give up their lives for some metallic rims that could be easily replaced.

The issue of replacement may be part of the dilemma, in that most automobile insurance companies will not replace the expensive rims, which can cost several thousand dollars. The insurance adjusters will replace stolen rims with standard retail rims that may be worth less than a hundred dollars. This may explain why owners of the expensive rims don't want to give them up without a struggle.

In the Compton Car Wash murders, the police were able to determine that the killers stole the owner's truck when they were in the process of leaving the Car Wash. And it didn't seem to be a situation where the owner resisted the taking of the rims. In this robbery-murder case, the victim was already dead when the robbers drove off in an all-tricked-out El Camino pickup with the stylish IROC rims.

The robber driving the pickup took it to an isolated industrial area, where he parked it. Since it was Super Bowl Sunday, there were no workers in the area. The two robbers left the pickup and headed to one of the robbers' relatives, where they were having a barbeque. The one robber was enjoying himself drinking beer and feasting on a rack of spareribs. When the game came on everyone was glued to the television. Most of the attendees were Bronco fans, and as Dick Enberg did the announcing they were pleased with John Elway's performance. However, it was running back Terrell Davis who scored the go-ahead touchdown and won the MVP for his record three rushing touchdowns. The fans enjoyed the halftime performances of none other than Boyz II Men, Smokey Robinson, The Temptations, Martha Reeves, and Queen Latifah.

The one robber had been telling several of his fellow gang members that he wanted to take the IROC rims off the stolen El Camino so he could install them on his Camaro. This robber talked several of his gangster friends into taking him to the alley where he had parked the pickup. In the process, they stopped along the way and grabbed four old tires and rims, which they would place on the El Camino.

They pulled behind the El Camino and one of them took a large auto jack and rolled it under the pickup and started removing one tire and rim at a time. After taking off the IROC rims, they replaced them with the old set of rims. Since these guys had done this before, they were quite proficient, and in less than 20 minutes they had a nice set of IROC rims and the poor El Camino looked sad with the junky replacements. A short time later it was decided to torch the El Camino. Although it was a great-looking vehicle, the robbers were concerned that their fingerprints might be on it. So the easiest way to eliminate that possibility was to completely burn it, thereby erasing any prints.

Later in the evening, around 7:25 p.m., a Deputy Cali responded to vehicle fire call and found the El Camino smoldering. When he ran the VIN, it came back to the owner of Wheel's N Stuff. Subsequently, it was learned that the owner had been the victim of a P. C. 187. When the victim's family members looked at the El Camino, they noticed it was missing its spiffy IROC rims. This information puzzled the homicide detectives. That was when they learned the astronomical price of a set of IROC rims. Then the question was, could the theft of the IROC rims be the motive for the killings? It didn't seem likely, but they put the word out to law enforcement that if anyone saw a set of IROC rims for sale to give the homicide detectives a call.

About a month later, a Long Beach officer stopped a man named Pops who was driving an older Camaro. The officer noticed that this old Camaro had a set of new IROC rims. The officer didn't have any information that the rims were stolen, so he merely gave the driver a traffic citation and the driver drove off. It wasn't until some time later that the traffic officer thought there might be a connection between the IROC rims taken after the murders and the IROC rims on Pops' Camaro.

This traffic officer began playing the role of Lt. Colombo portrayed by the late Peter Falk. The officer couldn't remember who was the owner or driver of this Camaro. He decided to look through the copies of hundreds of citations he had issued to see if he could find the traffic stop of the Camaro. In short order, he found the citation and made a copy of it which listed the driver's name as Aswad Pops with his Long Beach address. This information was related to the homicide detectives.

The detectives checked out the address but never saw the Camaro anywhere near the address. However, one day six weeks after the murders, the detectives went by the Long Beach address and spotted the Camaro in a driveway. They approached the car to get a better look and sure enough, the officer had been correct that the Camaro had an exact set of IROC rims like the ones that had been stolen. The detectives got a search warrant for the Camaro and had it transported to a police garage. There the detectives had a mechanic remove the rims. Just to get verification, the

detectives arranged for the original mechanic who had installed the IROC rims on the victim's truck to be present.

The detectives knew there were no serial numbers on such rims, but they hoped that there might be some markings that might make the IROC rims identifiable. The detectives had the original mechanic examine each of the rims. He rotated the rims and carefully scrutinized the back side of each one. After inspecting the last rim, he turned to the detectives and nodded his head, indicating that these were the same exact rims that he had installed on the victim's El Camino.

A smile came over the face of the one veteran homicide detective as he uttered, "How do you know?" Without any hesitation, the mechanic said, "Look here on the back of each rim. See this small drill hole. I had to drill a small hole in each rim in order for it to line up right on the tire." The other detective started chuckling in disbelief that anyone would have ever noticed such a small alignment hole in the rims.

The detectives now had the link they needed to connect this Aswad Pops to the IROC rims from the garage massacre. Everyone recognized that Pops couldn't have killed four guys at the garage on his own. Who would his partner in crime be? The word on the street was that Pops associated with a guy by the name of Bryon Wilson. The more the detectives looked into the backgrounds of Pops and Wilson, the more they saw a strong connection. As a result, the detectives obtained a search warrant for Bryon Wilson's apartment.

On the next page is a photo board exhibit showing the crime scene at Wheels N Stuff where the various victims were found. The lower photo board exhibit shows the stolen El Camino pickup with the IROC rims on it. Also shown is Pop's Camaro with the IROC rims on it.

GRAPHICS 1

The prosecutor used this exhibit to show the crime scene.

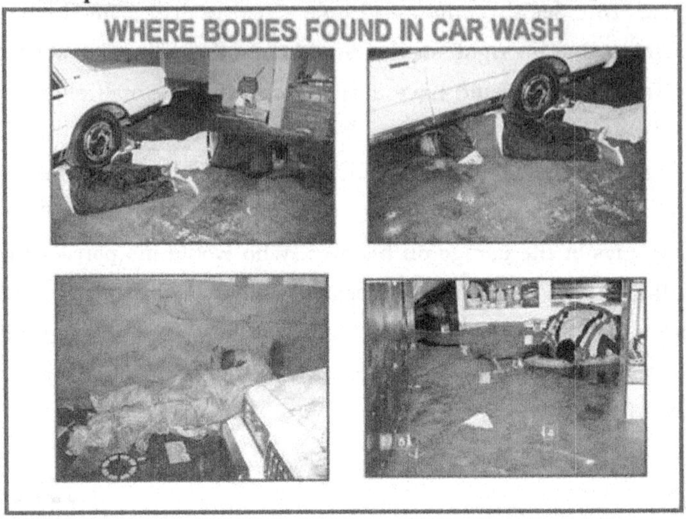

This chart showed the two vehicles with the IROC rims before and after.

CHAPTER 2-POPS—DISCOVERING EVIDENCE

The search warrant for Bryon Wilson's apartment was to obtain any evidence relating to the Car Wash murders. The police didn't know what they were likely to discover when they conducted the search. The investigators hoped to find the two weapons used in the killings. But most criminals are smart enough to hide the guns somewhere so they can't be easily traced back to them. Even though the apartment didn't contain anything like a "smoking gun" (a phrase originally used in the Sherlock Holmes stories), the detectives did find some very useful evidence that would later prove to be critical in the case. When the detectives started to conduct their search of the apartment, their attention was directed to a rifle on the sofa. They confiscated it hoping that it might be one of the murder weapons.

However, that would have made the case too easy to solve. Later forensic testing of this rifle determined that it was not used in the Car Wash Massacre. Next, the detectives checked out the sofa, and they found an unspent 9mm bullet that later would be matched up to the 9mm used in the murders. Next to the bullet on the sofa was a wallet that contained the identification of Bryon Wilson.

Also, in a shoe box labeled K-SWISS was a pair of athletic shoes that were examined and found to match the bloody footprints left at the crime scene. On the coffee table was a newspaper that had an article in the right-hand column with the headlines, "4 Bodies Found at Car Wash." This newspaper referred to the crime being investigated. The question was, why was this newspaper on the coffee table in Bryon Wilson's apartment?

What made it a piece of evidence was the fact that this newspaper was over a month old. The other unique feature of this newspaper was the fact that the entire apartment didn't have another newspaper anywhere. The significance of the newspaper was that someone who had been involved in the murders described in it might want to keep it as a trophy or something to brag about. It validated that the perpetrators had been successful and the killers had done something that was noteworthy in that it received the headlines in the local newspaper. Again, the newspaper wasn't the "In flagrante delicto" (expression for caught in the act), but it was just another piece of evidence that Bryon Wilson in some way was involved in the Car Wash murders.

Sometimes criminals leave, unbeknownst to them, cracker crumbs for the detectives to follow. When the detectives had thoroughly searched the living room, they started next with the kitchen table. On the table was a notepad with various drawings on it. To the investigator's surprise, there was a hand drawing of a person who looked very much like Aswad Pops standing in front of a car with IROC rims on it. The car looked like Pop's Camaro. Someone had written the words "THE MONSTER BEEFY" on the side of the drawing of the car. This was better than a calling card. This re-emphasized how the IROC rims were a reoccurring theme throughout the case.

Also, on this same notepad was a drawing of the same person resembling Pops holding what looked like a 9mm handgun. There was another drawing of an automatic weapon being fired with the casing flying out the side. It was unknown who the talented artist was who drew these sketches, but the detectives were going to keep them as pieces of a puzzle.

One additional item found in the notepad was a list of the gang members of the infamous "NIGGAS" gang. The names listed were the gang members' monikers such as "Nut," "Scrap," "Bird," "Snake," "Bone," "Smilie," and other typical gang names. The writer of this document had gone to considerable trouble to create a legend that referred to the various members. The star meant that a member was in Jail.

The detectives didn't know all the nuances of the list, but they did know that Aswad Pops and Byron Wilson were active members of a street gang and seemed to be proud of that fact. The detectives knew that Pops and Wilson were involved in the

Car Wash Massacre, but how were they ever going to be able to prove it in a court of law? There was no direct evidence of seeing the two doing the shooting or even being present at the Car Wash at the time of the shooting. All the detectives had were bits and pieces of circumstantial evidence to prove they did it. How was any jury going to follow the trail of all these little infinitesimal pieces to prove them guilty?

On the next page is a photo board showing the evidence found in Wilson's apartment. Also the lower exhibit shows the drawings and the list of gang members.

GRAPHICS 2

This is a chart of the items found in Wilson' s apartment including a live shell on sofa; shoe box; Wilson's id; newspaper article about shooting.

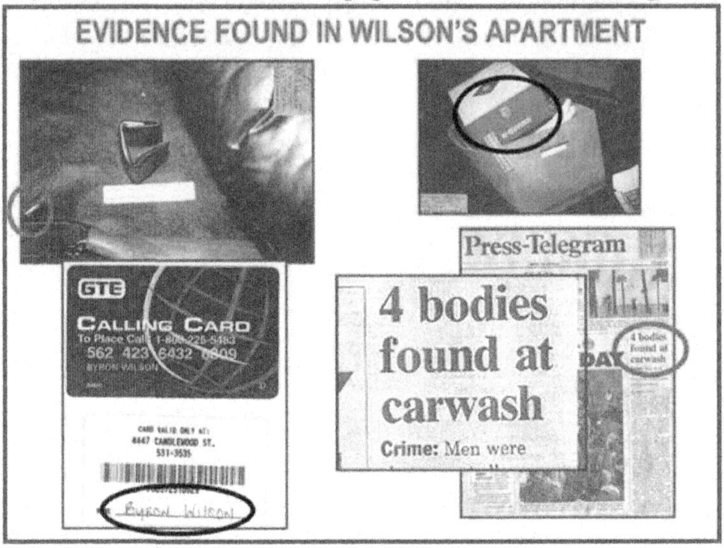

On the kitchen table in Wilson's apt. were these sketches found on a notepad showing IROC rims on Pop's car with guns and list of gang members.

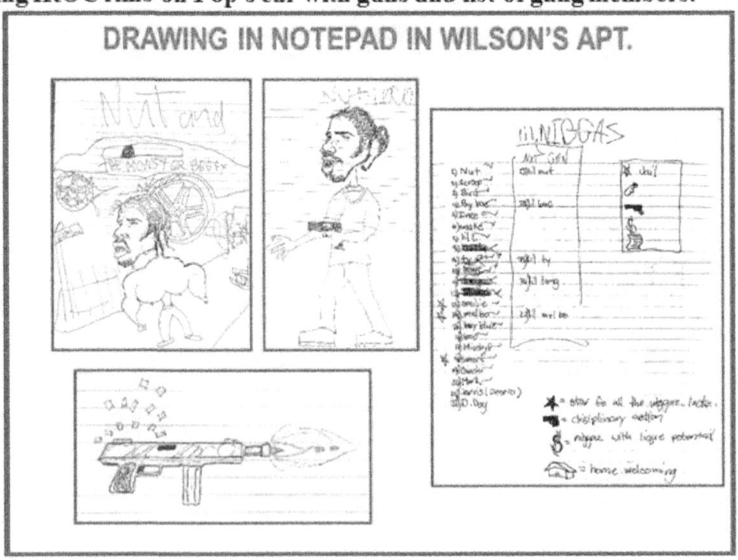

CHAPTER 3—POPS—CASE ASSIGNED TO MAJOR CRIMES

Since the detectives had both Aswad Pops and Byron Wilson in custody, they presented their evidence to the DA's Office to obtain a filing of charges. It wasn't long before the DA's administrators realized that this case was going to require an unbelievable amount of attention. Just by the mere fact that four persons had been murdered, this case was going to generate considerable news coverage, so a decision was made to transfer the case to the Major Crimes Division, where they had the time to give the case the amount of attention it would require if there would be any chance for a conviction.

Because of the bizarre facts of the case, it was clear that it needed a prosecutor who could work well with the detectives, since so much more investigation was going to be necessary. Deputy District Attorney John Monaghan was by far the prosecutor who had the know-how and patience to painstakingly work with the detectives to construct a strong foundation for any murder case. John had an incredible talent for taking the most complicated cases and organizing them in such a fashion to make them understandable to the jurors.

The key to this case was for the jury to grasp the significance of the stolen rims as well as understand the connection of the rims to the defendants. John Monaghan can best be described as a dead ringer for Dirty Harry Callahan, the San Francisco detective played by Clint Eastwood. He has no patience for crooks and sees it as his duty to bring lawbreakers to justice. Some might call John a 'Cops Cop,' who has ice flowing through his veins. But that isn't completely true; he does have a heart, but he doesn't wear it on his sleeve.

When you first meet John, your impression is that he is a military man who somehow wandered off the parade ground into a courthouse, shedding his uniform for a formal attorney suit with a stiff white shirt fully starched. When in court, he stands ramrod straight as though he was standing at attention. He addresses the court in concise terms, never wasting words on extra hyperbole. When he speaks, the words come out with a distinctive New Yorker accent.

His features rest on a slender six-foot frame topped off with slightly curly salt-and-pepper hair. His oblong face has a ruddy complexion accented by a chiseled chin. His deep-set piercing eyes are intensified by his gold-rimmed glasses. His face works overtime to suppress the slightest smile.

He projects the image of being fearless and acts confident as if he possesses all the answers. When addressing the court, it is clear that he rides the 'white horse' and clearly shows a disdain for any criminal who has crossed the line. He reminds everyone his job is seeing that justice is done.

His personality isn't soft and fuzzy around the edges. He is direct and expects everyone to do his or her job efficiently and promptly. He expects everyone to have the same determination as he exhibits in his job. His attitude is to fight for what is right. He sees the world in black and white and doesn't want to be bother with excuses of shades of gray.

Based on this description, one realizes the level of perseverance and perfection he expects of those he works with on his cases. John Monaghan is the type of person everyone would want on their team. You would know he had your back covered. You could always count on him giving 110% no matter what the battle was.

Seldom in life do we come across a person like a John Monaghan, who seems superhuman in fighting for justice but who shuns the limelight. He would walk a mile to avoid recognition for his accomplishments. He is one of those people who derives satisfaction from doing the impossible and doesn't need the news media to validate what he has done. Many humans seem to crave having the world tell them how great they are. John Monaghan approaches each impossible case he is assigned with the mindset that there is a path to success and it can be accomplished by unlimited preparation, incredible tenacity, and total dedication.

After John had read all of the police reports, he sat the detectives down and grilled them on every minute detail of the case. Even though the detectives normally do the questioning, when John was finished with them, they had to feel that they were being interrogated. John doesn't want any surprises when he is in trial, so he likes to get the complete picture from the outset. It's as though he is an artist starting with a blank canvas and he wants to see how all the pieces of the puzzle fit together.

John came to my office one morning and said, "Ron, you won't believe this case. It revolves around tire rims." I didn't quite understand what he was trying to say to me. In his Big Apple cab driver's accent, he said, "Ron, you know about IROC rims?" I didn't know how to answer since I didn't have a clue as to what IROC rims were. I didn't want to seem completely naive, so I pretended I knew what he was talking about. So I said, "Tell me a little more."

Then he dropped on my desk several photos of car rims, which I took to mean that they were the type of rims he was talking about. In a hushed voice he said, "Ron, those cost several thousand dollars." I pulled back as though I were impressed and said, "I didn't know that IROC rims were that expensive." I wondered, what's the big deal? I thought to myself at least I had learned something new today that I didn't know before. Up to this point in my life, I didn't have an inkling of what IROC rims were. Most likely I could have lived the rest of my life not knowing what they were.

Since I knew I was confused about the facts of the case, I told John to give me the various photos and I would create several photo boards he could use to show the jurors what he was talking about. The next step for John was to make sure that the jury understood the order in which certain events occurred. This included the various key witnesses' identifications and the various interviews of those witnesses. The investigation was conducted over 18 months, starting with the day of the murder, which was January 25, 1998, and ended at the time the trial commenced in June of 1999.

The murders at the Car Wash occurred at approximately 11:00 a.m., and it was important for the jurors to know that, later on that day, defendant Pops went to a Super Bowl party at his relatives'. There he persuaded two people to help him take the IROC rims off the El Camino and drive the pickup some distance away, where they set it on fire. The purpose of the fire was to destroy any fingerprints the parties might have left on the El Camino as part of stealing it and taking off the IROC rims.

John knew that the Timeline would be different for every witness who would be testifying. So he had Timelines created for each of the key witnesses. In this way, the jury could easily follow their testimony. **Randy's Timeline** was essential for the jury to believe his identification of defendant Pops as the passenger who got out of the Honda with a TEC-9 handgun and that defendant Wilson was the driver of the Honda and had a Glock 9mm handgun.

The Timeline spelled out the details of how the police showed the witness Randy numerous photos and that he didn't ID anyone until he came across a photo of defendant Pops. When Randy saw Pops' photo in the lineup book, he pointed his finger at the photo and said, "That's the Mother Fucker!" Later, when Randy attended a live Lineup, he was able to positively identify both defendants.

Another irony of the case was that this witness, one month after the murders, just happened to be driving around when he saw someone driving a Camaro with IROC rims just like the ones they had taken off the victim's El Camino. This provided the police with information that someone with a Camaro may be driving around with the stolen IROC rims. Undoubtedly, that was Pops' Camaro that Randy had seen. The detectives put this information out to all of the adjacent law enforcements. This was how the Long Beach traffic officer was alerted to look for IROC rims on vehicles they stopped.

To simplify things, we combined two other witnesses' (**Chris and Anthony) timelines** on one chart, since they both had seen the defendants coming to and leaving the murder scene. Chris' facts were listed on the top portion of the chart. He talked to the two defendants when they were in a dark Honda next to a side building to the Car Wash. The lower portion pertained to the other witness, Anthony, who got a good look at defendant Pops when he was driving the El Camino away from the crime scene.

On this page are the two charts that were created to show exactly when each witness was able to identify the two defendants, and the statements these witnesses made to the detectives.

GRAPHICS 3

Timeline of identifications and statements by witness Randy.

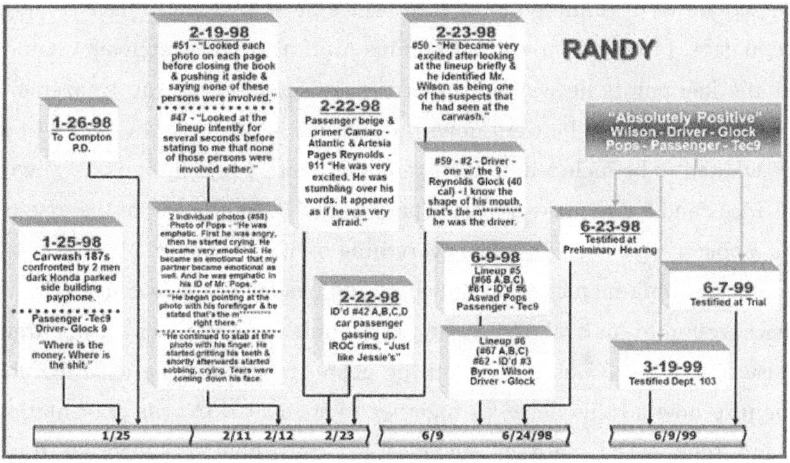

Timeline of identifications and statements by witnesses Chris & Anthony.

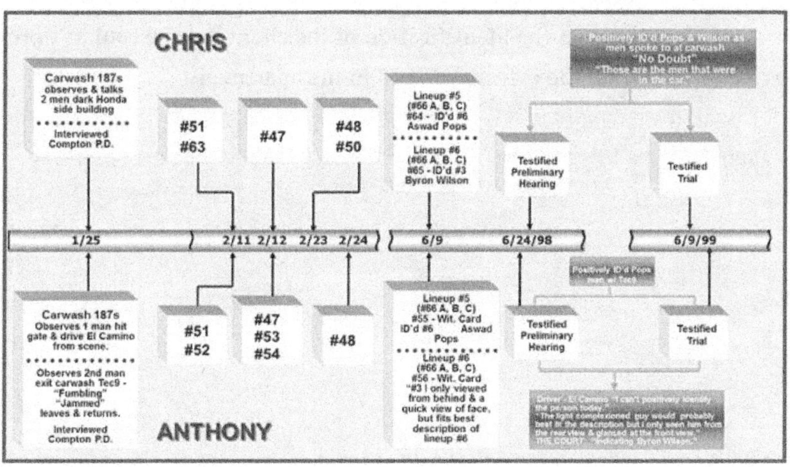

The key to the guilt phase of the case was how all the various pieces of evidence connected the two defendants to the killings and corroborated the testimony of these key witnesses. But the challenge was how to display all this evidence to the jury so they clearly understood where everything fit together. John Monaghan had a number of ideas how he wanted to explain the case to the jury. We created a number of drafts, but each time he would tweak it, ending up with a very cluttered visual that was too confusing.

I realized we were running out of time, since he was going to have to argue the case in two days. I told John to think about his Argument and sketch out on one piece of paper the key points he wanted the jury to understand. To my amazement, the very next morning before he went down to court he handed me the layout of all the items he wanted to be included on his Argument chart. I told him, okay we will take all of his ideas and try to make a 'Flow Chart' out of it. By the end of the day, we had prepared a poster-size chart that had everything on it.

The next morning he picked up the chart and headed down to court. John used it as the background to his oral Argument. John didn't use any notes for his Argument to the jury. Every issue was located on the poster board, and he used the chart to show the jury how all the pieces fit together to spell GUILTY. His presentation was logical and took every piece of evidence to show how it supported the three eyewitnesses. The Defense attorneys attacked the witnesses' identification of their clients. But Pops' attorney couldn't explain away the IROC on Pops' Camaro. Byron Wilson's attorney harped on the identification of his client, but he couldn't provide a cogent explanation for all the evidence found in his apartment.

The following page contains the Argument chart John sketched out which I used to prepare Argument chart titled CONNECTING EVIDENCE which he then used as the basis of his Argument to the jury.

GRAPHICS 4

Prosecutor's sketch showing what he wanted included on chart.

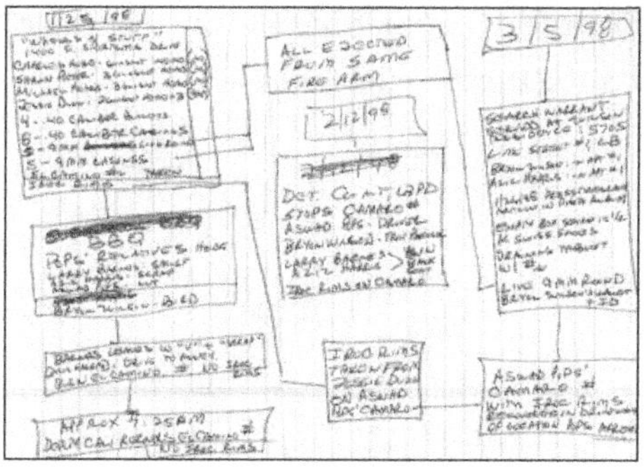

This is the final chart that the prosecutor used for his Argument to the jury. It contained all the facts of the case on one visual aid.

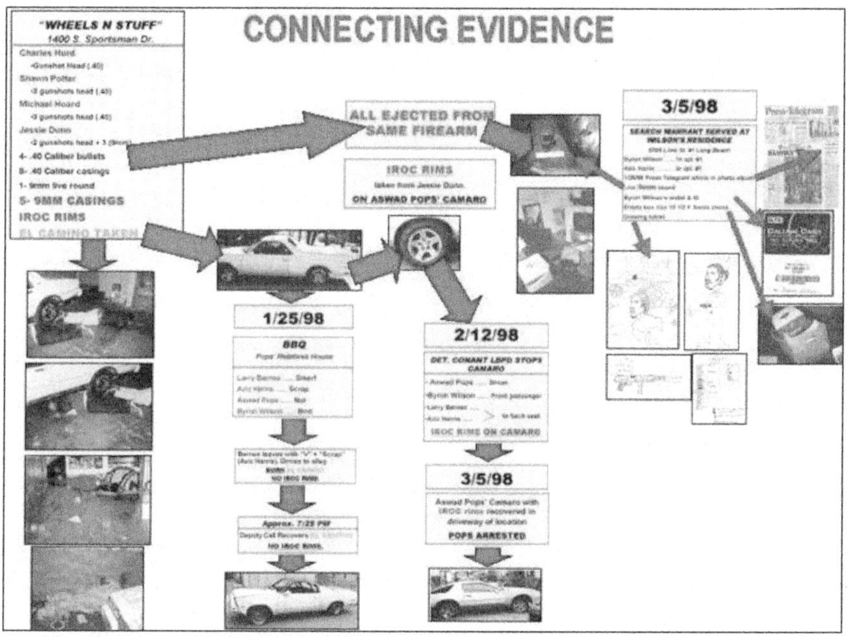

After both sides had finished their Argument, the judge read the final jury instructions. The jurors were excused to go to the jury deliberation room, where they reviewed the evidence. After considerable discussion, the jurors were able to reach a unanimous verdict on both defendants. The jurors came back with four First Degree Murder convictions on both defendants. The jury also found the special circumstance of multiple murders to be true. What that meant was that the case could progress to the next stage, which was the Death Penalty phase.

CHAPTER 4—POPS—CANDIDATE FOR DEATH PENALTY

John was pleased that the jury convicted both defendants; however, he knew the real challenge lay ahead of him. It's extremely difficult for a jury in Los Angeles County to unanimously agree to recommend the Death Penalty. There is always one or more of the jurors who just can't bring themselves to vote for the Death Penalty. In this case involving these two defendants, the Defense was going to paint a picture that this Car Wash was a front for narcotic dealings? This made the victims less than sympathetic in the eyes of the jurors. Some jurors could take the position that if you deal in dope you take a risk that you might get killed in your drug dealing.

However, John stood firm that he believed that a jury could be persuaded that the Death Penalty was the appropriate punishment for these two killers. John understood he had to develop a strategy that would direct the jurors' attention away from the victims and focus on how violent these defendants were. John liked to explain to the jurors that there are certain factors they could consider in determining if the Aggravating evidence substantially outweighed the Mitigating evidence. John knew that he had to concentrate on the factors (a), (b), and (c) in considering the Death Penalty.

Since most of these factors are hard to comprehend, let alone remember, John decided to have a chart prepared that spelled it out. In this way, the jurors had something to look at that explained exactly what John was telling them.

On this page, the chart on the top is the one John used to explain the factors the jurors were to consider when considering the Death Penalty. The lower chart is the one used by John to illustrate that the Aggravating evidence substantially outweighed the Mitigating evidence.

The prosecutor used this chart at the beginning of the Death Penalty Argument to explain what factors the jury could consider in deciding the punishment.

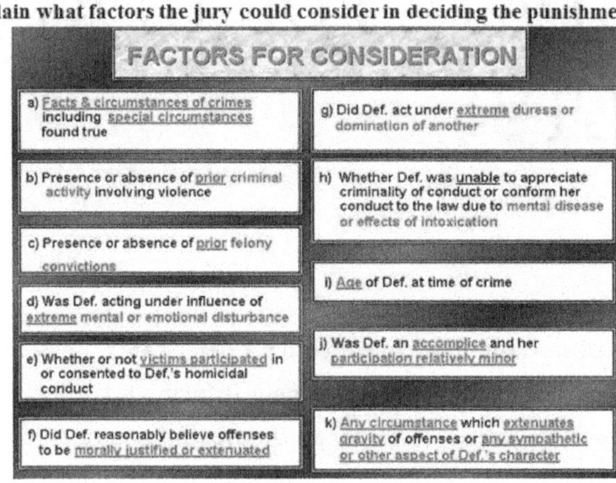

This chart was used to show that the Aggravating evidence outweighed the Migrating evidence.

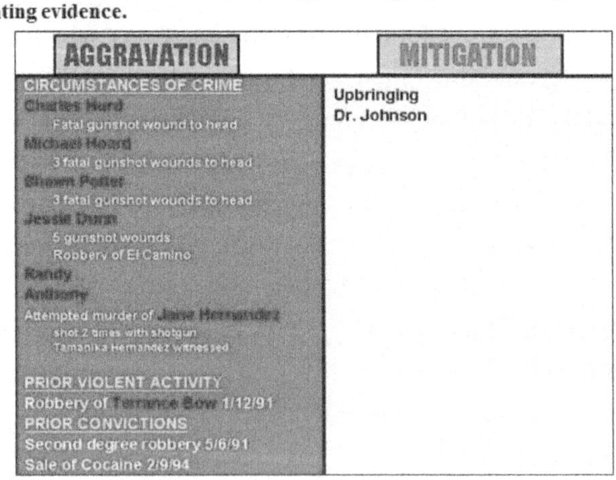

Since the jury's job is to consider whether the Aggravating Evidence outweighs the Mitigating Evidence, John had me prepare separate charts for each defendant. It's especially difficult in a Death Penalty case for the prosecutor to try two defendants before the same jury. What happens in this typc of situation is that the jury tends not to give the Death Penalty to the defendant who has less Aggravating evidence against him or her. Hence, the jury will start weighing the amount of evidence against each defendant and make a comparison decision. Of course, that isn't the way the jury is supposed to consider the evidence. Fortunately for John, both defendants had similar amounts of evidence that supported the three Factors that the prosecution could present Aggravating evidence on.

The main difference between the defendants was in the type of evidence that was presented by each defendant as to their Mitigating evidence. Both defendants wanted to blame the fact that they had a tough "Upbringing" that explained why they had such bad behavior. The Defense used this type of evidence in an attempt to sway jurors to feel sorry for the defendants.

The old debate is what influences a person's behavior most: Heredity or the Environment? The argument can be made for just about every criminal that their childhood environment was less than perfect. As to the Heredity part, the Defense called several doctors who claimed that the defendants were born with brain damage or some type of chemical imbalance. Because of these conditions, the defendants weren't able to conform their behavior to what society expected them to do. The Defense raised both the Heredity and Environment issues in hopes of trying to persuade just one of the jurors to concentrate on the Mitigating evidence. Since it requires a unanimous verdict for the Death Penalty, just one juror could cause a hung jury.

Even with the facts that the victims might be considered less than sympathetic, the jury was able to reach a unanimous verdict of Death as to both defendants. John had been able to keep the jurors focused on the Aggravating evidence and how it far outweighed the Mitigating evidence that the Defense had presented. It is very problematic for a prosecutor these days to be able to convince a jury to come back with a verdict of Death. But the defendants Pops and Wilson were by anyone's definition 'bad dudes' who executed four people who weren't harming them in any way.

If it hadn't been for the greed of these defendants, they might still be wandering the streets robbing people. If they hadn't taken the IROC rims and installed them on Pop's car, there wouldn't have been the compelling corroborating evidence to the eyewitnesses' identifications. Thank God the defendants had a love for IROC rims, which ultimately turned out to be the cookie crumb that led the jury to convict them and decide that the appropriate punishment was Death for both defendants Pops and Wilson

The big question is, what was the intent of the defendants? In this particular case, the robbers appeared to be intent on committing a robbery. The one eyewitness who initially saw the defendants heard one of them say, "Where's the money? Where is the shit?" There is no way of knowing whether they planned the robbery because of an expectation that there would be a large amount of Super Bowl cash on hand. Or was the thinking that there would be plenty of dope-dealing money because of all the Super Bowl partying? It isn't important why the robbers chose this particular day to commit the robbery.

However, the unanswered question was why the two robbers decided to shoot the owner and employees of the Wheel's N Stuff. It might have been that the victims weren't being cooperative in telling them where the gambling money was being kept. Therefore, the reason for the killing might have been the victims' lack of cooperation.

However, from reviewing the evidence it would appear that these two robbers were cold-blooded killers from the get go. They both came heavily armed with some very deadly weapons. Several of the witnesses said that Pops was using a TEC-9, which is an extremely deadly weapon because of its large magazine and rapid firing capability.

After killing the four people, they stole the owner's truck for the rims. Just think how many people would be able to calmly go about stealing this truck after all the noise and commotion that was created by the blaze of gunfire. These killers had to be devoid of any human emotion as the victims lay bleeding out on the cold concrete floor of the car wash.

It is difficult to find anything that is redeeming about Pops and Wilson. They had both been convicted of prior robberies and been to prison. They had the opportunity to learn that robbery was a crime and knew the consequences for committing robberies. This may be where some people would say that the killers were the victims. That society had failed to rehabilitate them when they were in prison and on parole. This case certainly illustrates that these graduates from prison had not been rehabilitated. These individuals became more hardened in that they didn't want any witnesses who could cause them to be sent back to prison.

What have we learned from this case of Pops and Wilson? When law enforcement investigators and a meticulous prosecutor like John Monaghan work together, they can bring together sufficient evidence resulting in the conviction of both murderers. If the DA's Office hadn't assigned this case to **Major Crimes Division**, this case wouldn't have received the attention it needed. Originally, the case would have been sent to the Compton DA's Branch Office, where it would have been stacked in line with dozens of other homicide cases. The local prosecutors would not have been able to work with the detectives to build such a complex case. I can state this with authority since the Compton DA Branch was one of the branches that years earlier, I had supervised.

I don't denigrate the local prosecutors; however, every organization needs to recognize that certain cases require special attention. When Major Crimes Division assigned the case to John Monaghan, he had the time to work directly with the detectives. With John's extensive experience, he was able to focus the detectives on what he would need in court to prove the defendants were the culprits.

The Defense attorneys argued during the Penalty phase that these defendants didn't have a proper childhood. Since both defendants grew up in the Compton area, one wonders whether the fact that gangster rap and NWA with their ***Straight Outta Compton*** lifestyle had an impact on the way these two grew up. When the youth of Compton hear and see their mentors bragging about shooting up the cops, would that not impact their future behavior? In this day and age, one can't criticize the wave of gangster rap, because the entertainment industry and the media claim that everyone has a right to express their own feelings, even if it glorifies violence. Maybe these defendants are the result of a warped culture that got started '***Straight Outta Compton.***'

I also want to spotlight the extraordinary police work, especially the Long Beach traffic officer who recalled giving a citation to someone whose car had IROC rims on it. What was amazing is that an officer took his own time to go through all his copies of his old citation looking for the one involving a Camaro. Furthermore, the fact that he worked for the Long Beach Police Department that had nothing to do with these homicides, which had occurred in the City of Compton. This case is an example of good police work.

To expand on the exceptional police work one has to include the detectives' ability to track down the person who had originally installed the IROC rims for the victim, who was the owner of the El Camino. This mechanic remembered that he had to drill a very small pilot hole on each of the IROC rims, which made these rims distinctive.

Another act of good police work was when the detectives obtained a search warrant for Byron Wilson's apartment. The detectives were smart enough to pick up an unspent 9mm bullet later linked to the crime scene. Also, picking up the SWISS shoe box proved to be useful since it was later connected to the bloody shoe print at the crime scene. Although the sketch pad on the kitchen table seemed more like trash, the detectives had the good sense to save it which proved to be extremely useful in showing the defendants were members of the 'NIGGARZ' gang.

Fortunately, John Monaghan had the smarts to take all these little cookie crumbs of evidence and weave them together to corroborate his three eyewitnesses. By creating his CONNECTING EVIDENCE chart, which he used in his Argument, the jurors could see with their own eyes how all the pieces of the puzzle fitted together. The bottom line was that John Monaghan, a member of the elite DA Major Crimes Division, truly exemplified the exceptional trial ability of the prosecutors that make up the ***DA DELTA FORCE.***

CHAPTER 5 RUN AND PAN-WAVE OF VIOLENCE

On July 27, 1995, Chhuon Run and Samreth Pan decided to commit a home invasion robbery of a family that kept a large amount of cash in their apartment. This family was in the business of selling things out of their apartment such as cigarettes, candy, and some jewelry. Within the Southeast Asian communities, it was quite common for sellers of small merchandise to operate their businesses out of their homes. These robbers understood this practice and knew that most victims of such robberies would not report the crime to the police. That was due to the fact that some immigrants were afraid to call the authorities because in their cultures there was a lack of trust of the police. The other reason for not reporting was that they may not be in the country legally and didn't want to attract the attention of any type of authority.

These robbers had their 9mm Glock semi-automatic weapons. The targeted residence was located upstairs in a large apartment complex. As the robbers proceeded up the stairs, they passed a young woman who was sitting on the stairs. The robber named Run told her "Shut Up". Run and Pan opened the door to the apartment and walked in as though they were customers. Upon entering the room, they saw seated in the corner a stoic elderly gentleman. The robbers turned to him and in a stern voice demanded money. They continued ordering the man to give them money and asked the other people in the room where they were hiding it. The old man recoiled and muttered something. The robbers took that as an affront and felt they were being ignored by him.

The natural reaction by Run was to take the 9mm Glock he was holding to his side and raise it up into a shooting position. Without showing any human emotion, he pointed it directly at the old man. Without any hesitation, he pulled the trigger and shot the elderly gentleman in the face. The victim's son looked in horror as he saw his father, in slow motion, fall to the floor. The tiny ramshackle apartment became chaotic with screaming and shouting. The apartment dwellers were reacting to the shooting of the old man and they were ignoring the demands for money.

Either the victims didn't have any cash or they were reluctant to hand over their hard-earned profits. Chhuon Run, frustrated by the lack of cooperation, raised his gun and pointed it at the old man's son and without any reluctance shot him. Everyone still alive in the apartment was frozen with fear. No one was handing over any money, and the three robbers didn't know what more needed to be done to motivate the remaining victims to cooperate.

The robbers had wasted two bullets on the two victims bleeding to death on the dirty, worn carpet. Run's patience had run out on these hardheaded people when he noticed a woman to his side. He swung his gun toward her and rapidly fired, and she fell like a fly to the floor. (However, she didn't die from her gunshot wound and later became a witness against them.) Run and Pan realized that this resistance had wasted the valuable time to commit the robbery. Based on all the shooting and yelling, they knew that police would have been notified and soon would arrive.

Run and Pan left the apartment without obtaining any cash or jewelry. They were very disappointed that for all their efforts they had come up empty-handed. As Run was leaving, he saw the woman who he had warned to "Shut Up" and glared at her. (Later, she would be able to identify the robbers).

What was interesting about the victims was the fact that they had survived the Killing Fields of Cambodia only to be slaughtered in their new country the 'Land of Opportunity' in the USA. On the refrigerator door in the kitchen, these victims had posted a picture of an American flag, which symbolized their dream of being able to live in America. Unfortunately for two of the immigrants, the American dream had evaporated as they lay dying from American gang violence.

The elderly victim had struggled long and hard to make his journey to come to America. His son, who was shot through the heart, was never going to enjoy the fruits of his father's labors. Everyone came out a loser in this Attempted Robbery. There were two dead victims, and the woman was critically injured. The robbers had tried unsuccessfully to find an easy target, someone who wouldn't resist and who had easy money to confiscate.

Besides leaving an apartment with shattered lives, the robbers had unintentionally left some clues to their visit to the apartment. The robbers looked upon themselves as 'Big Bad Dudes' who should be respected for their brazen attitude to terrorize immigrants. Packing Glock semi-automatics gave the impression that they were professional robbers who should be feared. However, it would be those shell casings from those Glocks that would be like cookie crumbs and would ultimately lead to their arrest.

Both Run and Pan somehow grew up with the attitude that if you fail at something, you pull yourself up by your bootstraps and try, try again. After this failed attempted robbery of the apartment, they set their sights on committing another robbery, one in which they would be successful. They immediately planned another robbery, but this time they would try to find a place where there would be fewer people involved. They recognized that the fewer the victims the less noise would be created.

They selected their next target and approached that residence. They had their Glocks ready for intimidation. As they walked to the porch, they saw an older gentleman. This unnerved them since they didn't want any witnesses who could identify them. Run turned to Pan with an inquisitive look and shook his head. They both agreed that the elderly man made this robbery too risky. They repacked their Glocks and left the area.

Things weren't going well for them in the Sacramento area, so Run and Pan got in their car and drove to the Southern California area, where they felt more comfortable since they were long-time gang members of the infamous ***TRG gang of Strong Beach.*** The initials stood for Ting Rascal Gang, and Strong Beach meant from Long Beach. This gang had a reputation for being violent and cold-blooded. Both Run and Pan felt duty bound to uphold the tradition of the TRG gang. Territory and respect were revered by them, and their gang had branched out to the far reaches of the San Bernardino area, which is 60 miles east of Los Angeles.

Ten days after they had committed the Sacramento home invasion robbery/murders, they wanted to visit an old-time gangster in the City of San Bernardino. Their gang was having trouble establishing a foothold for itself in this new territory. While driving the streets of San Bernardino, they noticed a red Toyota seemingly cruising around. The occupant appeared to be a rival gangster. For no apparent reason they pulled up alongside his vehicle and started shooting. They sprayed the vehicle with at least 32 rounds. The driver of this Toyota was Bunlort Bun After several shots had struck Bun, his dead body slumped to the side of the front seat. By the time they were finished, the car looked like Bonnie and Clyde's Model A Ford after it had been shot up by the cops.

Besides being deadly, the semiautomatics send a message loud and clear as to who is the new boss in that territory of San Bernardino. This time Run and Pan left two calling cards in the form of 18 shell casings from one 9mm and the other 14 shell casings from another 9mm semi-automatic.

It is hard to understand how this overkill in the San Bernardino community was adding to the prestige of the TRG gang. At least in the minds of Run and Pan they knew that any rival gang in the area would be scared to death and be less active, even though no one would know that this was the work of TRG.

Although they weren't accomplishing their purpose for returning to Los Angeles, at least in their minds their gang was gaining the respect it deserved. Two days later, Run and Pan were cruising in the Inland Empire. This time they were in the community of Pomona, slightly west of San Bernardino. They slowly traveled through the barrio area, their attention fixed on any teenage male who might be walking or driving around. They drove slowly down the street, and when they turned the corner, they saw two young Hispanic men, one carrying a rifle. He seemed to be placing it in the back-window rack of an old white Ford pickup truck. His name was Miguel Avina, and he had the day off from working at a local restaurant. Miguel and his friend Rodolfo were going to travel several miles to the local mountains to hunt for jackrabbits. Neither were gang members. They could best be described as hard-working immigrants on their way to have some fun. Some people might be offended at the fact that they were going to be hunting poor defenseless rabbits. However, ironically, they would be the ones hunted and the prey that would be killed by the gangsters Run and Pan.

When Run and Pan observed these two guys carrying a rifle, their conclusion was that these were gang members on their way to do a gang shooting. The natural response for Run and Pan was to pull alongside the pickup truck and stop. Without attracting attention, they both pulled out their Glock semi-automatics and pointed them at the two guys, who were totally absorbed with trying to place the rifle in the rack on the back window of the truck. Without warning, a volley of gunfire was shot in the direction of the pickup truck.

The cab of the truck was hit numerous times where both of the victims were seated. It appeared that most of the shooting occurred on the driver's side of the truck, since the detectives found numerous bullets exiting on the passenger side. With so many shots fired, it was remarkable that anyone inside the cab of the truck could survive. The driver, Miguel Avina, didn't survive; however, his friend Rodolfo was able to duck down on the floorboard, and luckily, he wasn't hit or injured.

What the detectives found strange about this shooting was that the murder victim, Miguel Avina, wasn't doing anything that could be considered threatening. He had gone rabbit hunting many times before. He had always placed his old rifle behind the back seat of the truck where it couldn't be a threat to anyone. He had many dreams of things he would do when he became an American. He wanted to have the opportunity to better himself through working hard. He had never been involved in any type of gang activities. He spent most of his time at his job, where he was well respected by his co-workers.

Miguel never knew what hit him or why he was targeted to be killed. It was hard to understand why Run and Pan thought it necessary to kill a person who was not posing any threat to them. Miguel was an immigrant to this country just like Run and Pan. The difference between these two types of immigrants was that Miguel believed that hard work would lift him out of poverty. However, Run and Pan wanted to use 9mm Glocks to shoot themselves out of poverty and gain the respect of their peers. There were at least ten 9mm shell casings recovered from the crime scene. Again, those ten casings were later going be crucial evidence connecting them to the shooting.

Eight days after the shooting and killing of Miguel in Pomona, Run traveled back up to Sacramento. He was driving a Toyota like the one described in the San Bernardino and Pomona shootings. However, this time he wasn't accompanied by Pan, his gangster bro, but he was accompanied by a young man by the name of CJ Edwards (Pseudonym).

Two gang officers were driving by one of the local schools when they spotted Run leaning into a car. They could see that he had on a baseball cap with the letters **TRG**. The officers remembered that after the July 27 shooting in the Sacramento apartment house, the word on the street was that the robbery-murders had been committed by **TRG** gangsters. Based on that, the officers approached and noticed that there was a young male inside the car. The gang officers had a photo of **CJ Edward** and realized that the person looked like him. They asked them questions as to what they were doing in the area next to the school.

One thing leads to another and the officer got permission from Run to search the car. While looking in the seat they found a spent shell casing in the fold of the cushion to the seat. With this and other evidence, Run and Edward were arrested. Little did the officers know the importance of what they had just found. That shell casing would be the beginning of the untangling of the web of violence that Run and Pan had spread over the entire West Coast. That shell casing would connect up the Pomona and San Bernardino murders. That one item was the biggest break in putting an end to this senseless reign of terror that ended up in the killing of so many innocent people.

The events of this case were unbelievably complicated, in that there were murders all over the state of California. Where should Run and Pan be prosecuted for these murders? The general rule is that the county where the crime occurred is where the case should be prosecuted. However, when serial killers move from county to county committing their murders, the result could be that numerous DA's Office would have to separately prosecute the serial killer, causing many costly separate trials. Since this was so cumbersome, the law in the state of California was changed to permit one county to prosecute all murders that occur in other counties within the state. All that was required was that the prosecuting county had a special circumstance murder that is connected to the murders that occurred in the other county.

Since one of the murders (shooting the victim in the red Toyota) occurred in San Bernardino County, that county's DA's Office could prosecute Run and Pan for the murders that occurred in their county. That was what was decided, so San Bernardino was given custody of both Run and Pan to prosecute them first.

When the San Bernardino case was over, Los Angeles County would get custody of Run and Pan for their murder. After Los Angeles was finished prosecuting them, then Sacramento had an opportunity to prosecute them on murders that occurred in their jurisdictions. However, the Los Angeles County DA's Office offered to prosecute the Sacramento murder at the same time they prosecuted Run and Pan on their Pomona murder. This was agreeable to Sacramento County, since it would save them considerable resources if they didn't have to have a separate trial in their county.

The only downside to such a decision would be if the defendants were acquitted, Sacramento DA's Office wouldn't later be able to prosecute these defendants in their county where the murders occurred. Apparently, Sacramento County DA's Office had confidence that LA DA's Office was competent to handle the prosecution of their case. The two DA's offices finally decided that Los Angeles could handle all the remaining murder cases against these two defendants.

The pressure was on the Los Angeles DA's Office to make sure that both Run's and Pan's vicious murder spree was over for good. The case was daunting not merely because it involved murders all over the state but that the witnesses were scared to death of testifying against any member of the TRG gang. The LA DA's Office had an outstanding Hardcore Gang Division, which was able to prosecute some of the toughest gang cases in the country. One of the alumni of that division was now in the Major Crimes Division; therefore, it seemed only natural to put John Monaghan on this tricky sensitive case. Later that proved to be one of the wisest decisions the DA's Office ever made, since the case proved to be an incredibly demanding and complex one that only an exceptional prosecutor could handle.

CHAPTER 6 RUN AND PAN—CASE GIVEN TO PROSECUTOR

Iremember when John came to my office trying to explain to me the Run and Pan case. The defendants' names confused me at first, so I grabbed my yellow legal tablet and put their names at the top and set up columns below listing the evidence pertaining to each one. Then I realized I was confusing the various crime scenes, so I reached behind my desk and thumbed through a stack of old Auto Club maps. When I found the California state map, I picked it up and started unfolding it; it covered my desk. Then I told John, "Okay show me on the map where the various shootings occurred." John's response was, "Don't you have a map of the entire west coast including Washington State?"

I was surprised when he mentioned Washington State. This was one time I wasn't well prepared. I glanced through my stack of maps I always keep for reference and found none for Washington State. Without missing a beat John said, "Okay, we don't need it now, but we will talk about the Washington murders when we discuss the Death Penalty evidence."

John then stood up and leaned over my desk, looking at the California map. His eyes zoomed in on the Sacramento area and he wrote in the names of the victims. Then he took his pen down the map, then flipped it over to show the area of Southern California. His pen moved from Los Angeles to the right until he came to

Pomona, where he wrote the names of the victims. Then he pointed over to the area of San Bernardino and said that was where the other murders occurred.

After John had briefed me on the case, I asked him to get me certain photos I would need to put the case together. After he left, I glanced down at the map and wondered what would be the best way to explain this case to a jury? I decided I needed to find a full map of the State of California and insert where the various murders occurred. It had to include the San Bernardino shooting, since the jurors would have to consider it as to the connecting evidence, although they didn't have to decide the question of guilt. So what John ended up using was a map with call-out boxes showing exactly where in the State that particular event occurred. This was more graphic and gave a more accurate picture of the various locations. At one glance, the jurors had the location with the date and some type of photo that represented what happened at that location. The other chart that John would use was one that listed the various crimes and special allegations that the jurors would have to decide.

On the following graphic page is the map that showed where the various murders occurred. Below on that page is a Charges chart used to help the jurors understand what they were going to be called upon to decide.

GRAPHICS 6

This is a chart using a map to show where various crimes occurred in State.

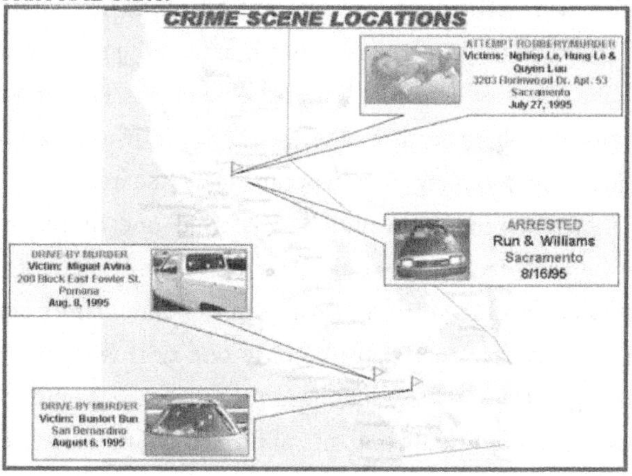

This chart illustrates what the jurors had to decide for each Charge.

CHARGES	ALLEGATIONS				SPEC. CIRCS.		
		Personal Use Firearms	Principle Armed	Street Gang	Robbery	Burglary	Multiple Murder
Ct. 1 Murder	First/Second Degree	✓	✓		✓	✓	✓
Ct. 2 Murder	First/Second Degree	✓	✓		✓	✓	✓
Ct. 3 Attempt Murder	Willful Deliberate Premeditated	✓	✓				
Ct. 4 Res. Burglary		✓	✓				
Ct. 5 Attempt Home Invasion Robbery		✓	✓				
Ct. 6 Murder	First/Second Degree	✓	✓	✓			✓
Ct. 7 Attempt Murder	Willful Deliberate Premeditated	✓	✓	✓			

Prior to the commencement of the trial, John had to make a decision regarding how he wanted to try the case. When the defendants were interviewed separately at different times, they made some slightly incriminating statements that could be used against them in court. John wanted to have the witnesses testify only once since he knew they were reluctant and may not be found for a later trial. From a strategy point of view, he could agree not to use any of the statements made by the defendants and have one jury hear the rest of the evidence. In doing so, he would be giving up some relevant evidence. The only way he could use their statements was if he could talk a judge into having two separate juries seated alongside each other during one trial. Each defendant would be assigned one of the juries. The only difference would be that each jury would hear only the statements made by their defendant and would be excluded from hearing the co-defendant's statements.

It was crucial to this case that there be only one trial with two separate juries. John passionately argued to the judge the need for two separate juries in the one trial of the case. He used the argument that this approach would save the court precious trial time. It would not inconvenience the court, since the only difference was that at the end of the trial the prosecutor would call a detective to testify what Run told him in front of the Run jury, while the Pan jury would be excluded from the courtroom. Afterward, the opposite would be done, as the Pan jury would only hear what Pan had told the detectives. The entire procedure might add an hour to the trial, while if they had to have two separate trials it would take three weeks of additional court time. This was critical for the prosecution, and John made a compelling argument that one trial would better serve the interests of justice in this matter. The judge was persuaded this would save court time and the witnesses from Sacramento would have to travel to Los Angeles only once to testify at the time of trial.

Now with the court agreeing to one trial, John would have to make it crystal clear which defendant was involved in which incident. That was when John created what was called the Relationship of the Parties visual to be used in his Opening Statement.

On the top of the visual were the names of two defendants, Chhuon Run and Samreth Pan, and next to them were two other individuals, Puppet and CJ Edward, who were involved to some extent in the underlying crimes. Although they could be considered suspects, the jury would not have to consider whether they were guilty of any crimes. They were merely witnesses who the jurors would hear from. However,

John knew that the jurors were going to be confused where these separate murders occurred and where Run was arrested. Originally, John thought he would use a separate chart that described each incident. John realized that the jurors needed one visual that combined all of the shootings. This way the jurors could see what similarities and differences existed between the incidents. It became apparent that words alone didn't give an accurate picture of what happened, where it happened and when it happened

Another visual that John wanted to use was a Timeline of Events, which listed the two murder incidents (Sacramento and Pomona) that the defendants were being charged with, plus the San Bernardino drive-by shooting crime (being used as a 1101 (b) incident) as well as the date and time of Run's arrest in Sacramento with CJ Edward.

On the following graphic page are the Relationship of Parties as well as the Timeline of Events visuals that were prepared and used during the trial.

GRAPHICS 7

This chart showed the parties the jury would be hearing about during the trial.

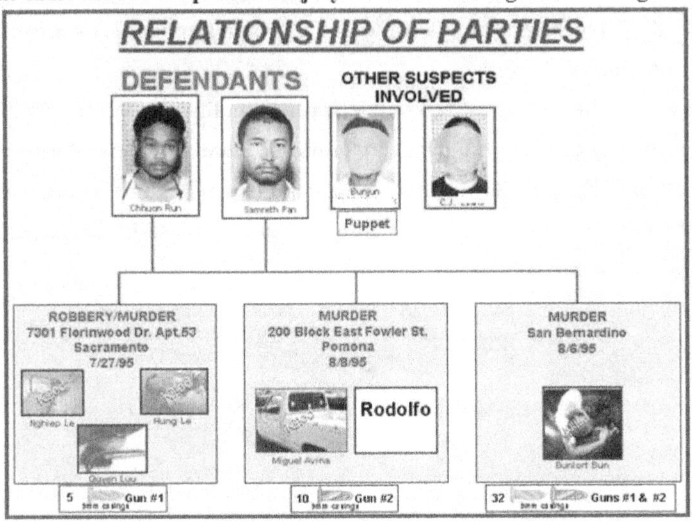

This chart showed the facts of each shooting in chronological order.

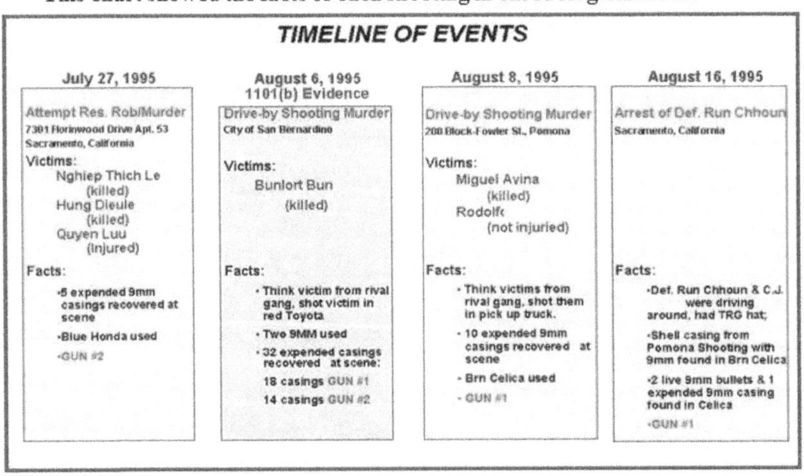

John knew the most difficult part of the case to explain was the Ballistic evidence. It was crucial for the jurors to understand how the shell casings connected these two killers to the shootings. This all rested upon the foundation that expended shell casings could be proven to have been fired by a particular gun. That was when John came up with a visual that showed how Run and Pan used two separate 9mm semi-automatics in the various shootings.

It was the shooting in San Bernardino that revealed that there were two different semi-automatics used. Puppet's testimony placed Run and Pan at the Sacramento shooting, and those shell casings matched one of the guns used in the San Bernardino murder. The ballistic tests came back that the shell casing found in the car in which Run was arrested was the same as shell casings found at the crime scenes in Pomona and San Bernardino. It was important that the jurors be able to follow the shell casings that connected the defendants to the various crimes.

On this page is a copy of a larger visual used to connect the shell casings to each shooting

This chart showed each shooting listing which defendant was involved. It showed the connecting evidence from eyewitnesses or ballistics. It was important that the jury understood there were two guns used and which one was connected to which defendant.

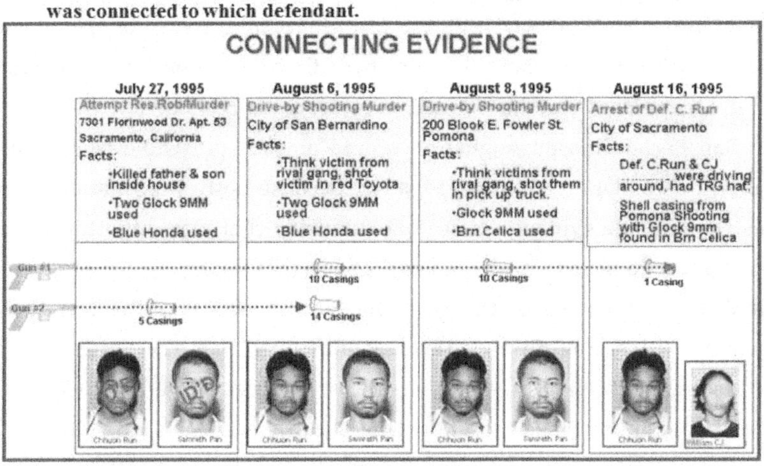

When it was time for the trial, John had laid a solid foundation. During his Opening Statement John showed the two juries his visual showing the map of California listing all the crime scenes. As John pointed to each murder site, the jurors seemed to be experiencing 'Shock and Awe.' (This is a tactic used by the military in which it uses overwhelming power and spectacular displays of force to paralyze the enemy's perception of the battlefield and destroy its will to fight.) The expression on the jurors' faces when they learned of all the murders was one of 'Oh my God.'

Next, John went over the various charges that each jury would have to decide. He used his Charges chart to try to simplify the process for the jurors. As the prosecutor continued to discuss the case, he used the Relationship of Parties to try to condition the jurors to keep track of who was involved in which murder. Several of the jurors could be seen writing down the facts so they would be able to understand the testimony of the witnesses.

The visual labeled TIMELINE OF EVENTS was where John spent considerable time talking about each unique shooting. He had listed all the major events in chronological order. However, he wanted the jurors to realize that the Drive-by Shooting in San Bernardino on August 6th would only be presented to this jury to prove these two defendants were tied together because both 9mm handguns were used. It was the ballistic evidence from that homicide that was important, but the jurors weren't going to have to render a verdict as to that event.

When it came to the trial of the case the biggest task was the fact that the witnesses would be coming from various counties all over the State. For most attorneys, this can be highly stressful, since the logistics of getting witnesses to court can be problematic. This is especially true of those witnesses who have to fly to Los Angeles Airport and require transportation to the courthouse. Often there are flight delays or cancellations and the witnesses don't arrive as expected. Judges don't like any type of delay that would waste precious trial time.

However, this is one area where John appears as cool as a cucumber. He always has a backup plan if a witness is delayed or missed their connection: John will call one of his detectives to fill in and give their testimony out of order. He always warns the jurors during his Opening Statement that some of the witnesses will be called out of chronological order because of witness logistic problems. In this way, John stays on the good side of the judge in not wasting court time. During this trial, there were several times when witness problems occurred, but the jury never was aware of it since John always had his 'Plan B' or 'Plan C' that he would immediately implement.

The other problem that John had to deal with was the fact that many of the civilian witnesses were scared to death to have to testify in open court in front of the defendants. But the fear factor wasn't the only problem. The witnesses from the Sacramento area weren't fluent in English. With those witnesses, John had to have a court interpreter ready to step in to translate those witnesses' testimony. Having to use interpreters can dramatically slow down a trial, making it hard for the jurors to stay focused on the facts of the case.

After a lengthy trial, John knew that his job was to pull all the witnesses' testimony together for the jurors. He knew that he could use some of the visuals he had used in his Opening Statement. However, he realized that his Argument to each separate jury would require a separate Argument chart, each having/showing/containing all the relevant evidence against that particular defendant, including the ballistic connection.

The main difference between the two Argument charts involved the statements made by each defendant. In Run's case, when he was interviewed by detectives, he waived his Miranda rights and was willing to talk. It wasn't clear why he wanted to talk, but possibly he felt that he was smarter than the detectives. He was sly enough not to make any major admissions. However, he was a little careless in what he actually said. He would admit to the shootings, but he made the following statement about the Sacramento robbery: "I told her to shut up." And he said, "You know it's true, that we, I was planning to rob the place." These weren't great admissions, but it was enough to place him at the scene of the Sacramento murder. The witness outside on the stairs would be able to fill in the details that **the person who made the statement to her was the person who did the shooting.**

As to defendant Pan, John used a similar chart, but he inserted Pan's photo with the statement he made to the detectives. When Pan was questioned about the murders, his response was, "It's not that. It's just I'm never going to see the world again." The inference was that he had done the murders and was going to be convicted and spend the rest of his life in prison for what he had done.

These are two of the Argument charts that the prosecutor continually referred to in the respective juries for each defendant.

This chart shows all the events with the connecting evidence plus defendant Run's statements to police..

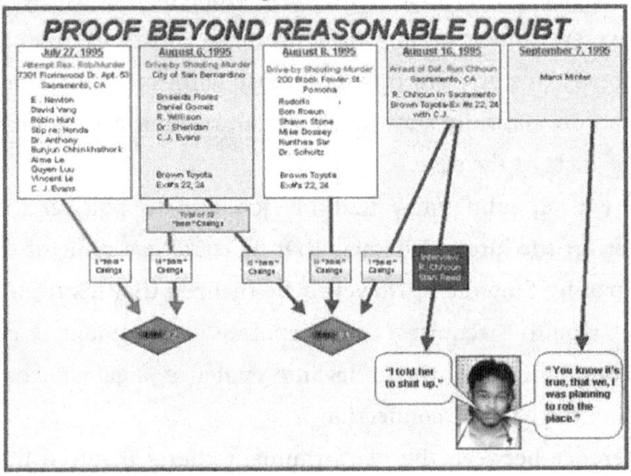

This chart shows all the events with the connecting evidence plus defendant Pan's statements to police..

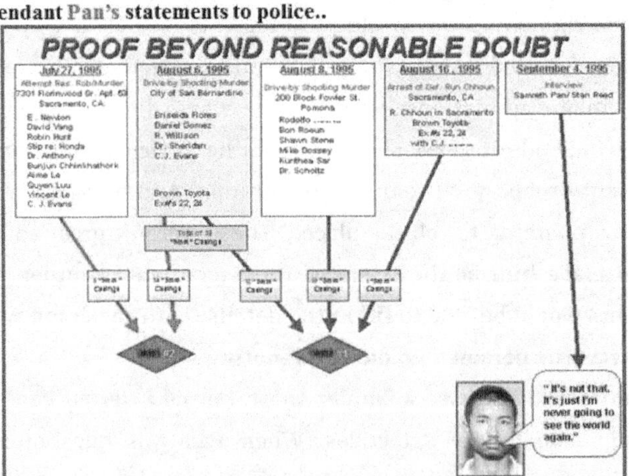

John Monaghan belongs to an elite group of prosecutors who epitomize the extraordinary skill involved in the art of arguing a case to the jury. At the beginning of the trial, he exudes confidence in his case. During the jury selection process, he spends time developing a rapport with the jurors. He projects the persona of a no-nonsense down-to-earth individual. His New Yorker accent paints a picture of a serious person who can be trusted. The jurors can detect his fearless attitude even when things go wrong.

He has a wealth of experience trying cases involving gangs. He knows that these types of defendants can intimidate his witnesses, who are concerned about possible reprisals from the defendants' fellow gang members. John knows what to say and how to put the witnesses at ease when testifying in front of the gang defendants. John knows how to handle witnesses who might change their testimony slightly, out of fear for their lives.

Likewise, in those cases involving deadly gangsters, the prosecution can't permit any of the jurors to feel fear of retaliation if they were to convict. The prosecutor has to make sure that the jurors feel safe in doing their job. John evokes strength and courage to do the right thing no matter what. He never flinches, and encourages the jurors to do their job no matter how unpleasant it may seem at the time.

John had done his job of having the witnesses testify in court, and he finished up by giving his final argument. His approach was that it was now up to the jurors to do their job. One jury panel came back earlier and was sent home until the second jury had finished their deliberation. When both had completed their deliberations, each jury panel separately rendered their verdicts. Each found their respective defendant guilty on all charges; they also found all the Special Circumstance charges.

CHAPTER 7 RUN AND PAN-DEATH PENALTY

John was greatly relieved that both defendants had been convicted and would spend the rest of their life in prison. However, the DA's Office had decided that both defendants deserved to receive the Death Penalty. John was one of the most experienced prosecutors in trying Death Penalty cases. He recognized that in the State of California it was an uphill fight to obtain a Death Penalty sentence. In order to have any chance of getting a jury to return with a death sentence, a prosecutor needs an overwhelming amount of evidence to convince all 12 jurors that this defendant has earned the ultimate punishment.

John had compiled considerable evidence against Chhuon Run. The big question was whether he would be able to amass sufficient evidence against Samreth Pan. This was one time that John was glad that both defendants had their own separate jury to consider the amount of Aggravating or Mitigating evidence. The reason being that both Run and Pan were charged with another homicide, but that was extremely vicious. It involved the killing of a family in San Bernardino two days after Run and Pan had killed Miguel Avina in the Pomona murder. However, when that case was tried in San Bernardino, Run was convicted but Pan's case was dismissed. John wasn't going to be able to present any evidence regarding Pan's involvement in that ferocious murder.

Also, as to Run, there was a murder in Spokane, Washington, in which Run was convicted with other people but Pan was not involved in it at all. So the evidence presented by the prosecution at Pan's Death Penalty trial mainly consisted of the same evidence that the jury had heard during the previous Guilt Phase of the trial. Of course, Pan's Defense presented evidence about him having a difficult childhood, especially because he was an immigrant. Without a doubt, Pan's Penalty Phase was going to be a much more difficult case for the prosecution.

In contrast, there was so much more Aggravating evidence to present to the jury in Run's case. John started out by using a different map for the Penalty Phase. He used a chart that included a map of the entire West Coast showing that defendant Run had been involved in brutal murders stretching almost from the Canadian to the Mexican borders. Besides the original crimes that the jury heard about in the Guilty Phase, they now heard of the killing of a couple in Spokane and another murder in San Bernardino, California, involving the killing of a family of three children and their two parents (this is a separate killing from the one in which both Run and Pan had been charged). Both crimes involved home invasion robberies where Run was looking for money and jewelry that was being sold from these victims' individual homes.

The San Bernardino family murders involved Run and some of his associates, who entered a house on Elm Street in the City of San Bernardino, on August 10, 1985. (That was four days after Run and Pan had done the drive-by shooting.) Run believed that this family had a large amount of jewelry and cash. Run had met up with several runaway girls who knew the family. He had one of the girls go to the house and gain permission to go inside. Then he and his associates barged their way in and pulled out their guns. Once inside, they demanded money and jewelry. They found a round red tin that had some jewelry in it. However, this didn't yield the stash that Run had expected, so Run thought he could get the mother to tell him where the valuables were hidden. He took the woman into one of the bedrooms and told her to start telling where the stash was. Run threatened to kill her children who were lying on the bed.

She claimed she didn't have anything, so the robbers shot and killed one of her young children. They asked her again to tell them where the valuables were or have another child killed. She said she didn't have anything and pleaded with them not to kill her child. Then they turned the gun on the other child in the bedroom and shot him several times. Then they grabbed the distraught woman and pulled her into the living room and repeated their demand, and again she shook her head indicating there weren't any valuables. They pointed the gun at her young son and shot him in the back three times, killing him on the spot. Finally, they turned to her again, and one more time she didn't say anything so they aimed the gun at her husband and shot him in the back and he fell dead on a blanket lying on the floor.

At that point, Run had heard that a good way to make people talk was by forcing toothpaste up their nose. So he had one of his associates go to the bathroom and get a tube of toothpaste. Then they squeezed it up her nose. She struggled while they did this, and still she wouldn't tell them anything. Her nose and face were covered with toothpaste. Then they began trying to pull her teeth out.

The only other person of her family that was still alive in the house was her very young son, who was less than three years old. Instead of shooting the young child, they tried another approach. One of them took a large butcher knife from the kitchen and placed it next to the throat of her last living child. They threatened to cut the child's throat in front of her if she didn't reveal where things were stashed.

When she didn't tell them what they wanted to hear, they started slowly to cut the child's throat in front of her. Either the knife was dull or they were growing tired. They stopped trying to slit the child's throat. Next, they took a gun and shot and killed the woman and then shot at the child. At that point, Run and his colleagues gave up in sheer disgust. They had wasted their time and several bullets and they had nothing to show for it all.

The young child was covered in blood from being shot in the hand and the cut on the throat. The robbers thought they had killed everyone inside; however, miraculously the young boy survived. When the police arrived at the crime scene, they found everyone in his family had been shot to death. While inside, they could hear a slight crying sound. When they went over to the bloody infant, they found he was barely alive. Some people would say the child was lucky to be alive; however, he might not have been so lucky in that everyone in his family had been slaughtered. Because of his age, it was unlikely he was aware of his mother being tortured to death. However, he had suffered from the bullet wounds as well as the knife cut around his neck, and had to be hospitalized for a considerable time.

These killings and the manner of the killings were definitely Aggravating evidence that John would be presenting against Run. However, as to Run, there was still more Aggravating evidence.

In the case in Spokane, Washington, where the husband and wife were murdered, Run used a similar MO by trying to rob a couple who sold jewelry out of their apartment. Run got the couple to let him and an associate into their apartment. Once inside, he attempted to rob the couple. They ransacked the place but couldn't find anything of value. They tied the two up with telephone wire. Since Run couldn't find anything, he got a kitchen knife and threatened them both if they didn't talk.

Neither would talk. However, for some reason Run thought that the victims had swallowed some of the jewelry. When the victims didn't cooperate, the robbers took the kitchen knife and slit both of their throats. They opened their throats and found a ring in the woman's throat. Run removed it and subsequently cleaned it up and gave that ring to a girlfriend he later met whom he was trying to impress as to what a 'Nice Guy' he was.

John finished presenting evidence to Run's jury, and the Defense started with their Mitigation evidence. The main thrust of their position was that the defendant had some type of brain trauma that made him the way he was. They had what they called an expert come into court to testify that he had given defendant Run a P.E.T. scan that revealed some type of abnormality.

John on cross-examination was able to show how unreliable the expert witness's opinion was in regard to the P.E.T. scan. John created a chart that was the basis for his attack on the unreliability of such a test.

On the next graphics page is the map that the prosecution used to show all the sites of violent acts which were committed by defendant Run. Below is the chart the prosecution used to attack the reliability of the P.E.T. test.)

GRAPHICS 10

For the Penalty phase of the trial a larger map was needed to show where all the shootings occurred throughout the West Coast.

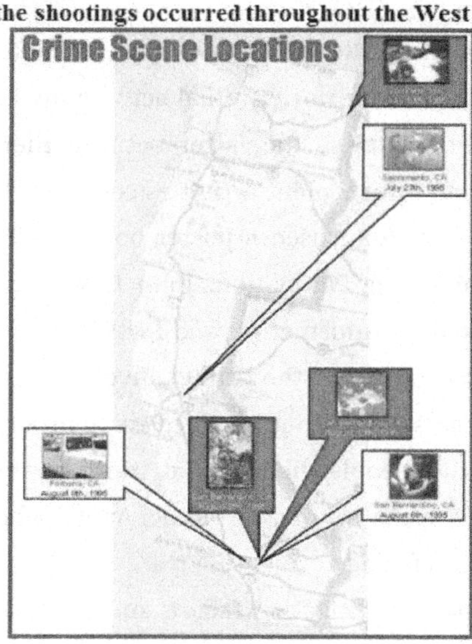

This chart was used to rebut the testimony of the Defense psychologist.

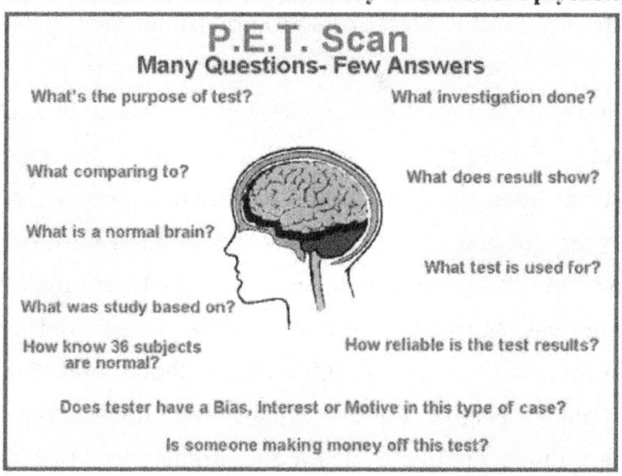

After all the additional testimony was completed, it was time for both sides to argue their case.

John had developed a special way to argue Death Penalty cases. He found it was most effect to explain the law that the jury had to follow. John knew that some jurors would have a hard time when it came to the actual act of recommending the Death Penalty.

John explained the factors that the jurors were to consider, such as the "circumstances of the crime" and other prior criminal activity involving violence. In the Run case, it was important to stress the latter because there was so much Aggravating evidence in regards to prior violent activities committed by Run.

To finish his Penalty Argument, John used a poster board with one side saying Aggravation and the other side saying Mitigation. John then began filling in the evidence in squares that included the information and facts about each incident. He started out discussing the Circumstances of the Crimes involved in the present case. He first placed on the board three squares that involved the murders in Sacramento. He talked about the fact that two people died in that incident and a woman was injured. Next, he discussed the Pomona murder of Miguel Avina, who was on his way to do some rabbit hunting with his friend.

Then John switched to the other Aggravation factor, and that was the other prior acts of violence. John began with the killing of Bunlort Bun, who was gunned down in his car as he was driving on the streets of San Bernardino. Next, he went into the facts of the murders of the couple in Spokane, Washington, and how Run had slit their throats to find jewelry. The final incident was of the family in San Bernardino in which three children and their parents were killed by Run as he attempted to rob the parents. That also included the fact that he was involved in the attempt to slit the throat of a three-year-old boy who they finally shot and left for dead.

On the right-hand side of the poster board, he tried to summarize what the Defense was claiming was Mitigation and should be considered to spare the defendant's life. John attached the words 'Difficult Childhood' and 'Brain Trauma.' He explained that many people have Difficult Childhoods but they don't automatically become a murderer like Run. He also argued that the issue of Brain Trauma was just an excuse being used by the Defense to try to save this cold-blooded killer's life who had no conscience in killing innocent people, especially children. John ended his Argument by saying that the Aggravation evidence substantially outweighed the Mitigating evidence; therefore, the only just verdict would be the Death Penalty.

The top chart is the evidence against Run and the lower chart is the evidence against Pan.

Graphics 11

This compared the Aggravating and Mitigating evidence as to Run.

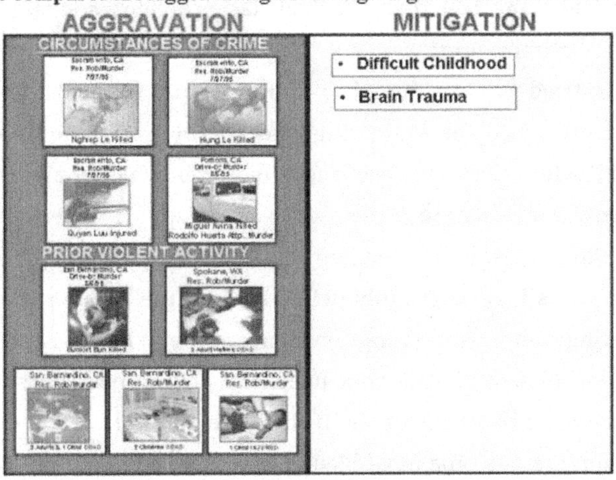

This compared the Aggravating and Mitigating evidence as to Pan.

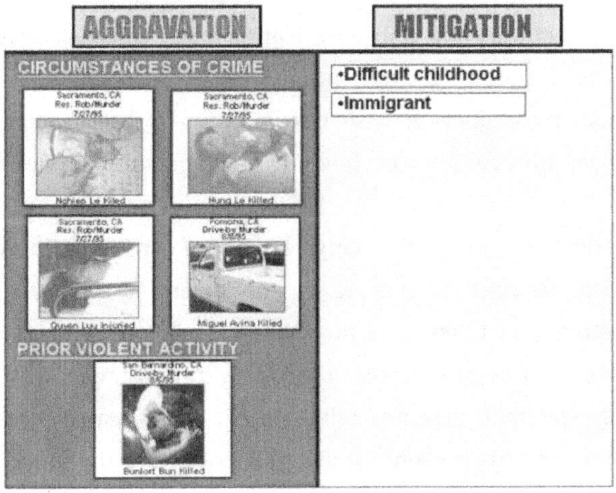

John made a similar Argument at the end of Pan's Penalty Phase. However, John didn't have much more to argue except for the Circumstances of the Crime. The only act of prior violent activity involved the San Bernardino drive-by shooting of Bunlort Bun. This evidence the jury had already heard in the Guilt Phase of the case. The Defense argued that Pan likewise had had a Difficult Childhood. The other issue the Defense raised was the fact that Pan had had problems adjusting in this country because he was an immigrant.

Again, John tried to put things in perspective and claimed that the Aggravation evidence far outweighed the Mitigating evidence. However, he had so much less to argue than in the Run case. This was one situation in which the prosecution was glad that there were two separate juries, since the disparity between the amounts of Aggravating evidence as to Run and Pan was enormous.

After both juries had thoroughly deliberated on the amount of weight to give to the Aggravating and Mitigating evidence, they both came back with a recommendation of Death. This concluded one of the most horrific cases that the DA's Office had seen in recent times. If this case had not been transferred to **Major Crimes Division**, the outcome most likely would have been different.

John Monaghan's persuasive skills came into to play when he did an remarkable job in convincing the judge to permit two separate juries in a single trial. When it came to jury selection, John had an uncanny sixth sense in predicting how people would react to different factual situations. By reviewing the potential jurors' questionnaires in conjunction with the answers to questions he would ask them during voir dire, John could sense how favorable or unfavorable they would be to his case.

John was flexible enough to change his approach depending on the type of jury that was finally selected. To him, it was important to relate to the jurors on their own level. John would make sure he didn't talk over the jurors' heads as so many attorneys do when trying to impress the jury with how smart they are.

John recognizes that 'attorney talk' doesn't always carry the day. He knows how to insert visuals into his presentations in order to keep the jurors interested in what he is trying to convey to them. As much as this case was based on circumstantial evidence, he took all the pieces of evidence and used them as building blocks that he continued to place on top of each other.

However, another area where he 'exceeded all expectation' was in regard to the Defense psychologist testimony. These expert witnesses are brought in by the Defense attorneys to try to explain the defendant's bad behavior. Many of these expert witnesses like to rely on the P.E.T. scans. Since this is a highly technical area, most attorneys don't feel comfortable cross-examining psychologists, in fear they might reveal how little they really know about psychology.

Without any trepidation, John will directly confront the psychologist by asking commonsense questions that the expert witness will give frivolous answers to. What John does is collect all those answers and later use them in his Argument to show how expert's opinion doesn't add up. Very few attorneys have the self-assurance to stand up to the hired expert witnesses from the other side. Before the expert is called as a witness, John ferrets out the transcripts where that expert has testified previously. John is prepared as to what he or she will testify to and what authority they rely on. Few attorneys can beat John in his cross-examination of Defense experts. This is just another reason why John Monaghan made a difference in the Run and Pan case. Unfortunately, Pan had gotten away with murder in the one case prosecuted in San Bernardino County.

However, in Los Angeles County, John Monaghan made sure that Pan as well as Run both were convicted and received the Death Penalty. There were few cases that were as horrific as this one; however, the news media hardly covered it. Even though the DA's **Major Crimes Division** was mainly set up to handle the publicity cases, sometimes there is a need to give special attention to tough cases the media isn't interested in. However, what the Run and Pan case showed was that this Division doesn't take on cases just because they generate publicity. This Division will take tough cases that fly below the radar, just like the Army DELTA FORCE often takes on operations the public never knows about.

Many times an elite group does a magnificent job that few people ever hear about. Why do they do this? The answer is that they are true professionals who do their job not for the public recognition but for the satisfaction of knowing that they did their very best at whatever task they are assigned.

CHAPTER 8 DUONG—NIGHTCLUB MASSACRE

The Anh the Duong' is the name of the defendant in this case and he is truly a 'Bad Dude.' Through his illegal efforts, he had assembled his own robbery crews that planned and carried out robberies throughout California. He and his crews targeted places that had large amounts of cash or items such as jewelry and computer hardware that could be easily converted into money. The defendant had no hesitation to take someone's life even for the slightest reason or in some situations when he had no reason. This case occurred on May 6, 1999, and involved the killing of four people as they sat in a restaurant booth in the International Club, which was located in the City of El Monte, California. This is a community located on the east side of Los Angeles County.

Even in LA, it is unusual to have four people gunned down at any one time. (Since you the readers have read about the Pop and Wilson case involving the shooting of four men in a carwash, you may think this is a common occurrence in Los Angeles County.) The immediate question was, how could this happen? The first thought was that it might be the result of some type of narcotics dispute between dealers. It could also be the settlement for infringing on someone else's narcotics territory. None of the victims were involved in drug dealing or anything related to it. The final consideration was that it must have been a hit, tied to some type of organized crime syndicate. Again, these victims weren't connected to any type of organized crime such as the Mexican Mafia or one of the Asian crime families.

So when four people were outright massacred in a nightclub there had to be some explanation for it. The police started asking questions and found that many people weren't talking, even though they knew something. Potential witnesses were scared to death to talk. Was it because what they had just witnessed scared them or was the killer a powerful person who could impose revenge on anyone who talked to the police?

The homicide detectives got the word that the killer may be a person by the name of Duong who had a shady past. However, solid evidence was hard to come by. The question was why did this Duong character want to kill these four people in the Club? There were bits and pieces of statements from various people that indicated that Duong had a dispute with one of the victims by the name of Minh Tram. Duong was connected to the Won Ching gang, and the word was that Minh Tram was associated with the Black Dragon gang. Apparently, there was a dispute over a woman they both knew. When the two of them saw each other in the Club, there was a rancorous exchange of words between them.

Several people observed the argument and indicated that the dispute tapered off as Tram walked all the way to the other side of the Club and left Duong by himself. Tram got together with a friend, Mr. Tang, and they sat down at one of the restaurant booths. The other end of this large table was empty, so a Caucasian male, who worked part-time as a DJ, decided to sit down for a moment. Then an Asian girl whose sister worked at the Club as a waitress decided to join the DJ after playing a game of ping-pong. To round out the group, the owner of the club sat at the far end of the table.

These people had very little in common except for the fact they were seated at this oversize booth. Duong 30 minutes later came and stood behind this booth. None of the occupants of the booth had seen Duong clandestinely approach and stand behind them. Suddenly, in one motion Duong pulled a gun from his waistband and pointed it directly at Tram's head. Without a word, Duong squeezed the trigger and Tam's head plunged forward. The roar of the gun drowned out the pool hall music. The detectable aroma of warm pizza was replaced by the pungent bitter smell of gunfire.

The others seated at the booth tried to turn their heads to see where this noise was coming from. At the same time, Duong moved around the side of the booth to the front, where he continued to shoot his .45 caliber semi-auto at everyone seated in the booth except for the owner of the club, who had dove under the table. The killer seemed to act methodically and shot each victim in such a manner as to kill, not merely injure, them. None of the victims were a threat to the killer, and none of the victims fought back. It all occurred within seconds, and it was like a nightmare that was occurring in slow motion. The killer had no hesitation in shooting Ming Tram, and the other innocent parties were merely collateral damage. The best way to describe this mass killing was that it was the "Nightclub Murder Massacre."

Defendant Duong appeared to be a pleasant-looking Asian man. But underneath it all, he was a cold, calculating individual whose occupation was that of a professional robber. Duong prided himself in amassing a group of meticulous robbers who had honed their craft to committing high end robberies throughout the state without ever getting caught. He and his group targeted establishments that had large amounts of money. Generally, he received information from insiders, so he knew when certain businesses were holding large amounts of cash for a business transaction.

That night Duong was the only person who used a weapon in the Nightclub Murder Massacre. When the other person, Tram, thought that the argument was over, Duong struck with vengeance, killing everyone that just happened to be near the person he had had the argument with. As the tony nightclub was transformed into a massacre site, Duong disappeared into the dark of night before the police sirens could be heard wailing in the distance announcing their arrival.

John Bugh (Pseudonym) was the owner of the International Club in El Monte. He was from Vietnam and had come to this country and become a successful businessman. His nightclub was a big hit with the young Asian set. The night of the shooting, Mr. Bugh was present in his club. He had noticed that defendant Duong had an argument with Minh Tram. He was seated at the table when Duong started shooting at Tram Ming. Perhaps due to good instincts from his days in Vietnam, when he heard the first shot he dove for cover and unbelievably was able to avoid being shot. He knew that Duong did the shooting and would reluctantly identify him.

He was extremely fearful of retaliation if he testified against the defendant. Because of his lack of cooperation with the prosecution, he was held in custody for a period of time, for his safety and to assure his appearance in court. The shooting wasn't good for business. The club had been operating on thin ice and this shooting was enough for the police department to close the place down for good. As a result, Bugh ended up losing this highly successful club.

Pedro Moreno (Pseudonym) just happened to be in the wrong place at the wrong time. He was at the International Club at the time of the shooting. When he heard the first shots, he looked for the closest pool table and crawled under it. He stayed under the table, scared to death as he continued to hear the gunshots and screaming from the victims and frightened guest.

All he could do was pray that he wouldn't be shot in the melee. The shooting stopped, so he thought the worst was over. Then he heard footsteps coming closer to the pool table he was hiding under. He saw two shoes appear and then the head of a person leaning down and looking at him. This person had a gun in his hand, and had an intent look on his face. Eye contact was made, and Moreno froze, believing he was about to die. For whatever reason, the defendant didn't shoot, and Moreno lived to tell about this encounter.

The International Club was an amiable gathering place. It could best be described as a giant pool hall with a bar. Everything was done on a large scale, as evidenced by the more than 25 pool tables available for patrons to use. One could play pool, billiards, or even snooker. If one wasn't interested in pool, there were arcade games to play or even a ping-pong room. If one wanted to have a drink and have something to eat, there were areas reserved for that. The actual bar was amazingly long and could accommodate dozens of customers. The Club catered to the Asian community, but many nationalities frequented the place.

People from all over the Los Angeles area came to the Club. Mr. Bugh had put in large amounts of money to fix the place up to make it appear trendy and attract a clique. It was obvious that this wasn't just an ordinary pool hall. This club was the place to go and be seen to meet the trendy people. There was another side of the Club, in that it could be a place where questionable people congregated. Although that was not its intended purpose, there was always the possibility for various Asian gangs to congregate, adding to the tension or possibly the excitement of the Club. The police were always concerned with the clientele of the Club and wanted to prevent any illegal incidents from occurring at the establishment.

This case had some similarities to the Run and Pan case that John Monaghan had successfully prosecuted. Both cases involved deadly Asian gangs that were committing robberies throughout the length of California. Both cases involved the killing of multiple victims, which merited the Death Penalty. There was no doubt that the DA's Office would send the case to **Major Crimes Division** earmarked for **John Monaghan**. Because of all the parallels between the cases, it seemed like deja vu for prosecutor Monaghan.

When he had absorbed all the facts from the police reports, he came by my Trial Support facility to discuss this new case with me. John said to me, "Ron, I've got another Asian gang robbery case." I envisioned another case involving residential robberies by Asian gangsters. When John said that this one involved a gangster killing four people in a nightclub in El Monte, I realized my first impression was completely erroneous. Then I said, "Let's start with the nightclub shooting." John handed me a stack of photos of the four victims on the floor next to a restaurant booth. The paramedics and others had moved the victims from the booth and placed them on the floor so they could perform CPR on them. They tried to see if anyone could be saved and quickly determined that the shooter had been unbelievably deadly in his shooting. When the paramedics had finished working on the victims, they tried to leave the crime scene intact for the homicide detectives.

After I had glanced through the horrific photos of the lifeless bodies contorted on the bloody nightclub floor, I realized that John needed the jurors to understand where each of the victims was seated in the booth. The four victims were seated in a large restaurant booth with a table in front of them. This made all the victims vulnerable to an attacker. Even if they were armed, it would have been extremely difficult for them to draw a gun from their pockets or waistband. Also, by sitting in the booth, there was no protection once the firing began. They couldn't duck behind anything because they were pinned between the booth and the table. I prepared on my computer a diagram showing the booth and table. Around the diagram I placed five photos depicting the booth, with wooden dowels inserted through the bullet holes in the back of the booth. *The next graphic page shows what that diagram looked like when it was used as evidence.*

John explained that what led up to the shooting was an argument that had occurred over by the pool tables. However, after the argument everything calmed down and that was when Tram went over to the restaurant booth. I tried to get a picture in my mind where the pool table was in relation to the booth. So I asked John where the pool table was and he said it was one of the 25 pool tables in the nightclub.

At that point, I realized that John was going to need some type of diagram showing the location. I asked John if there was an existing floor plan of the nightclub, to which John explained that there wasn't one. The city had an old building plan, but it wasn't up to date since there had been many modifications to the layout of the club.

Based on John's remarks and looking over the crime scene photos, I was able to make a rough draft of a diagram of the nightclub, which I asked John to have the detectives review. Several days later, John brought back the draft with a list of modifications that I incorporated in the final exhibit.

This exhibit was used by the prosecution during the trial to show the jury the long distance from where the original argument occurred to where the four victims were shot. When the eyewitnesses testified, John had them refer to the diagram as to where they were located at the time of the argument and later at the time of the shooting. These witnesses testified that the argument occurred way over by the eating area next to the kitchen. They described that after the argument, victim Minh Tram moved to the other side of the nightclub where he and three others sat down at the restaurant booth.

On the following page is the diagram of the International Nightclub showing where the pool tables were placed and the location of the booth where the victims were shot to death.

GRAPHICS 12

This visual was used to show where the victims were seat in the booth. Trajectory rods show path of the bullets in the cushions.

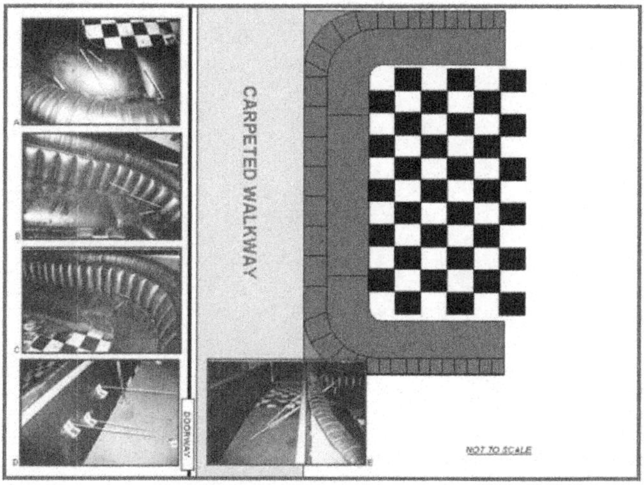

This diagram showed the floor plan of nightclub and where evidence was found.

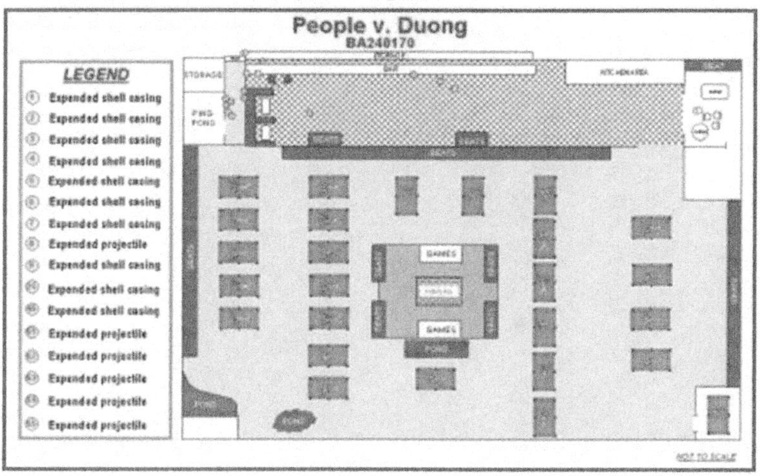

CHAPTER 9 DUONG—IMPORTANCE OF PHONE CALLS

John told me that he wanted the jurors to understand that the defendant had gone to great lengths to cover up his involvement in the shooting by trying to obtain all the security tapes from the nightclub. Shortly after the shooting, defendant Duong realized there were security cameras in the International Club. Duong was afraid that these cameras might have captured his image when he entered the Club or when he actually did the shooting. The defendant started calling people to ascertain if he could get the security tapes so he could destroy them. He used a friend as the middleman in the obtaining of the tapes. Then around noon, within 12 hours of the shooting, his friend arranged for the pickup of the security tapes from an employee of the International Club.

This was critical evidence in the case, in that it showed how the defendant and his associates worked frantically to obtain the security tapes. If Duong hadn't been involved, there would be no reason for him to obtain and destroy these tapes. This showed consciousness of guilt on the part of the defendant.

During the trial, the prosecutor had a representative from the phone company testify to making copies of Duong and his associates' phone records. John had a list of the relevant phone calls reproduced on a chart. However, he soon realized that by including all the calls on that exhibit he was making it difficult for the jurors to focus on the most incriminating calls.

John wanted a visual prepared that showed all the relevant phone calls between all the parties involved in obtaining the tapes. That visual showed the various callers and who and when they made these calls.

After reviewing that chart, John wasn't satisfied that these visuals clearly conveyed to the jurors the connections between all the parties making calls to each other. He wanted something that would graphically illustrate the calls between the parties at specific times. We prepared two flow charts showing the four parties who were involved. The first one showed all the phone calls that were made initially when Duong was trying to find out if there were security tapes. The second flow chart was of all the persons making calls about setting up the delivery of the tapes to Duong's associate.

The following graphic page shows at the top the visuals that showed all the phone calls, and below are the two flow charts of the initial contact about the tapes and later the delivery of the tapes.

GRAPHICS 13

These charts were used to show cell phone traffic between the parties.

These two charts were used to illustrate the phone calls made between the parties..

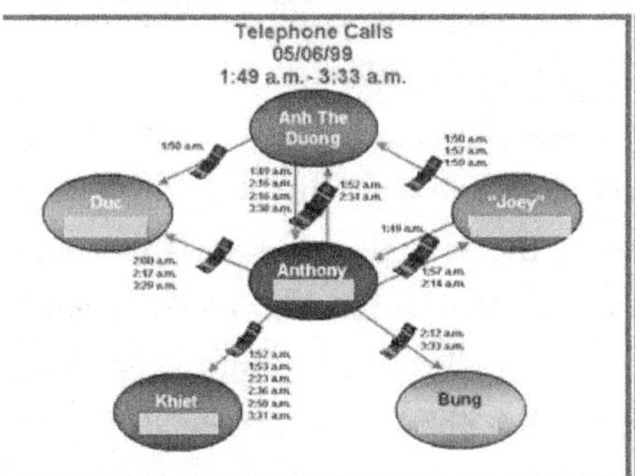

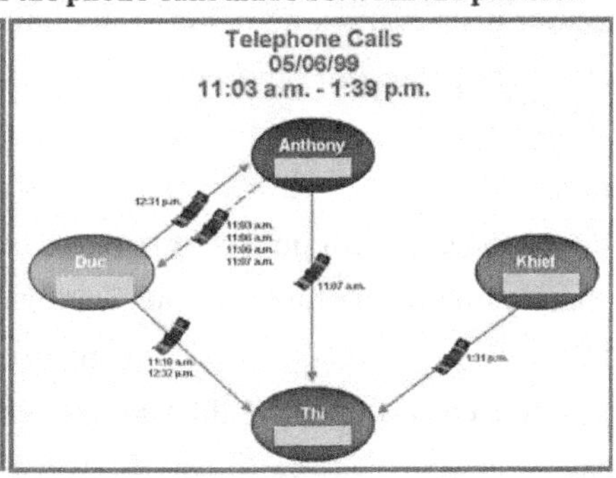

Although the actual trial wasn't very long, it was without any doubt one of the most challenging trials, since so many of the eyewitnesses were deathly afraid to testify against Duong. The defendant's reputation for killing anyone who crossed him made so many of the witnesses reluctant when forced to testify in front of him. Even though Duong was in custody, he had at his disposal his robbery crew, who were still out and about.

Mr. Bugh, the owner of the nightclub, had been sitting at the booth and had turned and seen Duong firing at the victims. By his quick thinking and his flexibility, he was able to take cover under the table. He had to feel that he was the luckiest man alive to survive all the gunshots fired at the booth.

By testifying, Bugh was setting himself up to be another target for Duong's crew to attack. John worked with this witness for hours to gain his confidence to be able to walk into the courtroom and identify Duong as the shooter. The other witness, who was hiding under one of the pool tables, was scared to testify after coming face to face with the shooter. The fear that he felt upon that encounter continued to haunt him. John worked with him so he gained the strength to testify to the jury even while the defendant was in the courtroom only a few feet away from him.

This is the time when a prosecutor feels the weight of the world on his or her shoulders. Obviously, the prosecutor doesn't want any harm to come to the witnesses that are called to testify. The appellate courts have held that prosecutors have a duty not to endanger the lives of witnesses. On the other hand, the entire judicial system collapses if witnesses aren't willing to testify in court. This is where a prosecutor does everything in his or her power to protect the witnesses from harm; however, every prosecutor knows there are no guarantees in life.

In order to persuade witnesses to testify, the prosecutor tries to give them reassurance that there will not be any retaliation, knowing that this is such a delicate balance. Based on the previous cases, the reader has seen that John Monaghan is one of the toughest prosecutors to have ever walked into a courtroom. He isn't afraid to stare down a defendant if the crook tries to give him the evil eye. John is well prepared, and it is like a chess game where he backs the defendant into the corner. He doesn't have to say the word 'Checkmate'; the defendant knows he has met his match.

At the end of the trial, it was time for the Argument. John knew he had several mammoth tasks. He needed to make sure that the jury understood all the evidence he had presented during the trial. He knew the best way to summarize the case was by categorizing the evidence into groupings. He decided to use a visual that he could continuously refer to. The first category he discussed with the jurors was titled 'Crime Scene Investigation.' This included the evidence that was introduced to prove that four people had been murdered. It was important in proving the corpus of the crime; however, it didn't provide much in the way of tying the defendant to the crime. The next category was 'Phone Records' which was important to show that the defendant was hurriedly trying to get the security camera tapes.

The 'Gunshot Wounds Inflicted' category was relevant in that the Medical Examiner could render an opinion as to the type of weapon used. Of course, the 'Witnesses at Scene' category was crucial to the case. With this category, John was able to review the testimony of each of the witnesses who testified to seeing the defendant at the Club that night, some of whom actually saw him do the shooting. What was ironic was that at the same time of the shooting there was a major drug deal being set up by other persons in the Club. The drug deal and the shooting were totally independent of each other. However, the operatives from the drug agencies were in a position to testify that they saw the defendant do the shooting.

The last category was at the bottom of the chart and it related to the three .45 Cal Semi-Automatic handguns that were owned or used by defendant Duong. The testimony as to the guns was confusing because it took so many witnesses to prove the connection of each gun to the defendant. By grouping the evidence regarding each gun in a separate box, John made it easier for the jurors to understand the testimony of all the witnesses regarding that particular gun. The connection was that Duong had three .45 Cal Semi-Auto guns and .45 Cal shell casings were recovered at each crime scene. The .45 Cal Semi-Auto which he had when he was arrested couldn't be matched to any of the recovered shell casings. It was believed that one of the other two .45s that he had owned was the one that was used in the actual crime scene.

John used another visual during his Argument to show all facts that proved that the defendant acted with Deliberation and Premeditation. That would become important when he was arguing that the Murder was that of First Degree.

This graphic page shows the Summary chart titled INTERNATIONAL CLUB MURDERS with all the evidence grouped into the various categories as well as the factual chart showing all the evidence of Deliberation and Premeditation.

GRAPHICS 14

This flow chart was used to show evidence pointing to defendant's GUILT.

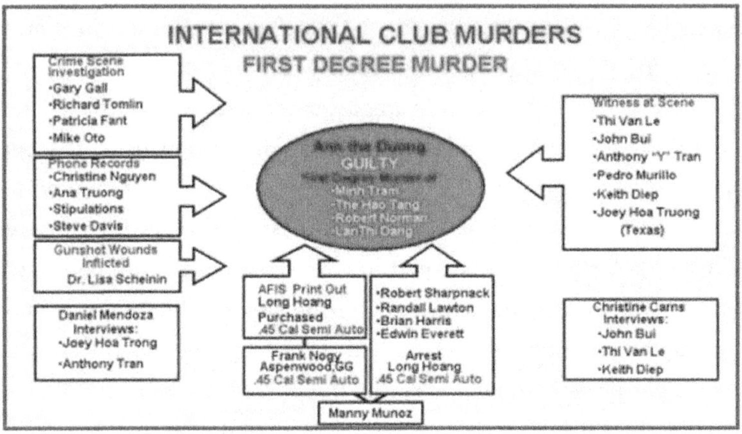

This visual showed the various acts of deliberation and premeditation.

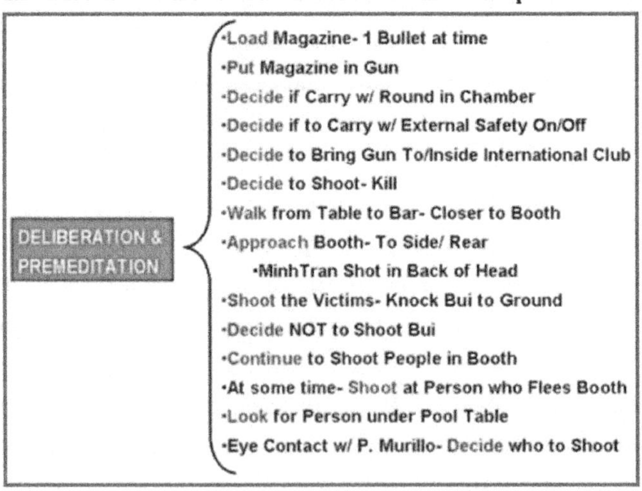

CHAPTER 10 DUONG—EXPLAINING THE LAW

What many attorneys forget is that the jurors aren't ATTORNEYS and they don't understand all the legalese that judges and attorneys keep spewing out assuming everyone is familiar with these terms. For years, John had been trying the most demanding cases, and he had learned that attorneys need to step back and make sure that all 12 jurors comprehend all these legal terms. (WARNING TO READER—*Some of you readers may not be as interested in the discussion of legal concepts. However, I have included them in the next several pages for those readers who are fascinated by the intricacies and complexities of the law.)*

In this case, the jurors needed to understand that they had three sets of decisions to make. John found the easiest way to explain this was to use a chart that showed three separate boxes. Pointing to the chart, the prosecutor said that first they needed to decide if all the elements of Murder had been proven. In this case, the victims were Human Beings, so the first element was met; next, the killing needed to be Unlawful. And the final element was whether the killing was done with Malice Aforethought.

Once the Murder elements have been established, the next question is whether it was a First Degree. This can be proved if there is evidence of Premeditation and Deliberation. Or this can be proven if there is evidence of Lying In Wait. John finished up by telling the jurors that they needed to decide if the Special Circumstance of Multiple Murder had been proved. In this case, that had been easily proven since there were four people who had been killed by this defendant.

John's manner of explaining all these decisions in three separate groupings seemed to give the jurors a 'Heads Up' of what decisions they had to make in this case. Since John had mentioned to the jurors that they could use Lying in Wait to prove the First Degree, he knew that he needed to explain to them exactly what it was.

This was important to this case because John thought some jurors might think that there wasn't sufficient evidence presented as to the Deliberation and Premeditation. It wasn't like Duong was planning to harm anyone on the evening of the shooting or even that he wanted to harm Minh Tram. Everything was peaceful until Tram and Duong got involved in some type of argument.

If the jurors found there wasn't enough evidence of Deliberation and Premeditation then John needed to use some other way to get to First Degree Murder. John believed that he could prove that Duong was Lying In Wait when he came up from behind and started shooting at Tram. Most of the shell casings were found on the floor behind the booth, indicating that the shooter had been standing and waiting behind Tram.

John used his old Lying in Wait chart spelling out the necessary requirements to prove it, which were: Waiting and Watching; Hid Purpose; and Made Surprise Attack. John gave a feasible argument that Duong's conduct could be considered Lying In Wait. After the original quarrel between Tram and Duong, Duong quietly came around behind Tram while he was sitting in a restaurant booth talking to friends. All the elements for Lying In Wait were present, which gave John another way of proving that it was a First Degree Murder.

The Murder Decisions chart and the Lying In Wait chart can be seen on the next graphic page.

GRAPHICS 15

This chart was used to show the jury what they needed to consider.

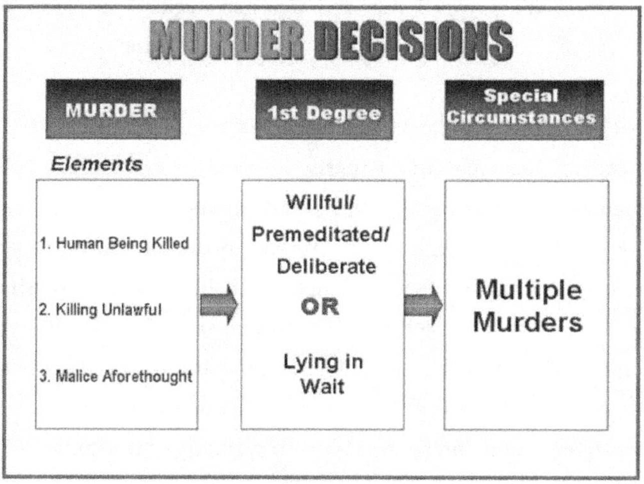

This visual was used to explain what constituted Lying In Wait.

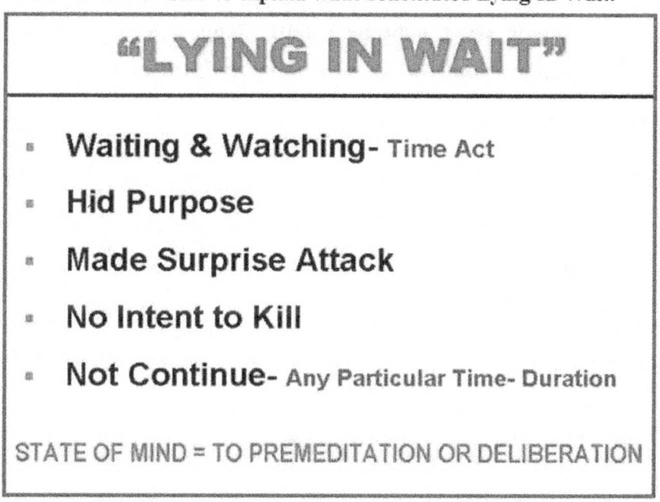

John had done a superb job and convinced the witnesses to come to court to identify Duong as the shooter. The Defense then changed their tactic and admitted that the defendant had done the shooting. The Defense's argument was the shooting was done in Self-Defense. When the defendant didn't take the witness stand, there was no evidence that the defendant felt provoked. This meant that the Defense couldn't rely on the Self-Defense argument. Also, the Defense knew that all the witnesses had testified that Tram was shot in the back without having any confrontation with Duong. That was when the Defense decided to claim that the shooting was done in Heat of Passion, which makes the crime only a Voluntary Manslaughter case.

The Defense tried to show that Tram had provoked the incident. If the Defense could convince the jurors that this was a mere Voluntary Manslaughter, then the defendant could be released from prison within several years.

After the Defense attorney had argued, the prosecutor had a chance to rebut his claim. John's response was that the evidence presented in court proved that there was no Heat of Passion since Tram's actions showed he was trying to get away from the defendant, Duong, and certainly wasn't trying to rekindle the argument. This helped the prosecution argue that the shooting was not done in the Heat of Passion because there was sufficient time and space separating Duong and Tram.

The next part of John's rebuttal argument explained that even if Heat of Passion did apply, it could only be used as to the shooting of Minh Tram and wouldn't apply to the other three victims who were shot by Duong. Those victims had not been involved in the initial argument, and therefore Duong couldn't claim he shot those three in the Heat of Passion.

The following page has a copy of the charts showing the language for Voluntary Manslaughter as well as Heat of Passion. Also shown is the chart highlighting the language showing that there must be sufficient Provocation that would arouse the passion in a reasonable person.

GRAPHICS 16

These charts were used to explain the elements for Vol. Manslaughter.

VOLUNTARY MANSLAUGHTER	HEAT OF PASSION
In order to Convict Mr. Duong of MANSLAUGHTER RATHER THAN MURDER: 1. PROVOCATION- Must be of the type to excite & arouse passion NOT only in Mr. Duong but in a Reasonable Person in the same Circumstances. 2. NO COOLING OFF PERIOD- If sufficient time passed for a Reasonable Person's Reason to Return so that reasonable person would NOT have shot the victims- THAN MANSLAUGHTER DOES NOT APPLY.	• Mr. Duong is not permitted to set up his own standard of conduct and • To justify or excuse himself because his passions were aroused • Unless the circumstances in which Mr. Duong was placed and • The facts that confronted him were such as also would have aroused the passion • Of the ordinarily reasonable person faced with the same situation.

This visual was used in the Rebuttal Argument to show insufficient Provocation.

VOLUNTARY MANSLAUGHTER (Heat of Passion)	DEFENSE ARGUMENT
• Murder can be reduced to manslaughter by Sudden Quarrel or Heat of Passion:	
• Provocation must be of the type to excite & arouse passion in reasonable person & defendant acted under that influence. • Naturally aroused passion, • In an ordinarily reasonable person, & • In the same circumstances an ordinarily reasonable person would have acted same way. • (ie. Shoot & kill the victims)	• So called Provocation "I know there was some fighting going on, you know, pushing, shoving, swinging, stuff like that" • Ordinarily reasonable person under this situation would come back later & shoot victims.

At the end of John's Rebuttal Argument, he could see from the juror's expressions that their brains were saturated with the dozens of legal terms. The jurors must have thought they had just attended a law school class in 'Crim Law.' At that point, John could have concluded his Argument and sat down. However, John knew that the prosecution couldn't afford to have the jurors make a mistake in rendering their verdict. The verdict form that the jurors had to fill out was so complicated that it made filling out a 1040 IRS Income Tax form a piece of cake.

John picked up his last chart and placed it on the tripod in front of the jury. The chart was titled JURY FINDINGS *(this can be seen on the next visual page)*, and John methodically went through each of the counts showing the jurors just what they had to decide. Some jurors crossed their arms as others leaned back in their chairs with an expression of "Oh, my God what have we gotten ourselves in for?"

John was well aware that the jurors were overwhelmed, but he needed them to see how count 1 involving the death of Minh Tram was different from the other counts. He pointed out to the jurors that the killing of Tram was the only one where they could consider Voluntary Manslaughter. The remaining three counts involved the three other people killed in which the jurors had to decide only as to First or Second Degree Murder and not Manslaughter.

Also, as to each count, the jury had to decide the 'Gun Allegation' as to whether a gun was Used and whether it was Discharged. This may seem redundant, since if the jury found it to be Murder, shouldn't that answer the question whether a gun was Used and Discharged? The answer is 'No.' The reason is that at the time of sentencing the judge has to give additional prison time if a firearm was found to be used in the killing.

Some attorneys take the approach that the jurors as a group are smart enough to figure out the jury verdict forms. John had learned over time that some jurors become so confused that they end up checking the wrong box on the verdict form. In this case, it would be a major mistake if the jurors forgot to check the box 'TRUE' under the Special Circumstance Multiple Murder. That would mean that the case could NOT proceed to the Death Penalty stage.

This JURY FINDINGS chart used by the prosecutor can be seen on the next graphic page.

GRAPHICS 17

The prosecutor didn't want the jury to make a mistake filling out the verdict form so he used this visual to explain what they needed to do.

JURY FINDINGS	
Ct. 1 Victim Minh Tran-	☐First- ☐Second- ☐Vol. Mansl.- ☐Not Guilty
Gun Allegations:	
Use-	☐True- ☐Not True
Discharge-	☐True- ☐Not True
Ct. 2 Victim The Hao Tang-	☐First- ☐Second- ☐Not Guilty
Gun Allegations:	
Use-	☐True- ☐Not True
Discharge-	☐True- ☐Not True
Ct. 3Victim Robert Norman-	☐First- ☐Second- ☐Not Guilty
Gun Allegations:	
Use-	☐True- ☐Not True
Discharge-	☐True- ☐Not True
Ct. 4 Victim Lan Thi Dang-	☐First- ☐Second- ☐Not Guilty
Gun Allegations:	
Use-	☐True- ☐Not True
Discharge-	☐True- ☐Not True
SPECIAL CIRCUMSTANCE:	
Multiple Murder-	☐True- ☐Not True
(True if at least 1 Count of First & Second Degree MURDER)	

Since the final Arguments had been completed, the judge read the final jury instructions and the jurors went out to start their deliberation. They spent considerable time weighing all the evidence but eventually buzzed to indicate they had reached a verdict on all the counts. When John heard the word GUILTY as to count one, involving the death of Minh Tram, he felt a deep relief. But when he heard the courtroom clerk say the words that the jurors found Special Circumstance of Multiple Murder TRUE, that meant that the case would proceed to the Death Penalty stage. The judge put the case over for one day so the prosecution could line up its witnesses to prove that Duong deserved to be executed.

CHAPTER 11 DUONG—DEATH PENALTY EVIDENCE

What the jurors didn't know about Duong was the fact that he was one of the most violent and prolific robbers that had terrorized the state of California for several years. Now it was the prosecution that had to bring in witnesses from all over the State to testify to the violent acts and robberies that Duong had been involved in. Defendant Duong had been implicated in the death or serious injury of numerous victims.

John knew that he had to somehow organize all of these violent crimes so the jury could keep everything straight. John in his Opening Statement of the Penalty phase of the trial used a chart consisting of a map of the state of California, with flag boxes inserted showing exactly where those crimes occurred. This was similar to the map he used in the Run and Pan case. *On the next graphic page is a copy of that chart.* Without a doubt, when the jurors heard John talk about all the other robbery shootings, they felt a definite relief that they had made the right decision in convicting the defendant.

This chart alone gave an overview of how widespread this defendant's crime spree extended. He had been involved in so many robbery murders that it painted a very different picture of the defendant from what the jurors had seen during the Guilt Phase of the trial. Some of the jurors might have believed that the International Club murders were a mere isolated incident. However, this misplaced belief was quickly changed when the jurors saw the big picture as to how many lives were snuffed out or ruined because of Duong's propensity for brutality.

John knew what a dangerous individual Duong had become. During the investigation stage, John and his homicide detectives wanted to create an accurate picture of Duong. The question was what could be proven in court. So they contacted dozens of police and Sheriff's departments throughout the State, trying to find out information about any violent incidents that Duong may have been involved in within their jurisdictions.

It became apparent that Duong had terrorized many communities. John had to determine which of the incidents of violence would be admissible in the Death Penalty phase of the trial. He also had to see which incidents he could find witnesses to who would be willing to come to court and testify about Duong's propensity for violence.

Chronologically, the first prior violent act that John presented evidence on was a robbery that occurred on May 3, 1997, at the Thien Thanh Supermarket in San Jose, California. Duong and his robbery crew had inside information that the son-in-law of the owner always received a large amount of cash from the bank on a certain day each week.

They waited across from the market next to a public telephone booth until they saw the son-in-law pull up in his Lexus and park at the far end of the store's parking lot. Duong and the robbers approached the Lexus and demanded that the driver hand over the money he was carrying from the bank. Duong and his robbery crew were amazed how easily they were able to obtain the $300,000 in cash from the son-in-law. However, the owner of the supermarket was standing near the car and saw the robbery take place. He was an elderly gentleman who didn't like being robbed, so he chased the robbers across the street. At that point, the defendant Duong took his gun and rested it on a parked car and shot at the owner. He was able to hit the owner, who fell to the ground wounded. The owner lay on the pavement in the parking lot until the paramedics came to transport him to the hospital.

At the hospital, the victim was treated for the gunshot wound. Initially, it appeared that the victim would survive the injuries; however, the victim had sustained extensive internal injury and eventually succumbed to the gunshot wound.

The police searched the area for slugs and shell casings. They were able to obtain a slug from the victim, and other slugs were found at the crime scene. These slugs were collected and placed in the evidence envelopes. The slugs that were recovered came back to the same type of gun that the defendant used, although not to the specific gun that he was carrying when he was arrested.

The following year, Duong and his robbery crew planned another robbery. This one occurred on August 28, 1998, involving an attempted robbery of the Wintec computer plant in Fremont, California. During that time, many computer and electronic companies were being targeted by robbers. Defendant Duong and his robbery crew knew that the owner of the Wintec Company often carried large sums of cash. Duong's crew had kept close surveillance of the place and knew that the owner would be leaving his office at the plant at a certain time. The owner followed a predictable pattern.

On Friday, August 28, the defendant and his crew were waiting for the owner to leave the office. When the owner came out, he was accompanied by his bodyguard and several other people. The Defendant and his crew drove up in two minivans next to the guard gate. The owner and bodyguard were suspicious of the two vans and started to run back into the office.

At that point, the defendant and crew couldn't carry out the robbery as they had planned. They were angry that they had been seen, so they started shooting at everyone in sight. The others that didn't get back inside the office ran to their cars for protection. One of these parties was a person who couldn't run very fast because he wore a leg brace. He got into the car and started to drive away. The crew continued to shoot in all directions and eventually hit the victim.

The victim of the shooting at Wintec was not a threat to the defendant or his robbery crew. The victim wore a brace on his left leg, which may have caused him to move too slowly to get away from the gunfire. He was shot once through the back, penetrating his heart and lungs. Unfortunately, he died at the crime scene in the parking lot of Wintec.

The investigators were able to determine the trajectory of the bullet in that it entered through the rear of the car and continued to go through the backseat and then entered the front driver's seat, where it struck the victim. It appeared that the car was driving away and was not a danger to the robbers. There could not be any justifiable reason for shooting at this innocent person leaving the scene.

The shooting was clearly an act of wanton disregard for human life of others. Obviously, the robbers were frustrated that they had not been successful in their robbery attempt. However, their indiscriminate shooting was unnecessary, and their conduct illustrated how callous the defendant and his crew were to total strangers.

The slug from the bullet that killed the victim was recovered and was able to be identified as coming from a .45 caliber weapon. However, it couldn't be traced to any particular gun that was recovered from the defendant. The best that could be said was that it was the same type of gun that the defendant always used.

In the Wintec attempted robbery, the robbers used two minivans. The owner and bodyguard were able to provide a good description of the vans. Not long after the shooting, the police spotted one of the vans and pulled it over. They were able to arrest several of the robbers. Duong was in the other van, which got away, so he had not been prosecuted for that murder. Nevertheless, Monaghan used the evidence from this Wintec shooting to show that Duong had committed prior acts of violence.

Inside the one van was duct tape that was brought along with the expectation that it would be used to tie up the victims. The expectation was to capture the owner and rob him of the huge amount of cash he usually carried on him. The duct tape was to be used to tie everyone up. Inside the office was a large amount of computer chips that the robbers were anticipating to load in the vans and haul away. These chips could be sold for hundreds of thousands of dollars.

Also found inside the van was a brochure about scanners of police radio frequencies. This type of scanner could alert the robbers as to when police were notified and began to respond to the robbery. Although the scanner wasn't found in this minivan, it may have been in the other minivan that got away with the defendant in it.

Not quite two years later, on January 16, 2001, in Newport Beach, California, the defendant and his robbery crew decided to rob one of the most exclusive shopping centers in Southern California. The wealthy residents of Orange County shop at the Newport Fashion Island Shopping Center. Traditional Jewelers is one of those prestigious jewelry stores in this high-end mall. It had the most expensive watches, rings, necklaces, and other jewelry only found in places like Rodeo Drive in Beverly

Hills. The defendant had cased the store and the immediate area of that shopping mall. Duong knew this was a great target because it was located near a parking structure where a getaway car could be parked.

What Duong didn't realize was that a half hour before closing of this jewelry store, the guards inside locked the front doors of the store for security purposes. The reason for doing this was to prevent robbers from rushing in just at closing time when the clerks are distracted by their closing procedures.

Duong and his robbery crew waited until just before closing to make their move to enter the store. They approached the large front doors and tried to push them open. They found them locked, and tapped on the door to get the attention of one of the clerks inside. One of the clerks said that they were closed. This infuriated Duong, who looked at his watch and could see that the store wasn't supposed to close for another 15 minutes.

Most good robbers would have accepted the situation and been willing to come back the next day. However, Duong's reaction was to pull out his gun and start firing at the door. He resented the situation and continued to shoot at the display cases in the front of the store. Duong then shot into the interior of the store. In the process of all the shooting, the security guards appeared. Duong was able to hit one of the guards even though he was wearing a bulletproof vest. As a result, the guard was seriously injured from three shots in the chest.

Fortunately, the other guard was not hit by any of the gunfire. This was truly a malicious act on the part of the defendant. Duong and his robbery crew didn't even attempt to take anything but just continued to shoot to do damage to the store and display cases. This was unprovoked violence for no rational reason. No one was resisting and nothing was to be gained by all the gunfire.

Those three types of robberies painted a picture of Duong being extremely violent; however, there was another robbery that occurred three weeks later that was just as aggravating. It involved the robbery of the Jade Galore Jewelry store in Cupertino, California. Duong had received information from his girlfriend that this little jewelry store carried large amounts of expensive jewelry. It was located in a small strip mall and would be easy to rob. This robbery occurred on March 13, 2001. Duong and his robbery crew entered the store after they were told that the security guard had gone into the back room to eat his lunch, which he did at the exact same time every day. They initiated their robbery when the guard came back into the showroom. At this point, Duong and his crew shot and killed the security guard as he walked back in. In this robbery, Duong was very successful in that he and his crew were able to rob the store of more than $500,000 in jewelry.

Defendant Duong was connected to the various robberies through witnesses who were able to identify Duong as one of the shooters. One of the most important witnesses turned out to be Duong's girlfriend. When he was arrested, so was his girlfriend. She wasn't a hardened criminal as Duong was. When the detectives talked to her, she was willing to explain the robbery. As to the Jade Galore Jewelry Store, she had provided Duong the information so he could know when and how to rob it. She indicated that she remained outside the store and wasn't directly involved in the robbery inside.

John wanted to use the girlfriend to testify to all the details regarding these robberies. However, the judge ruled that the girlfriend was an accomplice and therefore her testimony had to be corroborated before it could be received as evidence in front of the jury.

However, the girlfriend was not involved in the Traditional Jewelry store robbery in Newport Beach. John knew that he should be able to get testimony before the jury as to the Traditional Jewelry since he didn't need any corroboration.

John had a reputation for being a tenacious litigator. In this case, he lived up to his reputation in that he came up with a viable theory that the girlfriend was corroborated by the fact that the shell casings between the two robberies matched, which indicated that the same weapon had been used in both robberies. This was a brilliant bootstrapped argument. After several hearings before the judge, Monaghan was able to convince the judge that the ballistic match of shell casings supplied the corroboration that was necessary. As a result, the jury heard evidence that Duong was involved in both the robbery-murder at Jade Galore as well as the Traditional Jewelry attempted robbery and attempted murder.

Some attorneys might not want to put Duong's girlfriend in the difficult position of testifying before her boyfriend. She still loved Duong and didn't want to testify against him. Needless to say, prosecutor John didn't have any problem forcing the girlfriend to testify. John called her to testify to all the robbery-murders that she knew Duong was involved in. Although she was a hostile witness and didn't want to say anything to incriminate her boyfriend, John would use the prior recorded statement that she had given the detectives to refresh her memory. Through this tedious process, the jurors heard all about these prior robbery-murders.

It was ironic that she was supplying the prosecution with the most devastating evidence against her boyfriend. This was the evidence that was going to guarantee that her boyfriend would receive the Death Penalty. After begrudgingly testifying, she stepped down from the witness stand and walked by Duong, her boyfriend. Sitting at the counsel table, and he held up a handwritten note for her to see that stated, "I forgive you." Without a doubt, this was very touching and said something about true love and what lovers go through.

John finished with his last witness, and it was time for the Defense to put on whatever Mitigating evidence that they had. The main thrust of their evidence was that the defendant had a difficult childhood and that he was a Vietnam immigrant. This argument was geared to touch the jurors feeling of guilt that many Americans have regarding the Vietnam War. Many of the jurors were of the age who remembered the angst that people had about whether America was the cause of all the suffering that many of the Vietnamese children went through.

It was then time for both sides to make their Arguments. It all came down to whether the prosecution had presented enough Aggravating evidence to substantially outweigh the Mitigating evidence. John used his map of California to show where all the prior violent acts had occurred. John wanted the jurors to visualize how the defendant's criminal activities had taken place all the way from Northern California to Southern California.

John leaned over and placed on the easel a large visual poster board chart with the word AGGRAVATION. He used that chart to go through the cold-blooded way in which Duong killed the four innocent victims at the International Club. He had placed four photos on the chart showing how each victim had been massacred while innocently sitting in a restaurant booth.

Then, right below those four photos, he had four boxes that illustrated the prior violent acts of the defendant, including the Thien Thanh Supermarket, the Wintec Computer plant, Traditional Jewelers, and the Jade Galore Jewelry store. John reviewed with the jurors how just about everything that Duong did resulted in human carnage. He concluded by pointing to the chart and relating that defendant

Duong, by all his violent activities, had earned the Death Penalty, since it was clear that the Aggravating evidence by far outweighed any Mitigation evidence presented by the Defense. The defendant was involved in so many senseless killings. It was amazing how he was able to impose the sentence of death on so many of his victims. He was so devoid of any human feeling for his victims. Duong wasn't a mentally disturbed person who had difficulty knowing the difference between right and wrong. Duong was just an outright "Cold Blooded Killer."

The following graphic page shows the map of the State illustrating where these other robberies occurred. The chart below was a list of the Aggravating evidence that the prosecution had presented during the Penalty phase of the trial.

GRAPHICS 18

This map was used in the Penalty phase to show where all the shootings occurred within State of California.

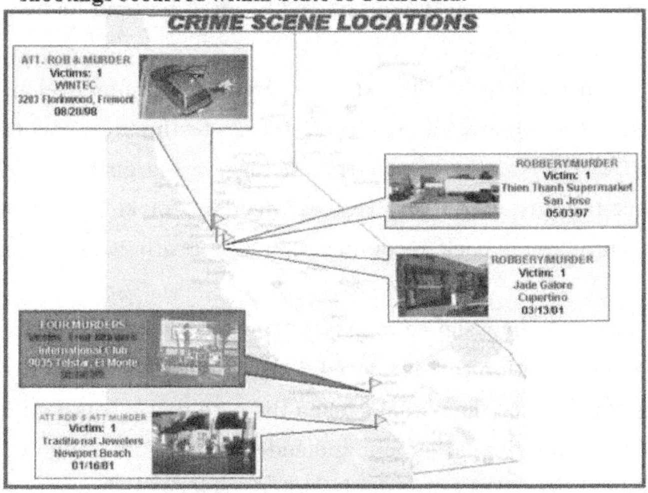

This chart was used during the Penalty phase showing the amount of Aggravation.

What was interesting about this case was that Duong's girlfriend was the critical witness who sealed Duong fate as to persuading the jurors that Duong deserved the Death Penalty. Even though she begrudgingly testified for the prosecution against her boyfriend, Duong didn't hold this against her. When she stepped down from the witnesses stand, she had to walk by Duong who was seated with his attorney at the counsel table. As she walked by Duong, he looked up at her and he held up a paper note he had written which stated, 'I FORGIVE YOU.'

As her eyes glanced down at the note a surprised look came over her face. Was this an expression of true love in which one lover's testimony cemented the other lover's fate of DEATH? Maybe the defendant forgave his girlfriend for testifying against him, but the jury didn't forgive the defendant for killing all these people. Ultimately, the jury came back recommending the Death Penalty for ANH THE DUONG.

If this case hadn't been assigned to **Major Crimes Division**, it case wouldn't have received the special attention that it needed. Without the diligent effort and tenacity of **John Monaghan**, this case could have taken the path that it was a crime of heat of passion caused by the original argument and ended up as a Manslaughter case.

Whatever one thinks about the merits for or against the Death Penalty, this defendant by his antisocial conduct had earned the ultimate punishment. Maybe it takes a special prosecutor like John Monaghan to spend the time to build a case to prove to a jury how evil some human beings can be. However, as to Duong, maybe there would be some question whether he truly deserves to be called a human being. He seemed to be totally devoid of any moral compass.

Like the Run and Pan case, there was little or no media interest in Duong's case. Many critics like to claim that District Attorneys are political animals who crave publicity. However, John Monaghan again put his heart and soul into the Duong case, and not for the notoriety, as there was none. There was no monetary reward, nor a perk such as a larger county office.

Members of elite groups such as the DELTA FORCE do their thankless job not for the high fives, they don't receive but for the self-satisfaction they get by doing something important for the good of society. The prosecutors in the **Major Crimes Division** like John Monaghan do a remarkable job for reasons that most of their fellow countrymen don't understand. They do it because it is the RIGHT THING TO DO.

CHAPTER 12
RADEMAKER-WANNABE A STAR

Every society has myths that are passed down from one generation to another. The elderly learn that these myths aren't true, but the young eagerly embrace them. Then we tend to combine these myths with other myths we end up with a gigantic myth.

One of these myths is that anyone can be successful if they just persevere. Another myth is that celebrities such as movie stars and models live a much better life. When you combine these two myths, you get the big myth, which is that if you want to be a famous movie star you have to continually persevere. Celebrity seekers take chances in order to be discovered so they can live the celebrity life.

When a young woman with stars in her eyes meets someone, who promises that she can advance her dream of being a model or movie star, she becomes hypnotized. She truly believes when she is told, "With your good looks you should be a movie star and I can help you make it."

How many guys have used that line to be the Pied Piper, with an endless stream of young women following their every step? Since guys have used this worn-out line for so long, it would seem that women would have caught on, that this was just an old 'pickup line.' Mothers should teach their daughters to be leery of the 'lounge lizard' types who make such a flattering comment.

One reason such myths get started is that for years there have been stories that Lana Turner was discovered when she was at Schwab's Drugstore in Hollywood. An unknown Norma Jean Baker posed for photos that made their way to Hugh Heffner, who published them in the first edition of his Playboy Magazine. Afterwards this Norma Jane changed her name to Marilyn Monroe. From that moment in time a star was born which eventually blossomed into a famous movie star. There is no end to the stories how photographers have been the key factor in the discovery of some young women.

In reality, there is no one way to become a movie star in Hollywood. It isn't like one stands in a line and waits for their number to be picked. They have to wait for their opportunity to be auditioned for a role. To understand the process of being discovered, one has to understand the economic theory of supply and demand. On the supply side, there are thousands of young women who want to become stars, and on the demand side, there are only a limited number of positions to be filled.

With such a wide gap between supply and demand, most young women become desperate to do something to be noticed, or stand out from the pack of wannabes. That is where the famous "Casting Couch" comes into play. Many young women learn that one way to be noticed is to date or sleep with people who they believe are in a position to better their career. The more direct line is, "If you sleep with me, I will make you a star."

In many cases, it is a pervert who is taking advantage of star-struck women. In a jaundiced way, that may be the way the world of Hollywood operates. People taking advantage of the young and naïve is nothing new. One might say that the young starlets are also trying to use the other person to open doors for them.

Over the years, an even lower form of the "Casting Couch" has evolved, and that involves 'snakes in the grass' who advertise themselves as photographers claiming to have connections in the entertainment industry. The young woman meets with the photographer for a photo shoot and is persuaded to go to a secluded area where some photos are taken and some sex play is expected. In some cases, the woman is very vulnerable, since she is all by herself with no escape. Many go along with the requests of the photographer, hoping for the best. Others may resist and are never heard from again.

Kimberly Pandelios was a Cuban native who grew up in Florida. Her mother was well established and a highly educated lady. Kimberly met Peter Pandelios in Pennsylvania, and they fell in love. Before long, she convinced Peter to move back to Florida with her and call that their new home. A short time later, she became heavy with child and a baby boy was born. For many women, being happily married and having a healthy baby would be enough.

To describe Kim, one would start by saying she was a petite Latina with attractive blondish hair. When people met her, they were impressed by her adorable face, which was framed by long, curly hair. However, deep inside that small frame was a woman who had a burning ambition to be known as a celebrity. When she started out, she took every opportunity to model, even if it was for swimsuits and lingerie. Every job boosted her confidence in thinking that she was someone special. After reading enough magazines and listening to others' advice, she knew that she had to position herself in a place where she could be discovered.

She persuaded her husband that they should move to California, where she would have more opportunities to find modeling jobs. It wasn't long before they were living in a tiny cozy apartment in Northridge, which was at the north end of the San Fernando Valley. To advance her modeling career she poured over magazine advertisements and knocked on agents' doors. She quickly learned that talk and promises were easy to come by but money-paying modeling jobs were infrequent. Most contacts wanted her to spend her money on glamor-photo resumes to illustrate her photogenic qualities.

Her desperation in finding a break led her to glance through the LA Weekly and LA Express. These magazines might be described as the last resort, since their emphasis was more on jobs in the soft porn business.

Kim noticed an ad about a modeling opportunity, and she called and left her number for someone to call her back. Within a short time, she received a call from a man named "Paul." He indicated that he had been in the business for a long time and needed a model for photos for an off-road magazine. He explained where the photo shoot was to occur and how much she would be paid.

Kim said that she would have to think it over but it sounded interesting. Kim, after evaluating the phone call, felt that this Paul seemed to sound sincere and seemed to have connections. She didn't like having to go to a distant location for a photo shoot, especially with a stranger. However, Paul didn't sound like the type that was going to take advantage of her. They had further conversations, and she talked herself into believing that it would be okay. She had done a number of photo shoots with other photographers and everything worked out. She thought now that she was 21 that she was invincible and could handle any situation.

She talked it over with her friend Michael Hayes (Pseudonym), who wasn't quite as keen about this off-road photo shoot. He warned her that it sounded too vague and there were too many illegitimate people who claimed to do photo shoots. Even with this warning, Kim didn't want to pass up a chance that might be the big break she was waiting on. She decided to accept this opportunity and felt it was worth the risk.

Early that Thursday morning on February 27, 1992, Kim reminded her husband that she had a photo shoot with Paul for an off-road magazine. He was happy for her, since she was so enthused about this chance. Around 8:00 a.m. she picked up the keys for her 1990 Plymouth GTX and went by her baby son's room. There she gave Nicolas a kiss on the forehead and hurriedly walked to the kitchen, where she gave her husband a peck on the cheek. Peter turned toward her and wished her well, uttering the words, "Please be careful." Peter remained at the apartment to take care of their son, who was 15 months old. Kim went directly to Angelo's Beauty Salon in Sherman Oaks, where she had her hair done. She trusted them to do a good job on her hair. Kim knew the importance of looking good, especially for outdoor photo shoots. With all her high hopes riding on this job, she wanted to look radiant in order to impress Paul, whom she hadn't personally met.

The night before, Kim had arranged for her babysitter, Peggy Grimm, to come over at 11:00 a.m. to care for their son. Peter had to leave around then to give him enough time to get to work. The cold weather and dampness in the air of February could make Kim's hair go frizzy if not sprayed perfectly. The hairdressing took a little longer than planned, and she finally left around noon. Kim knew that she was running late, so she called home to tell Peggy, her babysitter, that if Paul called to tell him that she was running late but would soon arrive where they had agreed to meet.

It was after 12:00 noon, and she stopped to grab a bite to eat. By 1:30 p.m., Peggy received a call from Paul asking about Kim's whereabouts. Peggy conveyed the message that Kim was running late but was on her way to meet him.

Peggy spent the rest of the day taking care of Kim's baby. Kim had told her that she would be back home by 5:00 p.m. As the afternoon turned into evening, she was concerned as to what had happened to Kim. It was around 8:00 p.m. when she heard the phone ring. Thinking it was Kim, she rushed to the phone to discover that it was Paul. He told her to tell Kim that she had left her "Appointment Book" at his place. He explained that he and his wife had gone out for dinner and when returning home he noticed the book. When asked about Kim, he said that she had left his place around 4:00 p.m. This surprised Peggy since Kim should have arrived home. She didn't know what else to say to Paul, so she said goodbye and hung up.

Peggy waited and waited, but Kim never arrived. Peter came home and took care of the baby, bur Kim didn't return home. Peter started making some phone calls to friends to find out if she had stopped by their place. No one had heard from Kim, and Peter didn't know what to do. He started to retrace all the comments Kim had made about this Paul who she was supposed to meet with. Then he remembered that Peggy had said that Paul had called and said that Kim had left his place at 4:00 p.m.

Eventually, Peter called the police department to see if they had any word of Kim being in an accident. He was told that the police department's policy was not to take a Missing Persons Report until the person had been missing at least 48 hours. Peter was beside himself wondering if there was some type of misunderstanding or if an accident had occurred preventing Kim from calling to advise where she was. Needless to say, this was an agonizing night for Peter, not knowing what to do or where to turn for help. It was a very long night for him.

The following graphic page shows a chart that summarized this case and is followed by a Timeline showing all the crucial events.

GRAPHICS 19

This summarized who was involved & where the killing occurred.

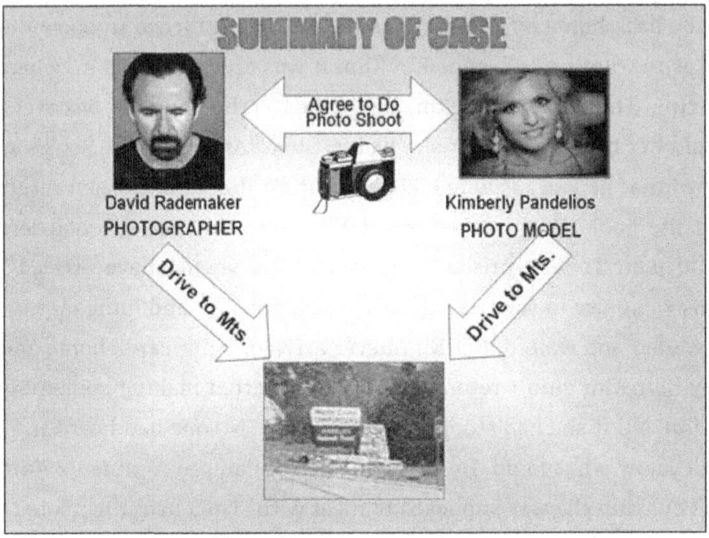

This Timeline showed when various events occurred.

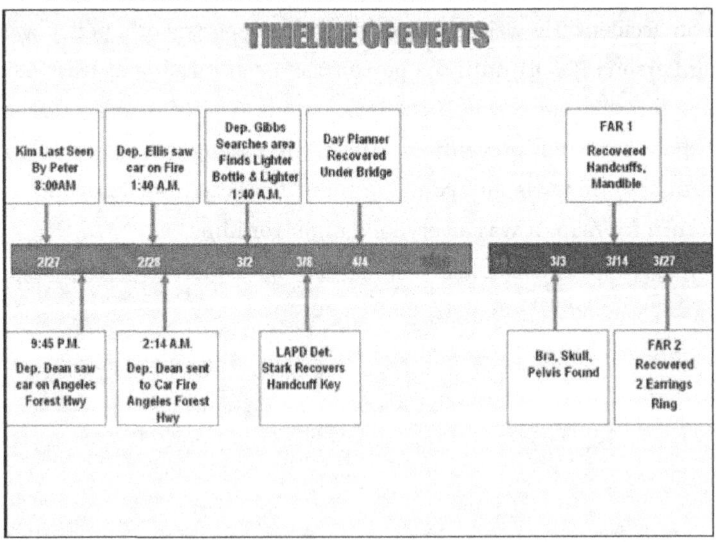

While Peter was racking his brain trying to figure out where Kim was, Deputy Dean of the Los Angeles County Sheriff's Department was in her own car driving down Angeles Forest Highway. It was around 9:45 p.m., and she was on her way to report for the "graveyard shift" at the local Sheriff's station. She had driven this mountain road so many times it was like her car could anticipate the next curve before she got there. At night in February, this area is not heavily traveled. It might be one of the most isolated highways in all of Los Angeles County. One of the reasons why it is so deserted at night is that it is so dangerous with so many twists and abrupt turns.

As the deputy started descending the mountain, she noticed a Plymouth vehicle parked in one of the turnouts. She slowed down briefly, wondering why anyone would park their car there. It wasn't against the law, but the question was why. There wasn't anything near where the car was parked; however, it was a quarter mile from the entrance to the Monte Christo Campground. The deputy didn't want to be late for work, so she continued down the hill to the Sheriff's station.

Around 1:40 a.m., Deputy Ellis was driving home going up the Angeles Forest Highway, which is even more deserted at that hour. Outside his car there was total darkness except for his headlights. His eyes fixated on a bright object in front of him that it looked like a giant bonfire, but this was wintertime and there were no campers around. He continued to drive up the roadway and couldn't figure out what this all meant. Eventually, he was close enough to recognize it was a vehicle fire.

He stopped and checked to see if anyone was trapped inside. He called to have a firetruck come and extinguish the fire before it spread to the nearby brush. Since it was February, the fire danger wasn't as critical as in the fall, but he didn't want to take any chance of it expanding. Deputy Dean overheard the call for a fire truck so she headed up the mountain highway. When she got to the site of the burned car, she recognized that it was the same car she had seen earlier when she was coming to work. It was strange that the car was deserted when she went by four hours earlier and there was no sign of a fire at that time. The question was, how did this car catch on fire in the middle of the night without anyone around? *The following graphic page shows where the burnt car was found as well as where other items of evidence were discovered.*

GRAPHICS 20

This visual showed where the car was located and human remains were found.

This map showed where key items were found along the mountain road.

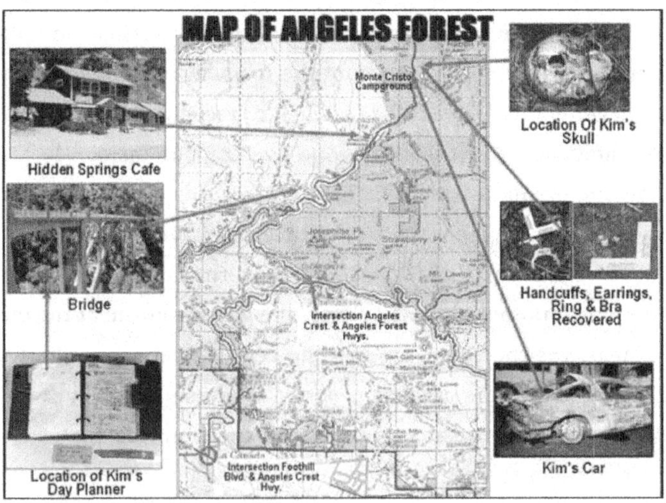

The Sheriff's Department ran the license plate and discovered that the car was registered to Kim Pandelios. At the same time, her husband had tried to report her missing but the police insisted that he wait for 48 hours before filing a formal Missing Persons Report. The Sheriff's Department had the car towed to a garage for investigation and for photos to be taken of it. Two days later, the investigators went up to the site of the fire and checked the area out. About 15 feet over the side of the embankment, they found a 32-ounce metal container of Kingsford Charcoal lighter fluid. Also not far away, the investigators found a cigarette lighter.

It seemed peculiar that the driver of the vehicle had disappeared and the car seemed to have been set on fire by someone. Six days later, an LAPD investigator from the Missing Persons Unit stopped by the site where the car had been burned to check out the area. Since his main concern was trying to figure out why Kim Pandelios was missing, he truly didn't know what he should be looking for. He could easily see the outline of where the Missing Persons' car had caught fire. He was staring at the burn marks in the soft soil when his eyes zoomed in on a metallic object. He slightly kicked it to get a better view then all of a sudden, he could make out the object. It appeared to be a handcuff key in the dirt several feet behind where the car had been parked. The initial reaction was that the deputy sheriffs who had been at the scene two days earlier must have dropped it. As a result, all the deputies who had been in the area were contacted and they verified that they hadn't lost a handcuff key. No one was missing a handcuff key, so why would such a key appear at the scene of a car fire?

A month later, a hiker contacted the Sheriff's station indicating that he had found an 'Appointment Book' under one of the big bridges that span the gorges running through the mountainside. The hiker said that he was hiking along the side of the stream when he noticed this book. He picked it up and saw that several pages listed modeling agencies and decided to leave it where he found it. The Sheriff's investigators indicated that they were interested in it, so the hiker took them back to the location. There they found the 'Appointment Book' right where the hiker had seen it. The investigators showed it to Kim's husband, Peter, who identified it as being Kim's. Her husband related that was one thing that Kim never parted with. All her contacts and appointments were listed in this book.

The following graphic page shows Kim's burnt car and the Appointment Book that was found down the road next to a stream.

GRAPHICS 21

This visual illustrated where victim's car was burnt.

This was chart showing the exhibit of the victim's appointment book.

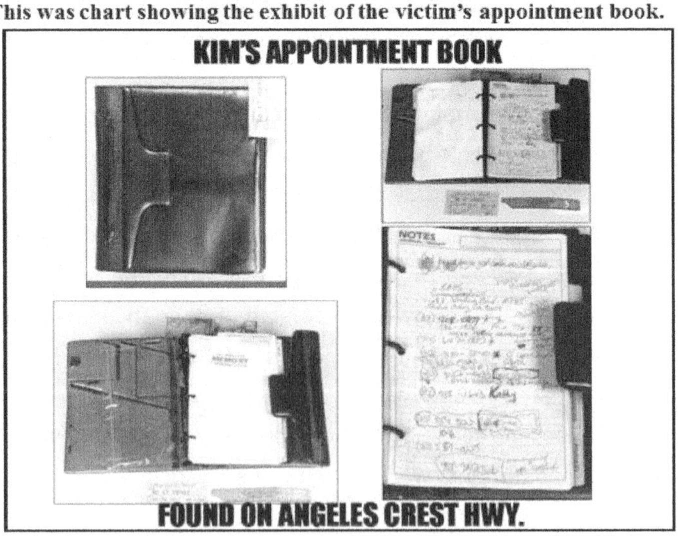

At this point, the only information that the Sheriff's investigators had was that a young Northridge woman had disappeared and her car had been burned and her Appointment Book was found several miles down the mountain highway. The investigators had more questions than answers. Peter, the husband, had found a piece of paper in their apartment which had the name "Paul" written on it next to a phone number. The LAPD Missing Persons Unit investigators checked it out and determined that the phone number had been called several times shortly before Kim's disappearance. When they checked on whose number it was, it came back to the American Voice Retrieval service.

Less than a month after Kim was reported missing the number was disconnected. The investigators were able to indirectly connect the number to a David Rademaker. However, there was no person by the name of 'Paul' who used that phone number. There weren't any leads that were developing into anything. LAPD was treating the matter as a Missing Persons Report.

Of course, in any situation where the wife disappears, the first person who is considered a suspect is the husband. In this case, the investigators didn't even have a dead body. This could be just like the runaway bride situation, where Kim may have wanted out of the marriage. But what negated that theory was the fact that Kim was so close to her son that it was highly unlikely that she would run away without him. The investigators couldn't find anything to support the theory that Peter, the husband, would have any reason to harm or get rid of his wife.

CHAPTER 13 RADEMAKER—FINDING THE SKULL

A year went by without any word as to the whereabouts of Kim. By then her family thought the worst had happened, but they clung to the hope that possibly someday she would reappear. There had always been stories about people who had amnesia and were later discovered living their life somewhere else. As unrealistic as those stories are, they kept hope alive for the family members.

In this type of situation, the love ones are ambivalent about their feelings. One segment would be continuing to believe that the missing person may still be alive but living apart from them. Or would it be better to know that the missing person is in fact dead, at which point the family accepts their loss and moves on with their lives?

Less than a year later, on March 3, 1993, there were two hikers who were exploring the north end of the Monte Christo Campground. This was within a short distance from where law enforcement had conducted a search for Kim. In this area, the mountain stream gently carved its way around the hillside covered in pine trees. The hikers weren't on any trail but just wandering through the high brush. One of them kicked something and glanced down to see what his foot had struck. It didn't look like any of the rocks in the area. He leaned down to get a better look. It was covered in dirt and decomposing leaves. It had the appearance of some type of bone structure.

The hikers' initial reaction was that these were from some type of wild animal. This aroused the hiker's interest, so they started looking around the area to see if there were more bones. To their surprise, they came across a skull. Things started running through their minds. The more they examined it, the more it looked like a human skull than an animal's. What started as an adventure of blazing a trail through the hillside now became more sinister. This was the closest these hikers had ever come to seeing a human skull. Their only point of reference was when they were kids at Halloween, they used plastic skull like buckets to collect their trick-or-treat candies in.

They didn't know what to do. They had never found human body parts before, so they didn't know whom to contact. Should they pick up the items they had found, or should they leave them where they found them? They didn't know the proper protocol for such a situation. They looked around some more, thinking they might find something that would help them to know what to do.

Under some brush they found a turquoise cloth-like material. They didn't want to touch it with their bare hands, so they took a stick and tried to toss it into the air to get a better view of it. The thing had straps, and after a few seconds it was something that every adolescent male should be familiar with: a woman's bra. It appeared to be in good condition except for the straps being cut.

The hikers eventually did the right thing and contacted the authorities. The Sheriff's Department went to the site and took photos of the exact locations where the hikers pointed to the items. There wasn't anything else that was readily observable. The authorities wanted to conduct a thorough search of the immediate area. However, they needed to contact the Coroner's Office to have them assemble a group of people who would have the time and know-how to check for more body parts and possible evidence.

Eleven days later on March 14, 1993, the FAR (**F**orensic **A**nthropologic **R**ecovery) team started their meticulous search. The team consisted of a Pathologist, an Anthropologist, and others from the Coroner's Office. As they dug, a documentarist was in charge of making a record in writing and photographing everything that was uncovered. These searchers were aware that whenever a dead body is left out in the forest that it is eventually pulled apart by wild animals. After the body is dismembered, the animals generally drag the body parts as far as they can to where they can consume the remains down to the bones.

These Graphic shows the area where they began to search looking for more items and found more bones and evidence.

GRAPHICS 21

This was diagram showing where various human bones were found..

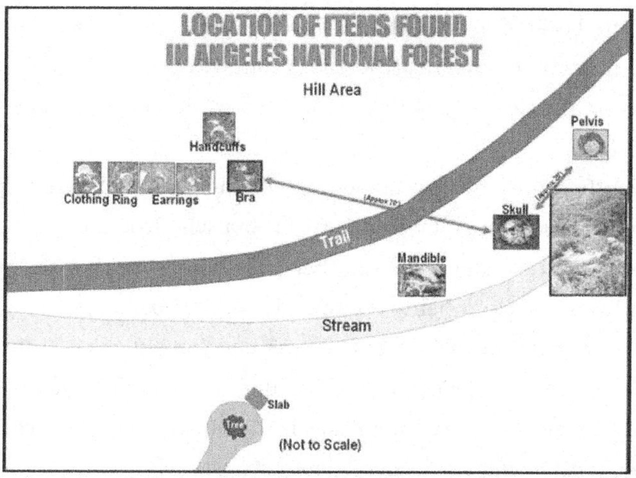

This visual showed photos of search party looking for evidence on the hillside.

The searchers knew that body parts could be found a considerable distance from the original site where the skull was found. Some 25 feet away, they found the lower jaw or mandible. This was a great find, since there were a sufficient number of teeth that could be used to identify the victim through dental records. The team continued to look around and found a clump of hair and some clothing. They dug the soil out from under the material and found a pair of handcuffs buried several inches in the ground.

The handcuffs became a link between the dig site and the location where Kim's car was burnt and where a handcuff key was found. The investigators obtained the key and tried it on the newly found handcuffs. They found the key did, in fact, open the handcuffs.

Most handcuffs are carried by law enforcement personnel. It was possible that they were accidentally dropped by some officer, but why would any officer be in this isolated location far from any trail? Another possibility was that the person whose body was found was somehow being restrained or kidnapped.

After closer examination of the bra, it was determined that the bra straps had been cut with a sharp object such as a knife. But why would a bra would be cut on both straps? One explanation would be that if the person were handcuffed, the only way to get the bra off would be by cutting both straps.

The clothing that was found was examined and it appeared to have cuts in it, possibly from a knife. That might mean that the person was stabbed with her clothes on. The Coroner's Office didn't have much to go on, so they weren't able to determine the cause of death.

The following graphic page shows where the various items were found, including the bra that was identified as Kim's.

GRAPHICS 23

This visual showed the photos of where items were found.

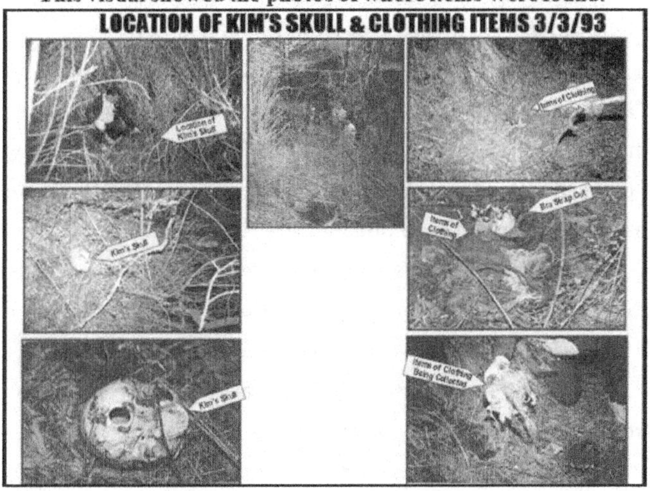

This visual showed where the bra was found & where it had been cut.

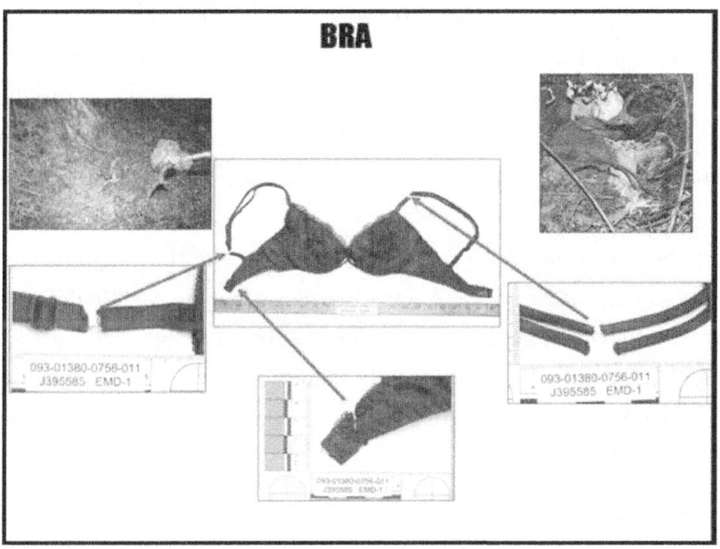

The FAR I team had done well in their findings. The picture was emerging that this could be a homicide. The size of the skull and mandible were likely those of a female. The bra helped to confirm this. It seemed like this hillside was a puzzle with only a few of the pieces visible. Everyone thought that there must be more hidden on the hill that might unlock the mystery of what happened here.

Two weeks later on March 27, 1993, there was another team of searchers who were named FAR II. They were hoping that they would discover more pieces of the puzzle. This time they concentrated on trying to find anything that might be buried in the dirt. They used sifters to pour the soil through to see if there were any small objects that they might have missed during the previous search.

After considerable digging and sifting, the team found a pair of earrings and a green stone gold ring. They photographed them and then cleaned them up to see if they could be identified by anyone. The investigators didn't know for certain what they had; however, they were well aware that Kimberly Pandelios may have disappeared from this general area a year earlier. The amount of deterioration of the body parts would be consistent with a body being left in the woods for over a year.

The investigators had two ways of identifying the body. One was from the possible comparison of the dental records and the other was showing the bra, ring, and earrings to Kim's relatives. The Coroner's Office obtained the services of a forensic Odontologist who examined the skull and mandible and determined that they were from the same person. They obtained Kim's dental X-rays and compared them to what had been found in the mountains. It appeared that this was one in the same person.

The detectives showed Peter the bra, the ring, and the earrings. He said the bra appeared to be the same size and type that his wife did wear. He definitely identified the ring and the earrings as ones that Kim wore. Although this wasn't the same as identifying a person by fingerprints, nevertheless it was fairly strong circumstantial evidence that the body parts that were found at the dig site were the remains of Kimberly Pandelios.

The following graphic page contains two of the exhibits that were used in the trial to connect the items found to the victim.

GRAPHICS 24

This visual showed the victim wearing earrings later found in mountains.

This visual showed photos of the victim's ring later found on the hillside.

Both the Sheriff's Department and LAPD were stymied by the lack of progress in solving the case. A Sheriff's Homicide investigator was working a similar type case. It involved a person by the name of Linda Sobek, who was a model and a Raider's football team cheerleader. Her body had been found in a remote area of the Angeles Forest not far from where Kim's body was found. A Charles Rathbun was charged with murdering Linda Sobek by hiring her to go on a photo shoot in the mountains. In that case, the photo shoot was for off-road pictures of the new SUV Lexus. Charles Rathbun had tried to have sex with her and she resisted. Rathbun strangled her and later buried her body in a shallow grave in the mountains.

While investigating the Charles Rathbun case (this becomes confusing since both names are similar—**Rathbun** and **Rademaker**), the detective received numerous clues. One of the clues came from an anonymous caller on November 25, 1995. That person indicated that the detectives should be checking out a guy by the name 'Rademaker,' since he had been involved in lighting a car on fire back in 1992 after murdering someone in the mountains. It was then March of 1998, when the detectives checked on the name David Rademaker. The investigator found that person was in state prison. With a little checking, the detective found out that the person had been convicted of molesting a young girl. This stirred the detective's interest, so he tracked down the law enforcement agency that was responsible for sending Rademaker to prison.

He learned that it was the Burbank Police Department, and the detective in charge of that case was contacted. It was learned that the young victim was a person by the name of Mona (Pseudonym). The Burbank detective indicated that the victim Mona had told him about being molested by Rademaker. Mona had made the off-handed remark that Rademaker had told her that he had sex with a woman in the mountains and then killed her. The Burbank detective didn't follow up on the statement about Rademaker's involvement in a possible murder, since there wasn't enough information to follow up on.

However, the Sheriff's Investigator decided on his own to contact this young victim, Mona. When he interviewed her, she wasn't able to add anything to the Charles Rathbun case. So the Sheriff, as well as the LAPD investigators, did nothing with the information, primarily since they were focused on finishing up the investigation on Charles Rathbun for killing Linda Sobek and were not conducting any follow-up on the Kimberly Pandelios matter.

Time went by without any break in Kim's case. Then towards the end of 2003, the Sheriff's Unsolved Homicide Unit was going through Kim's case. They noticed Mona's name listed in the file and decided to track her down. On January 19, 2004, this new group of investigators contacted Mona to see what she knew. She didn't know Kim Pandelios, but she remembered David Rademaker telling her that he had killed a model up in the mountains. He explained on one occasion to her that he wanted to have sex with this model and she refused. He overpowered her and had anal sex with her.

Rademaker went on to say that she had begged and pleaded for her life. She kept saying that she had a child she wanted to get back to. She promised not to bring charges against him if he would let her go. Rademaker described her as blonde with a "nice pink ass hole." Finally, after he had anal sex with her he pushed her head into the water and drowned her.

On a separate occasion, Rademaker was watching a TV program Unsolved Mysteries and he told Mona that the program had indicated that the killers had been a biker group. He told Mona, "that wasn't the way it happened." Rademaker went on to tell her that the police had originally contacted him because some of the phone calls had been traced to his phone. He indicated that he knew the police were trying to trick him by claiming that some tattooed bikers were involved.

To corroborate her statement, she indicated that she had gone up the mountain many times with Rademaker. She remembers one time when they stopped along the road. Rademaker went down the embankment and later told her that he saw some bones of the woman he had killed, and that he broke apart some of the bones and threw them in the bushes.

CHAPTER 14 RADEMAKER—SEX SLAVES

The detectives were ecstatic that they knew what had happened to Kimberly and how she was murdered. The mystery was solved, but now the difficult part was trying to build a case that would stand up in court. As convincing as Mona was, the detectives wanted to know more about her and her relationship with Rademaker.

Mona told the detectives that she met Rademaker in September 1993, through a so-called "party line." Rademaker would post flyers around the schools with a phone number on it. The young person would call the number and talk to Rademaker. She was 14 years old and he was 29 years old. Rademaker started having sex with Mona, and the relationship lasted for several years. She indicated that he liked to use handcuffs during the sexual acts. He got her hooked-on drugs and particularly on heroin. She tried to leave him, and he threatened to kill her. Mona's parents got a restraining order against him contacting Mona. When he continued to contact Mona, her parents called the police, who then came out and arrested him.

When the detectives interviewed Mona, they found that Rademaker had been having sex with a minor and providing drugs to a minor. The DA's Office prosecuted Rademaker. In 1997, he decided to plead guilty to the charges. He received a sentence of 12 years in state prison. He served about six years and was released in January 2004.

The detectives heard more than they wanted to know. They realized that any defense attorney could make Mona out as being vindictive and just trying to get back at him for all the bad things he had done to her. As informative as Mona was, they needed someone who would be unimpeachable.

The Sheriff's detectives had a difficult situation. They didn't want Rademaker to come after Mona and harm her, or at least dissuade her from cooperating with the authorities. On the other hand, they needed time to come up with evidence that would stand up in court. It was decided for the safety of Mona and community that the Sheriff's Department would place Rademaker under surveillance.

Two weeks later, the investigators had come up with a woman named Cheryl (Pseudonym) who was Rademaker's girlfriend between 1990 and April of 1993. (Mona hadn't come on the scene until September 1993.) The detectives were able to track Cheryl down and went to interview her on February 3, 2004. She was cooperative and told a story very similar to Mona's. She said that in 1990 she met Rademaker on a "party line." She said that it was a ruse in which Rademaker claimed to be a photographer for producers. He used the ploy to meet young girls for sex. She said the first time she met Rademaker he took her over to his house and gave her wine coolers. She was all of 14 years old and he proceeded to have sex with her. He supplied her with various drugs. She eventually moved in with him and helped him with his phone sex business.

Cheryl remembered that around February 27, 1992, when Kim disappeared, that Rademaker picked Cheryl up from work around 11:00 p.m. They went to Denny's Restaurant to get something to eat. Then, out of the blue, he told her that he had a fantasy to set a car on fire. Around midnight, Rademaker drove Cheryl up the Angeles Forest highway looking for a car to burn. They drove a long distance up the mountain until he pulled in behind a parked car and got out. Cheryl remained in the car.

He took a can of charcoal lighter fluid and poured it all over the car. Then he took a lighter and set the car on fire. He ran back to his car without the lighter fluid container. The car seemed to have a golden glow like a well-lit barbecue. Within minutes the car was a total blaze. He made a wide U-turn and headed down the mountain highway. Cheryl shook her head in wonderment as to why her boyfriend had a craving to set a car on fire. This was a memorable event for Cheryl, something that she didn't forget.

This information seemed to be good corroboration, but it would be difficult to prove that this occurred on the exact date that Kimberly had disappeared. The detectives showed her the photos of Kim's car and her response was that it looked similar to the car that was set on fire. She also was shown photos of the Monte Christo Campground area near where Kim's car was parked and burned. She said that she recognized the area, since Rademaker had taken her up there at least 20 times.

The detectives had to make a tough decision. They wanted to build a strong case against Rademaker. One way was to have Cheryl call and talk to Rademaker to see if he would make any incriminating statements. The detectives came up with a cell phone that Cheryl could use to have conversations with Rademaker. This was a special phone that would record both parties' conversations. She was advised not to use it to talk to any other person.

Using the cell phone, Cheryl talked to Rademaker on nine occasions. She told him that the Sheriff's detectives had contacted her about the burnt car in the mountains and she didn't know what to tell them. By the tone of Rademaker's voice, he was suspicious of Cheryl's phone calls, but he continued to talk.

On March 1, 2004, Cheryl was able to persuade Rademaker to have a face-to-face meeting- one that would be secretly recorded. In police parlance, this is called a "Pretext" meet. Cheryl arranged to meet Rademaker and she drove to the meeting place. He got in her car and she asked him what she should say to the detectives who were asking about the missing model in the mountains. When Cheryl pressed him by saying "Did it happen to be the car?" Rademaker whispered, "Yes." He continued to tell Cheryl to lie about the burning the car.

After an hour, this one-on-one 'Pretext' conversation in Cheryl's car came to an end with Rademaker saying goodbye to Cheryl. He told her that she had been the love of his life. He hoped their relationship could be rekindled so they could once again make mad passionate love like they used to. Cheryl's response was something like, "I don't think so."

Cheryl had to be thinking that she had just gotten admissions from Rademaker that could send him to Death Row. The body wire that she had on got every word of their conversation. The tape recording might not be classified as a 'smoking gun,' but it had enough admissions on it for the detectives to take the case to the DA's Office for possible filing of charges.

On March 3, 2004, Rademaker was arrested for the murder of Kimberly Pandelios. The next day the detectives obtained a search warrant for Rademaker's place and conducted a search. They seized his computer, which showed there had been numerous attempts to locate Mona. Also, there had been many inquiries on the internet regarding models being used for sex and later killed. It was bizarre how many inquiries he had made regarding similar types of killings. It appeared that the detectives acted quickly enough to prevent Mona and any potential model from being harmed.

Because of the long delay in the case and the limited amount of evidence, the DA's Office assigned it to the DA's Office **Major Crimes Division** for prosecution. Since John Monaghan had recently won some extraordinarily difficult cases, he got the nod to handle it. Monaghan had no fear of losing. He knew the rules of evidence and would find legitimate ways to build a case. When considering how best to describe John Monaghan persona, many use the term that he has True Grit. (This is a trait based on an individual's passion for a long-term goal coupled with a powerful motivation to achieve their objective. This perseverance of effort promotes the overcoming of the obstacles in order to accomplish their goal.)

What comes to mind for most readers is the old ***True Grit*** movie from 1969 starring John Wayne as the one-eyed, hard-nosed U.S. Marshal and Glen Campbell as a Texas Ranger whose job was to track down a murderer in the Indian Territory. However, others may focus on the more recent ***True Grit*** movie made in 2010 starring Jeff Bridges as the U.S. Marshal. In that movie, it was Matt Damon who plays the Texas Ranger. In either of these movies, the characters were tested to show their True Grit. Likewise, in this case Monaghan's True Grit can be seen as he takes on the toughest of the tough desperados, whom he ultimately is able to track them down years later in order for justice to prevail.

John lined up all the witnesses for a Grand Jury hearing. The essential witnesses were called, including Mona and Cheryl, who told how Rademaker bragged about killing a model in the mountains. After hearing all the evidence, the Grand Jury came back with an indictment for the Murder of Kimberly Pandelios. The case consisted of one count of murder with two Special Circumstances. One being that the murder was committed during the commission of a kidnap and the other being murder during the commission of sodomy. This seemed simple enough, but Monaghan knew the hard part was going to be trying to prove that Rademaker committed these offenses.

The hurdle that seemed 100 feet high was the fact that the Defense had a witness that claimed that he saw a group of motorcycle bikers with a woman who looked like Kimberly Pandelios who was in handcuffs within a few feet from where the body parts were found near Monte Christo Campground. This witness was named Brian (Pseudonym), and he seemed to be sincere and genuine as to his observation. On March 10, 1993, only seven days after the hikers had found the body parts, Brian contacted the Sheriff's Department. He indicated that he had seen the TV reports about the bones being found in the area of the Monte Christo campground. The news program showed a photo of Kimberly Pandelios, and that jogged his memory of having seen a similar woman handcuffed near a van at that Campground.

He explained that he was driving around in the mountains in his off-road vehicle when he came to a campsite. He saw this blonde-haired woman leaning on a van and she appeared to be handcuffed. He drove closer to see if the woman needed assistance. All of a sudden, three bikers with tattoos came from around the bushes. They looked menacing, and he decided that he was outnumbered and left the area. He didn't give much more thought to the matter until he saw the TV program almost a year later.

From that point on, the Sheriff's detectives who worked the case believed that Brian was correct and that Kim was killed by a group of bikers. As a matter of fact, the Sheriff's Department worked with a TV program, Unsolved Mysteries, to recreate the crime so anyone who had information might come forward. That segment was the most watched of any of the crimes that the TV show had aired.

John realized that this was going to be a formidable Defense to overcome. He recognized that Brian believed what he was saying. Instead of attacking Brian as a busybody, Monaghan decided that he would accept the fact that Brian did see some bikers and there was a blonde woman handcuffed and wearing high heels. There was the possibility Brian had seen something; however, he was wrong either as to the date or the location. He was trying to recall something that occurred over a year earlier.

The one fact that illustrated that Brian must be wrong was when he insisted that he made this observation on February 29, 1992. That date was two days after Kim's disappearance and her car had been set on fire. Monaghan's approach was that no one who kidnapped Kim and set her car on fire would have remained in the area with her for three more days. The deputy Sheriffs who had been at the scene of the vehicle fire and had checked out the area didn't see any biker group anywhere near the Campground.

Being a prosecutor teaches one to be versatile. Prosecutors learn to prepare their cases so they are ready for trial. But invariably at the last minute the other side comes up with a reason why they can't proceed. This is similar to what soldiers always complain about, which is the 'hurry up and wait' scenario. In order for a case to start trial, a number of things have to occur. The Defense attorney has to be ready as well as available for trial. It is hard for Defense attorneys to schedule their cases without having a lot of downtime.

The other problem is that the court where the case is to be tried has to be open for the trial. Often a case takes longer than expected and the cases that are following that trial have to back up or be rescheduled. John diligently schedules his case for trial. He and Defense counsel had set the case for a date certain in February 2006. Then at the last minute, John found that one of his prior cases had to be delayed and would have to start trial in February. John now had two major trials scheduled at the same time in different courthouses. John realized he wouldn't be able to try the Rademaker case. Who could he get to try this case for him?

John's supervisor was Pat Dixon. Pat had tried many of the major cases in the DA's Office. Five years earlier, he had become the supervisor for the Major Crimes Division. He had tremendous respect for John in the manner in which he prepared and presented his cases. ***Pat Dixon agreed to take over the Rademaker case for trial with only days to prepare.*** Only a highly experienced prosecutor could step into such a convoluted case. There were legal motions that had to be argued and witness interviews had to be dealt with all at the same time.

This was a disappointment for John, who had put his heart and soul into building the Rademaker case in order to reach a just verdict. He wanted to bring closure for the Pandelios family. Although he was in trial in another courthouse, he still tried to make himself available whenever issues arose in the final preparation of the Rademaker case. John Monaghan and Pat Dixon had their own distinctive styles of trying a case in front of a jury. However, they were forced to find a way to jointly present the Rademaker case to its jury. It wasn't easy for these two strong-willed prosecutors to decide on tactics and strategy for the case.

Although from the courtroom perspective the presentation of the case seemed flawless, behind the scenes there was tension and fervent debates how to best proceed with the case. John was available to give the Opening Statement to the jury. He used a slide show which I, the author, had worked on for months with John just to get it precisely the way he wanted it. Because of the built-in Defense (Bunch of Bikers Who Did It), John had a well-orchestrated approach to minimize the impact of that Defense.

John's Opening Statement set the stage for the jurors to understand what happened, when it happened, and where it happened. It was now going to be up to his boss, Pat Dixon, to call all the witnesses to prove that it was David Rademaker who actually killed Kimberly Pandelios in the Angeles Forest on January 29, 1992.

The trial had its unique difficulties, since the witnesses had to testify to things that had occurred twelve years earlier. The first hurdle in the case was to convince the jury that the person who was killed was in fact Kimberly Pandelios. If the prosecution wasn't able to prove that the person was in fact Kim, then the Defense would raise issues as to whether there was an actual murder. It doesn't require that an actual body be found. There are cases in which the victim's body was never recovered. However, the prosecution has to present sufficient evidence to convince the jury that a specific person had been killed.

The critical part of the case was going to be the testimony of two witnesses, Cheryl and Mona, whom the defendant, Rademaker, had told about killing a model in the National Forest back in 1992. These women had never met Kim or even been aware of her name. That was why it was important to tie the burnt vehicle to Kim. By doing that, it established that Kim was likely in the general area where the bones were found. Fortunately, technology had advanced sufficiently so that the bones could be tested by using DNA. A sample of DNA was taken from Kim's mother and was tested against the bones that had been recovered. DNA experts were able to determine that in fact the remains were those of Kimberly Pandelios.

The Defense approach was that Kimberly may have run away and still be alive somewhere. With the new DNA evidence, the Defense didn't have a very strong argument that she might have run away and taken up a new life somewhere else. To make sure that the jury understood that Kim was dead, the prosecution presented DNA expert testimony.

Having established that the body was Kim's, the prosecution called the two young women, Mona and Cheryl, to tell their stories. It was incredibly difficult for them to testify in front of the jury. They didn't relish having to tell in open court about the darkest part of their lives. They had both gone on with their lives and didn't want everyone in the general public to know that when they were 14 years old they were associating with David Rademaker. They weren't proud of how he got them into using heavy drugs such as heroin and used them as sex toys. This was a chapter in their life they preferred to forget.

CHAPTER 15

RADEMAKER—PRETEXT TAPE

The key piece of evidence was a recording of a Pretext meeting between Cheryl and Rademaker that occurred on March1, 2004. The detectives wired up Cheryl and she drove alone over to a restaurant to meet Rademaker. There she persuaded him to go outside to her parked car where they could talk. She told Rademaker that the police had contacted her about the so-called 'burning a car on a mountain road.' She asked him what she should tell the police. He was very cagey and kept telling her to say nothing, since it didn't happen.

Since she had gone up to the mountains and seen him pour charcoal lighter fluid on a car, her next question was: Did that car belong to the model whose deteriorated body was found nearby? Rademaker didn't want to make any incriminating statement, but he slipped up and admitted that the burned car belonged to the dead model.

The relevant part of the Pretext tape between Cheryl and Rademaker is as follows:

Cheryl: They're asking about a car though.

Rademaker: No.

Cheryl: . . . a murdered girl.

Rademaker: Okay. The murdered girl was the girl's car.

Cheryl: The car that we went up to the – the one that we did?

Rademaker: Uhm-hmm. The one that we just happened—uh, obviously it never happened.

Cheryl: Okay. Obviously, when I talked to them, it never happened, but that happened to be—did it happen to be the car?

Rademaker: (Whispering) YES.

During Cheryl's direct examination, she did her best to recall everything about the incident in which Rademaker had taken her up the Angeles Forest Highway, where he set a car on fire. When Mona testified, she did her best to recall Rademaker's statements about how he went up to the mountains and burned up a car. Both Cheryl and Mona did well in testifying. The Defense attorney was able to cross-examine both of them at length; however, they both survived the intense barrage of questions. The Defense tried to paint a picture of two women who were out to get Rademaker. The purpose of their fabricated testimony was to punish Rademaker for what he had done to them when they were very young. The prosecution knew that both women had to be corroborated to show that they were telling the truth. To a large extent, the two witnesses corroborated each other. The prosecution used other pieces of evidence to prove that both witnesses were being truthful.

As for as the rest of the prosecution's evidence, the two deputies were called who saw Kim's car on the Angeles Forest Highway. Further witnesses that were called to testify were the officer who found the charcoal lighter fluid can near the car, and the other officer who found the handcuff key. The detectives were able to find the hiker who found the Appointment Book, and he testified to finding it.

Then the detectives were able to track down the hikers who stumbled across the bones and skull which were later identified as the victim's. Then a group of witnesses testified to doing the methodical searching for personal belongings and eventually coming across the earrings, ring, and the cut bra. Also called as a witness was Kim's husband, Peter, who testified that Kim was excited to go on this photo shoot with a photographer who went by the name 'Paul.' Peter was able to identify in court the earrings and the opal ring as being Kim's. As to the cut green bra, he indicated that was the same size that Kim wore and she had one that looked similar.

The babysitter came to court and testified to receiving a call from Kim as well as two calls from a person named 'Paul.' There were phone records introduced which showed that Rademaker used a phone that Kim had called regarding the photo shoot. After the prosecution had called their witnesses, they rested their case.

Then Defense wasted no time in calling on Brian as a witness. He testified that he believed he saw Kim being restrained by three big tattooed biker guys right near where her body was later found. He was definite and came across as a person who believed in what he was saying. On cross-examination, he wasn't as certain on the exact date and varied a little as to the location. However, the Defense was counting on him to be their ACE witness.

The Defense called several additional witnesses to cast some doubt on the stories told by Mona and Cheryl. All this testimony was vague, since the events had occurred over 12 years earlier and there were numerous inconsistencies as to when and what happened.

The Defense tried to explain away the recorded Pretext statement that Cheryl had obtained from the defendant. They tried to emphasize all the times Rademaker had said, "It was if it didn't happen." At no time did he come out and clearly state that he killed Kim.

But for the Defense to be able to totally attack the Pretext, it would be necessary for Rademaker to take the witness stand and explain what he really meant when he acknowledged that the burnt car belonged to the missing model.

For whatever reason, Rademaker refused to take the witness stand. Without him testifying, the jury would infer that what they heard on the tape was true. This was a big gamble on the part of the Defense. However, Rademaker was caught between a rock and a hard place. He was no dummy, and he didn't want to be cross-examined by the prosecutor. Tactically, it might have been a wise decision by the Defense, but it was going to limit what his Defense attorney would be able to say during the final Argument.

Both sides had put on all their evidence, and it was time for Argument. Pat Dixon argued for the prosecution and laid out the People's case. He relied on a slide show that fortified his oral Argument. He reviewed with the jury the testimony of Mona and Cheryl and showed the evidence that corroborated them. The strength of their testimony was that the burnt car belonged to the murder victim. However, what was vague was how the victim got to the area where she was killed. Mona was the one who said Rademaker had mentioned how he had anal sex with her before he drowned her.

In order to prove up the Special Circumstance of Kidnapping and Sodomy, the prosecution had to supply proof beyond a reasonable doubt that Rademaker did in fact kidnap or sodomize the victim. The Kidnapping was supported by the fact that bones were found a substantial distance from where Kim's car was parked. What became crucial was the fact that a handcuff key was found behind Kim's car that matched a pair of handcuffs that were found under Kim's bones. The inference was that Rademaker handcuffed Kim up by her car. Then he forcefully made her walk the short distance to where her body was found. Pat argued to the jury that, according to the jury instructions regarding Kidnapping, that would be sufficient movement to constitute a Kidnap.

Pat's argument for the Special Circumstance of Sodomy was that Kim's bra's straps had been cut with a knife. This would be consistent with a person trying to sodomize Kim from behind. The prosecution had put on a witness who testified that Rademaker preferred sodomy sex in place of vaginal sexual intercourse. The witness said that Rademaker had a nickname as 'Butt Buster.' Both Mona and Cheryl confirmed that Rademaker had claimed that he had killed Kim after he had anal sex with her just before he drowned her in the stream.

On the following graphic page are the slides that the prosecutor showed the jury about the elements required to prove Kidnap and Sodomy.

GRAPHICS 25

It was important for the jury to find that a felony was committed in the commission of the killing in order to prove First Degree Murder.

The prosecutor used these charts to show that there was a kidnapping and an act of sodomy.

KIDNAPPING

Person unlawfully and with physical force or fear carries away that person without consent, a distance that is substantial in character, is guilty of Kidnapping.

MOVEMENT OF VICTIM

Distance that is substantial in character

- Not slight or trivial
- Look at the totality of circumstances
  - Actual distance moved
  - Increased risk of harm
  - Decreased likelihood of detection
  - Increased danger to victim if tried to escape
  - Enhanced defendant's opportunity to commit additional crimes

SODOMY

Every person who participates in an act of sodomy when the act is accomplished against the victim's will by means of force, violence, duress, menace, or fear of immediate and unlawful bodily injury on the alleged victim, is guilty of the crime of unlawful sodomy.

"Sodomy" is sexual conduct of contact between the penis of one person and the anus of another person. Any sexual penetration, however slight, is sufficient to complete the crime of sodomy. Proof of ejaculation is not required.

When the Prosecution was finished with their Argument, Rademaker's Defense attorney didn't waste any time reminding the jury of Brian's testimony. The attorney with glee recited exactly what Brian said he saw, which was three biker dudes holding a handcuffed curly-haired blonde woman who looked like Kim next to a van very near where her body was ultimately found. With a broad brush, he tried to paint Mona and Cheryl as vindictive women who had it in for his client. He hammered on the jury instruction that discussed Reasonable Doubt and that Brian's testimony was a perfect example of such doubt.

During the prosecution Rebuttal Argument, Pat tried to let some air out of Defense's claim that 'The Big Bad Bikers Did It.' Pat tried to point out how illogical it was for people who kidnapped the victim to remain two more days within feet of where the victim's car was burned. Both sides had finished their Arguments, and it was time for the jury to commence their deliberation.

CHAPTER 16 RADEMAKER—DEATH PENALTY PHASE

The jury deliberated for several days and indicated that they had reached a verdict. When they were brought back into court, they announced that they had found Rademaker guilty of Murder in the First Degree. This was the good news for the prosecution, but the jurors had trouble with one of the special circumstances. They found that the Murder was committed during the commission of the crime of Kidnapping but not during the crime of Sodomy. The prosecution had all along known that both special circumstances were going to have to rely on what Rademaker had told Mona and Cheryl. For whatever reason, the jury didn't find the Sodomy allegation to be true.

Fortunately for the prosecution, the jury had at least found the Kidnap Special Circumstance true, which permitted the prosecution to continue to seek the Death Penalty. The jury was ordered to come back the next day to hear evidence for the penalty phase of the trial.

The Penalty phase is like a new trial while using the same jury. The next day, Pat gave a short Opening Statement explaining what evidence would be presented to the jury. The prosecution was mainly relying on the Aggravating nature of the Circumstances of the Crime. The prosecution called members of Kim's family to provide the Victim Impact evidence. Her mother explained how much she missed her daughter. Then Peter Pandelios testified how difficult it was to raise their son without Kim. Then the dramatic moment was when Kim's son Nicolas took the witness stand. He told how hard it was to grow up without having a mother. After the Victim Impact testimony, it was hard to find any dry eyes in the courtroom. Kim's family represented everything that was good about America, which was a far contrast from Rademaker, the registered Sex Offender, who was every parent's nightmare.

The prosecution had hoped to use Rademaker's prior felony convictions, for which he had gone to state prison. The law states that the prosecution can present evidence of a defendant's felony convictions as part of the evidence in the penalty phase of a trial. However, the appellate courts have ruled that the only prior convictions that can be used are those that occurred prior to the time the defendant committed the present offense. Rademaker's felony conviction involved the child abuse of Mona, which occurred several years after he had murdered Kimberly Pandelios.

The prosecution can present any **prior act of violence** committed by the defendant. The detectives were able to find a prior violent act involving Rademaker. It was a situation in which a prostitute had gone to Rademaker's house to have sex with him for money. When she went to the door and saw him, she had second thoughts of going into the house to have sex. When she hesitated, Rademaker grabbed her arm and tried to drag her inside the house. The prostitute was in fear for her life and pulled as hard as she could to break his grip on her wrist. He fell back and she took off running. The prosecution realized that the prostitute's testimony wasn't going to have too much impact on the jurors, but this was all the prosecution was able to come up with as to prior acts of violence by Rademaker.

The Defense presented witnesses who indicated that Rademaker had had a difficult childhood (it seems that you the reader have heard this one before). They called a psychiatrist, who tried to explain all the problems that Rademaker encountered in growing up. John Monaghan had a break in the other case he was trying in the other courthouse. He told his boss Pat Dixon that he was available to be back on the Rademaker case. John had recently had the opportunity to cross-examine a psychiatrist on similar issues.

He cross-examined Rademaker's psychiatrist and got her to admit things that were detrimental to the Defense. John's technique in questioning psychiatrists reveals his utter contempt for the excuses they give for their clients' antisocial behavior. By the time John had finished his cross-examination, the Defense had to wonder why they had ever called this psychiatrist.

Finally, the Penalty Phase of the trial was over and it was time for both sides to make their Argument. Although John had just come back, he was completely familiar with all the evidence that had been presented during this penalty stage. He used a slide show to walk the jurors through the evidence. One slide showed a scale with MITIGATION on the left side and AGGRAVATION on the right side.

First he discussed the Aggravating evidence, which he listed in three categories: Preying on Vulnerable; Brutal Manner of Killing; and finally, Victim Impact. John started discussing how Rademaker preyed on 14-year-old girls, getting them addicted to heroin and involved in torrid sexual activities.

John then moved on to talking about how Rademaker brutalized Kim. She was isolated in the forest with no one around to help her. She was sexually violated on a cold day on a hillside. Her last thoughts were that all she wanted to do was go home to her baby. She promised not to go to the police if only he would let her live to raise her son. The defendant's answer was to take her head and push it into the water to drown her.

John Monaghan ended his Argument discussing the Victim Impact. It wasn't merely Kim being a victim but her entire family and the hell they had lived through all these 14 years not knowing what happened to their loved one. Kim was robbed of being able to see her son grow up. But her son was robbed of having a mother to be with him as he was growing up. John stressed that the Aggravation in this case far outweighed the Mitigation, which was merely the defendant having a less-than-desirable childhood.

John finished his Argument by clicking on the screen a slide showing two photos of Kim with her dear son Nicolas. This was what John wanted the jurors to remember when they started to decide the defendant's fate.

The next graphic page shows the two slides the prosecution used in their Argument regarding the Death Penalty.

GRAPHICS 26

The prosecutor wanted to show that the Aggravating evidence outweigh the Mitigating evidence.

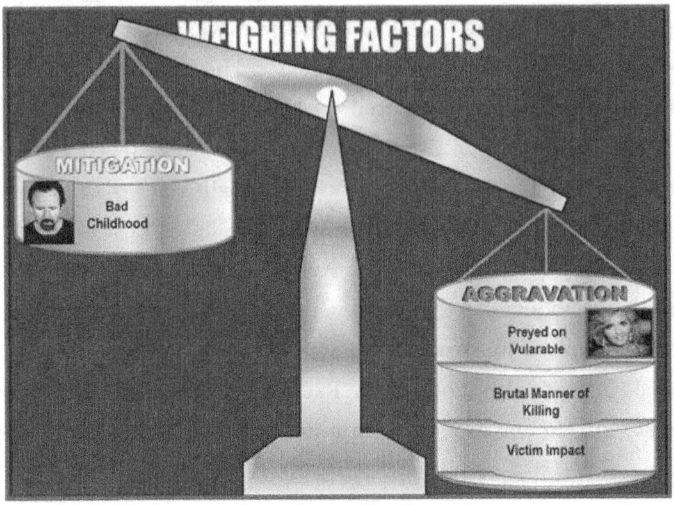

This was a Victim Impact exhibit used in the Penalty phase.

The Defense gave their Argument, which was to save Rademaker from the Death Penalty. They argued the concept of "Lingering Doubt." The prosecution knew that it would be hard to overcome the possibility that Rademaker might not have actually done the killing. The Defense continued to remind the jury that Brian had testified that he had seen Kimberly alive two days later being held by several bikers. He had always maintained that he was certain that it was Kimberly who he had seen in the same general area where her body was later found.

After the Defense had argued, the jury went out to deliberate. It took them a little over a day to come back with the verdict of Life Without the Possibility of Parole. This jury, with all the Victim Impact evidence and the callousness of the crime, was NOT persuaded to come back with a verdict of Death. In this case, Lingering Doubt won out over Victim Impact.

John disagreed with the verdict but accepted it. Was it the fact that he wasn't available to try the case from start to finish? We will never know. But John, aka True Grit, gave it all he could under the circumstances. He only hopes that he didn't let Kim's wonderful family down by not getting a Death Row address for David Rademaker.

Your author has had the opportunity to work with hundreds of attorneys in my 43-year career with the DA's Office. When I saw how John Monaghan and Pat Dixon basically did a tag-team job on the Rademaker case, I was amazed how well the two of them handled the incredible pressure of a Death Penalty case. Most attorneys would be begging for some type of continuance so they had sufficient time to prepare. However, there is a breed of human beings who quickly assess situations and respond by doing an unbelievable job in the limited amount of time available.

The answer may be that those individuals are incredibly brilliant, well trained, or intensely dedicated. However, it might be that they possess a sixth sense that sets them apart to accomplish incredible deeds. After working closely with both John Monaghan and Pat Dixon for years, I have learned that they are a rare breed of attorneys. I don't mean to sound like I am nominating them for a Nobel Prize or a possible sainthood, but they demonstrated an incredible talent for making sure that the murder victims aren't forgotten. I marveled how they never were too busy to try to make sure that JUSTICE WAS DONE.

CHAPTER 17 HILL—WHO'S CALLING?

January 12, 1994, Pomona Police Department dispatcher received a phone call at 5:13 a.m. It was a typical Wednesday morning. The caller told the dispatcher in a calm composed voice:

Caller: *I did it again.*

Dispatcher: *You did it again?*

Caller: *Yeah the* ***strangler****.*

Dispatcher: *The* ***strangler?***

Caller: *Yah. At uh, at San Antonio, San Antonio and D Street in Ontario.*

Dispatcher: *San Antonio and D Street in Ontario?*

Caller: *Yeah. At the park, on the grass, that's where I left her, good night.*

Dispatcher: *Ok...*

Caller: *I did um, what—what's this number five or six, I forget, but she's out there.*

Dispatcher: *Okay. Who is she?*

Caller: *I don't know.*

Dispatcher: *You don't know?*

Caller: *A prostitute.*

Dispatcher: *Oh.*

Caller: *Okay?*

Dispatcher: *Okay. Uhm, where—*

Caller: *Good Night.*

Dispatcher: *he left, he hung up.*

The caller hung up and the dispatcher was in total wonderment as to what she had just heard. What was she to do with this information? What did this all mean?

She sat there for a moment to collect her thoughts. As a dispatcher, she was used to callers who were so excited about reporting a gangland shooting or automobile accident they forgot to give sufficient information. With most calls that she received she knew exactly what to do. Her primary task was to figure out if she should transfer the caller to another authority or dispatch police units to a certain location.

This caller gave an address that wasn't even in her jurisdiction. San Antonio Park was in Ontario, several cities over from the City of Pomona. In other words, this wasn't her problem to worry about. She could contact Ontario Police Department and convey to them the information. The dispatcher had had calls in the past from pranksters and drunks who would report crazy bizarre things that were totally untrue. But could this all be a hoax? What seemed strange to her was the fact that the caller claimed to be 'the strangler.' She was aware that in the last two months in the Pomona area there were several prostitutes strangled. Could this phone call be related to those crimes?

As to this call, the dispatcher made several contacts as to some direction as to how the Pomona Police Department should respond. Then at 5:13 a.m. the phone rang in the dispatcher's room. When it was answered, the caller seemed irate and started complaining to the dispatcher:

Dispatcher: *Pomona Police Department*

Caller: *What's taking so long to get over there?*

Dispatcher: *Pardon?*

Caller: *San Antonio and D Street.*

Dispatcher: *Okay. What—what did you say? What's taking so long to get over there?*

Caller: *Yeah.*

Dispatcher: *Okay. What —what do you mean, sir?*

Caller: *Y' all better catch me before I kill again.*

Dispatcher: *Are you—*

Caller: *Good Night.*

Dispatcher —are you watching the . . .

The dispatcher recognized the caller as the same as the original caller. Ontario Police Department was informed of this second call and immediately dispatched units to San Antonio Park.

The responding officers didn't know what to be looking for. Since it was still early morning, the park appeared dark and gloomy. No person could be seen anywhere in the play area or the picnic table section. Since the caller used the term that he was the 'strangler' and said that there was a body in the park, the officer exited his unit and did a quick scan of the grassy area. He couldn't see any figure that looked like a dead body. Then he used his flashlight like a beacon to illuminate shadowy areas. This city park is wide open, without any fences surrounding it, and consists of fields of grassy areas.

The officer had to trade personas and try to think like a 'strangler.' Where would such a person place a dead body? His first reaction was the body must be around the picnic tables because that was where the gang members hung out. As the officer was shining his flashlight in the picnic area, other officers arrived and they moved over to the baseball diamond as others went to the restroom building. Eventually one of the officers was shining his flashlight near several pine trees when he stopped to get a better look. All that officer could see was a shadowy figure of what looked like a woman lying down on the grass area. He directed the beam from his flashlight toward the head of the subject. He could see that it was a female lying face down. She had on a full-size blue blouse as well as a blue jacket. Her lime-green skirt was pulled up, exposing her crotch and bare legs.

At first, the officer called out to the woman to see if she had passed out or was sleeping something off. Since it was during the dead of winter, the officer couldn't fathom a live person lying exposed in the middle of the park. When he heard no response, he stepped up closer to the woman, shining his bright flashlight on her face hoping to see some sign of breathing. The body lay perfectly still. What caught the officer's attention was the fact that there was a blue cloth that seemed to be tied around her neck. The officer cautiously approached and could see long corn rows of her hair that seemed to be entangled in the knot of the cloth around her neck.

The officer slowly stepped backward as his eyes focused on what now he believed was a dead body. He notified his fellow officers as to his finding and asked them to join him between the baseball diamond and the tennis court in the middle of the park. Within moments, he was surrounded by other officers as they all stared at the motionless body. By this time, everyone was numb from the bitter cold and the horrible sight of a human being who had been strangled to death. What did this all mean? Then the word came not to touch the body and to preserve the area around the body as a crime scene.

After an hour or more, a detective arrived and took over the investigation. He tried to make an assessment of what this all suggested. The victim was a middle-aged black female who had been strangled. Since the victim had her skirt pulled up to the point that the detective could see that she had no panties on exposing her private parts, the natural inference was that she was a victim of some type of sexual assault. His next observation was that she had the sticky portion of what looked like duct tape around her ankles area as well as on her face. When he examined her fingernails, there appeared to be something under several of them. It appeared that the victim had been in some type of struggle.

As the detective was making the observations, his mind was trying to remember what he had been told about the recently named '60 Freeway Slayer.' He was aware of a number of bodies being found in the neighboring cities of Pomona, Diamond Bar, and Chino, which formed a corridor along the 60 Freeway. Those victims were black prostitutes who had been strangled. His next thought was, could this be the work of the '60 Freeway Slayer'? Could this victim be a prostitute?

There was no purse or any form of identification on or around the victim. How could he find out who this victim was? If she was a prostitute, it might take weeks before someone would put out a missing person report on her. Maybe her fingerprints would reveal her identity, especially if she had been arrested for prostitution.

The detective didn't know for certain what he had, but he wanted to talk to any one of the detectives who were involved with the '60 Freeway Slayer' cases. Had the other cities had a phone call announcing where to find their dead women? When the caller said this was number five or six, the detective had to believe that this had to be some type of serial killer even if it wasn't connected to the '60 Freeway Slayer.'

Then the detective got busy assigning others to search every inch of the park before the park goers converged on the park with the morning joggers and exercise buffs. The searchers were told to look for any pieces of the blue cloth that was used to strangle her. They also were alerted to look for pieces of duct tape.

After several hours of searching, nothing worth noting was found. Other searchers scoured the adjoining streets to look for possible pay phones that the suspect could have used to call the police. It had to be close enough so the caller had a clear view of the park and could see that the police had not arrived at the location. It wasn't long before someone found a pay phone nearby and right below it was a strip of duct tape lying underneath. Was this something relevant to the case or not? It was photographed, and the duct tape was carefully placed in an evidence bag to be analyzed if needed.

The next day an autopsy was conducted where the blue cloth was cut off around the victim's neck. Since it was so intertwined with her dreadlocks, several of them were cut off and saved. After the cloth was removed from her neck, there was a clear strangle mark that went around her neck. This line was very clear and deep, and the coroner had no difficulty classifying that the cause of death was strangulation.

The coroner's office took several swabs from the victim's vaginal area and placed them in separate vials to be saved in a so-called rape kit. This was1994, and law enforcement was just beginning to use DNA as a forensic tool. The DNA databases were very limited, and one could say that scientists still had their doubts about DNA becoming a useful forensic tool. (This was one year before the O. J. Simpson murder trial, in which the public became acquainted with DNA evidence.)

The other detectives who were working on their own '60 Freeway Slayer' cases were most interested in hearing all the details about this case in Ontario. The information came in that the victim had a hard-luck story, and some believed that she was using prostitution to support her drug habit. They agreed to add this new case to the list of five other murder cases. However, the wrinkle with this new case was that it had occurred just over the county line in San Bernardino County. This meant that the local police department couldn't turn the case over to the Los Angeles County Sheriff's Department, which worked the serial crime cases that take place within their own county.

Whoever was going to head up the investigation had to recognize this was a hot-button type case. For years, the news media liked to criticize law enforcement for not being more aggressive in solving the 'black prostitute rape-murder cases.' The news media tried to make it look as though law enforcement doesn't value the lives of **black prostitutes**. This feeds the narrative that 'Black Lives don't matter' in the eyes of the police.

However, those critics don't factor in why these cases are so factually difficult to solve. I, the author, have worked on many 'Black Prostitute Serial Killer' cases and have learned firsthand why these cases are so perplexing. Before DNA became a forensic tool, I worked on the case of ***People vs. Louis Craine*** which was called 'Southside Slayer' case. This 1988 case involved an unemployed black male who murdered at least four black female prostitutes. The only evidence we had against Craine was statements he had originally made to the police which he later retracted. We had to use the defendant's family to corroborate the statements. It was a tough case, and eventually prosecutor John Watson, in 1989, was able to convict Craine and get him placed on Death Row. The judge at time of sentencing said, "The victims fought frantically for their lives . . . and he manually strangled each of them to death and discarded their bodies in abandoned houses, vacant lots, and an alley like so much trash."

Also, I worked on the first trial of the case of ***People vs. Michael Hughes***, the so-called 'Southland Slayer,' for killing four women. In that case, the jury didn't recommend the Death Penalty. However, several years later Hughes was connected to three more rape-murders by the use of DNA analysis. This time he was prosecuted by Beth Silverman, who was able to get him convicted, and this time the jury agreed on the Death Penalty. Hughes' signature act on his victims was to leave them with their legs spread apart, showing their pubic area. It was unknown why he did it, but the detectives believed he wanted to shock whoever found the body as well as to try to demean the victim.

When the case of ***People vs. Chester Turner***, also called the 'Southside Slayer,' came along, my job was trying to organize all 10 murder cases so a jury could understand all the evidence. Tuner was thought to be the most prolific black prostitute murderer. Bobby Grace was the prosecutor on this first case, which resulted in Turner receiving the Death Penalty. However, a few years later DNA testing connected him to four more rape-murder cases. This time it was prosecutor Beth Silverman who got the jury to again give Turner the Death Penalty. At time of the sentencing, one of the family members made an astute comment when she said,

"He will never be around to do anything to anyone else again, and thank God for the modern technology that helped convict him."

Just as Turner was convicted, the DA's Office was faced with another similar case, ***People vs. Lonnie Franklin Jr.*** 'Grim Sleeper,' for the killing of at least ten women. Again, Beth Silverman prosecuted this case and got him convicted. The jury recommended he receive the Death Penalty. When he was arrested, a search warrant was obtained for his house, where the detectives uncovered hidden in his house nearly 1,000 photos of women or teenage girls, many nudes, some of whom appeared to be unconscious or dead. The scary part is that many of those depicted have never been identified and may be additional murder victims.

What I learned from all these cases was how the news media likes to hammer law enforcement. The media will constantly run headlines claiming that the law enforcement had a 'blind eye' to all these murder victims just because they were black. Unfortunately, what the news media knows but glosses over is that these cases are inherently difficult to solve because the prostitutes work alone at night in dark, isolated locations. There are seldom any eyewitnesses around, and if there are, they are pimps or other prostitutes who don't want to talk to the police. Until DNA came along, prostitute killings were very difficult to solve whether the victim was black or white.

In 1993 and 1994, DNA was on the horizon and samples were collected. But the obstacle was that the DNA databases were very limited. In the '60 Freeway Slayer' cases, the police obtained vaginal samples from all the victims, but there were no DNA matches to anyone who was in the DNA databases. Month after month and then eventually year after year, this case remained unsolved. By that time, it had turned into a decade that had gone by without a suspect being charged.

In the meantime, considerable activity was going on that would eventually reveal that the culprit was a person by the name of Ivan Hill. It all started when Hill was convicted as an accomplice in a Glendora liquor store holdup on January 24, 1979, in which a man was killed. Since this was a robbery and someone was killed, the felony murder rule applied and Ivan Hill was convicted of murder and was sentenced to state prison. By February of 1993, Hill was released from prison. It wasn't until October 1993 that he began committing the murders that became labeled the '60 Freeway Slayer'. The last murder occurred in February 1994. Shortly after that, he committed a number of robberies for which he was arrested in March 1994 and placed in custody. He was convicted and sentenced in 1994 to a new term in state prison. Before Ivan Hill was to be released on the robbery convictions, the Department of Corrections took a sample of Hill's DNA and had it listed in the statewide DNA database.

In September of 2002, the Los Angeles County Sheriff's Department started to reexamine many of their 'cold cases.' The detectives pulled the Betty Harris case from September 1993 and submitted the vaginal swabs for DNA testing. In March of 2003, the detectives received the word that the DNA on Harris' vaginal swab came back a match to Ivan Hill. This was shortly before he was about to be released from state prison. As a result, samples from the other victims of the so-called '60 Freeway Slayer' were sent in for testing and compared to the sample from Ivan Hill.

CHAPTER 18 HILL—THANK GOD FOR DNA

In 2004, big things were happening in the world of DNA. Back in 1994, the OJ Simpson case had introduced the American public to the fact that DNA could be used to connect an accused to a crime. At that time, law enforcement had to obtain a DNA exemplar from the suspect either by consent or by the use of a search warrant. Then law enforcement could see the potential for solving 'cold cases' if they had a large enough database to compare to evidence that had been collected at crime scenes.

Nowhere was there more excitement about the forensic use of DNA than in the area of rape and sexual assault cases. In these types of crimes, the suspect often ejaculates, leaving a calling card in the form of his DNA in the victim's vagina or on the panties. The logical conclusion was that if the DNA of sexual predators or sex offenders were placed in a database, then that could be used to compare with evidence obtained from new unsolved sex cases.

A DNA database of 'criminal types' seemed like a good idea, since it would catch criminals (rapists) before they commit additional crimes (rapes) in the future. However, the Right to Privacy groups said, "Wait, not so fast." Law enforcement has not obtained any search warrant for the accused's DNA. Therefore, placing a person's DNA in a database to be used in future unsolved cases is a violation of unreasonable search and seizure and an invasion of the Right of Privacy.

Many liberal groups fought vigorously to prevent any type of DNA database from being created or ever used to catch criminals. Also, there were conservative groups who looked upon a DNA database as a government incursion into everyone's private life. The question was, would all these liberal and conservative groups be able to fight off the DNA tsunami that was about to change the world of fighting crime?

The sexual assault groups and the Victim's Rights groups had logic on their side. For over a hundred years, fingerprints were collected and stored by the FBI and other state agencies. Those stored fingerprints were used to compare to latent prints that had been collected at crime scenes. The public had accepted the fact that everyone who was arrested had his fingerprints rolled for identification purposes. The side benefit was that those prints were afterward stored by law enforcement agencies. When there were future crimes, law enforcement would refer back to the old fingerprint cards to see if there was a match.

I, the author, was involved with the creation of the statewide fingerprint database (Cal ID), in which we used computers to store the fingerprint data. In that way, all the fingerprints from LAPD, LASO, and any law enforcement agency in the state had everyone's fingerprints who had ever been arrested by any of the agencies. The liberal and conservative groups either were asleep or didn't realize how the computer was going to change the fight against crime.

However, when it came to DNA, the liberal and conservative groups were awake but they were up against Women's groups who saw the potential for saving thousands of women from being raped if only there was a DNA database. The 2003-4 years were the battle years. Several years earlier, Congress enacted a federal law that required any federal parolee to provide a blood sample for a national DNA database used to solve crime. Most of the federal circuit courts went along with it, except for the 9th Circuit of Appeal, in which a three-justice panel objected to the use of a DNA database.

The justices who objected were Justice Stephen Reinhardt and two other justices, who held that parolees couldn't be required to provide a blood sample whose results could be placed in a database. Eventually, in August 2004, the full 9th Circuit Court of Appeal disagreed with the first findings and ruled that a parolee could be required to submit a blood sample to be taken for DNA testing and the results placed in a national DNA database.

After the full panel reversed Judge Reinhardt's original holding, he said, ". . . all Americans are at risk of having our DNA samples permanently placed on file in federal cyberspace. Even governments with benign intentions have proved unable to regulate or use wisely vast stores of information they collect regarding their citizens." Other justices who opposed DNA databases said, "It is important to recognize that the 4th Amendment intrusion here is not primarily the taking of the blood, but seizure of the DNA fingerprint and its inclusion in a searchable database."

The dissenting justices continued to complain how a DNA database would destroy American's freedom. One claimed, "The Bill of Rights restrains government power, including law enforcement efficiency. In a world unrestrained by our 4th Amendment, every citizen, convicted or not, might be forced to supply a DNA sample. More crimes would undoubtedly be solved . . . but that is not the world Mr. Madison and the First Congress created for us.

Some predicted that bad things would result from the opinion of the 9th Circuit's ruling allowing DNA databases by saying, "The ruling establishes the legal groundwork for the government to take DNA samples from the general population. What this opinion by the 9th Circuit does is really a dangerous thing. It just becomes a slippery slope. Where do you stop?"

However, the majority of the 9th Circuit held that parolees have only limited rights of privacy and can be forced to give blood samples even if there is no specific reason to suspect they are involved in additional crimes. The court went on to say, "Taking a blood sample is only a minimal intrusion that is justified by the need to keep society safe. The DNA program helps minimize the pain and suffering recidivist offenders sow in our communities."

On November 2, 2004, Californians voted by 62% margin to approve a DNA database. Proposition 69 required the collection of DNA samples from all felons, and from adults and juveniles arrested for or charged with specified crimes. The DNA samples must be submitted to the state's DNA database.

After the passage of Proposition 69, there were numerous attacks indicating that it was unconstitutional. Then in 2013 the U.S. Supreme Court ruled in the opinion of ***Maryland v. King*** that a similar DNA law in Maryland was a valid form of police identification of suspects, analogous to fingerprinting and photographing.

The California Supreme Court is in the process of deciding whether to follow the appellate court decision in ***People v. Mark Buza***, which ruled: We conclude that the DNA Act, to the extent it requires felony arrestees to submit a DNA sample for law enforcement analysis and inclusion in the state and federal DNA databases, without independent suspicion, a warrant or even a judicial or grand jury determination of probable cause, unreasonably intrudes on such arrestees' expectation of privacy and is invalid under the Fourth Amendment of the United States Constitution.

In the Ivan Hill situation, he was arrested and convicted for various robberies within a month of the last victim being killed. While he was in prison, a DNA sample was taken from him and its results placed in the state's DNA database. In 2002, the LASD had Brenda Baker's vaginal swab tested and the result was sent to the state's DNA database. When her swab was run against the database, it came up with a match to Ivan Hill.

After LASD ran the other victims and received confirmation that they also matched Ivan Hill, the homicide detectives took the case to the DA's Office for the filing of a criminal complaint. On November 3, 2003, the DA's Office filed six counts of murder on Ivan Hill. Since this was a year before Proposition 69 was passed, the legality of the DNA sample taken from Ivan Hill was based on the fact that DNA samples could be taken from anyone serving a sentence in state prison. Therefore the '60 Freeway Slayer' case wasn't affected by the controversy regarding samples from arrestees that weren't convicted felons.

Back in 2003, the DA's Office had what was called a DNA Coordinator who oversaw the cases relying on DNA evidence. She didn't prosecute each of the cases involving DNA issues, but she tried to provide uniformity of filing of such cases and to provide advice as to how to handle all the myriad of motions that the Defense attorneys filed in every DNA case. The DA administrators recognized that this Ivan Hill serial murderer case was going to require a top-level prosecutor. Not only were there going to be cutting-edge technology issues but the DA, Steve Cooley, made it quite clear that this case merited the Death Penalty.

The DA's Office had tried to train several deputies to specialize in the DNA cases; however, there was no one in the department at the time to take on the complexity involved in the Ivan Hill case. The DA administrators turned to **Major Crimes Division** to absorb such a heavyweight case. The 'King of the Death Penalty' was John Monaghan. The attitude was, why not just add this case to the long list of cases he was working on? The belief was that Death Penalty cases take forever to get to trial and maybe someone else could be assigned to this case during the interim.

The DA administrators didn't quite comprehend what they had done. Once John sinks his teeth into a case, he thoroughly prepares it the way he thinks it should be tried. Once he assimilates the facts of the case, he determines the best way to handle the DNA issues. Back in 2003, the Defense attorneys in DNA cases were demanding all sorts of records from the Crime Labs in hopes of finding some crack in the crime labs' procedures. At that time, the Certification of the crime lab became a big issue for the Defense. In order to comply with the Defense discovery request, it could take weeks for the crime lab personnel to find and copy all the documentation the Defense attorneys were demanding. This would bog down the crime lab in trying to comply with the endless requests from the Defense attorneys.

The DA's DNA Coordinator had her way of handling these discovery requests, and John had his expeditious way of doing it. To put it mildly, John and the DNA Coordinator clashed. Yet a better way to describe the disagreement would be to imagine the finale of all the Fourth of July fireworks shows, the Sydney New Year's fireworks, the Beijing Olympics fireworks all going off at the same time. The fallout wasn't pretty. Over time, things subsided, and undoubtedly everyone learned a lesson. Most of all, the DA's administrators discovered that placing two strong personalities together in a centrifuge situation can cause the equivalent of an atomic explosion that may take years to settle.

John Monaghan was a litigator who understood the thinking of jurors. He recognized that it was going to be next to impossible to get 12 jurors to impose the Death Penalty strictly on the basis of the results of DNA tests. His belief was that, as great and wondrous as DNA was, there has to be something more to convince a jury to convict and go the next step of recommending that the accused should die for what he did.

This is where John went the extra mile: he was determined to find something besides the DNA results to prove to the jury that the defendant committed the murders. He started looking at each of those murders to see what *other evidence* could link Hill to those killings. Back in 1994, when Hill was arrested for the robberies, they found in his wallet various business cards which referred to sites near where some of the bodies were discovered. This needed to be explored to see how useful it could be in supplying corroboration.

Another piece of evidence that came to the detectives' attention was a letter that Ivan Hill had written to his cousin explaining that he knew he would eventually be connected to all the murders. This wasn't as good as a smoking gun, but it showed the defendant's mindset that he eventually would be found out. The other thing that the detectives needed to do was see if anyone could identify Ivan Hill's voice on the tape of the call that was made to the Pomona dispatcher on January 12, 1994. Could anyone recognize the voice on the tape? Another possible corroboration might be revealed by the type of knots the killer used to strangle the victims. John had examined all the knots from the ligatures to see if they were all the same.

In August of 2004, it was time for the preliminary hearing in the case. John called the necessary witnesses to testify to each killing. He could use the detectives to testify to much of the facts, since hearsay evidence is permitted to be introduced at a preliminary hearing before a magistrate who is a judge. However, there were certain witnesses he wanted to put on the witness stand to see how well they would do testifying in a courtroom setting. He brought in two women who had claimed it was Ivan Hill's voice on the Pomona Police Department dispatcher tape. Since ten years had elapsed, the question was how definite would they be?

What John learned was that one witness was terrific and said that she had no doubt the voice was that of Ivan Hill. However, to his surprise the other woman got cold feet when she had to testify in open court in front of the defendant. Her answers turned from definite to "That it sounds like him but I can't be certain." Originally, when she listened to the tape, she was absolutely certain it was her old friend's voice. John was glad this came up during the preliminary hearing and wasn't in front of a jury. He could try to have the detectives find someone else to identify Hill's voice, or have this witness reconsider her change in testimony.

The Defense attorney didn't put on any witnesses or evidence but seemed more focused on objecting to the DNA sample that Hill was required to provide while a state prisoner. The Defense attorney's only hope was to have the judge throw out the DNA evidence, since the other evidence connecting Hill to the murder victims was extremely weak. The magistrate wasn't about to toss out the DNA evidence and allow Hill to walk out of the court a free man. The question of the legality of requiring a prisoner to supply a DNA sample, the magistrate ruled, was an issue for the appellate courts. Hill's attorney had a good argument, but it wasn't going to prevent the magistrate from holding Hill to answer to the charges.

After the preliminary hearing, it took two long years before the Hill case would be ready for trial. There were endless challenges regarding the DNA. If the Defense lost the DNA battles, their next line of attack was the mental and emotional health of the defendant. They made a concerted effort to find psychological experts who would say that Hill didn't have the intent to kill or ability to premeditate and deliberate the murders because of mental disabilities.

CHAPTER 19 HILL—TIME FOR TRIAL

In October of 2006, the jury selection for the trial began. This is where John has an uncanny ability to size up potential jurors. He first scrutinizes the jurors' questionnaires and rates their answers. When it comes time to voir dire the jurors in open court, John doesn't waste time with the standard questions. He has specific questions he wants to ask based on their answers to the questionnaire. Sometimes John isn't as interested in the juror's answer to his questions, but he may be more interested in the manner in which the juror answers the question. John looks at all the jurors and divides them into two groups: either 'leaders' or 'followers.' Some potential jurors have strong personalities and often become the foreperson or the ones who do most of the talking. Those are the jurors that John is most concerned about. The 'follower' types are not as much of a concern since they are generally influenced by the 'leader' types.

During the jury selection both sides used several of their peremptory challenges, and the final composition of the jury was six men and six women. When Judge Fiddler asked John if the 'People' wished to make an Opening Statement, he replied in a fervent voice, "Yes we do, your Honor." John stood up and walked over to the lectern, and his first words were that he wanted to thank the jurors for their service. He stated, "You are the conscience of the community and it will be you who decide this case."

Since this case involved six counts of murder, he wanted the jurors to become familiar with the various victims' names and the locations where their bodies were found. In order to orientate the jurors, he used a PowerPoint slide show instead of his poster board visual aids. He felt that since there were so many murders involved, a slide show was a more effective way to convey all that information to the jury.

When he clicked the remote control his first slide projected on the screen mounted on the courtroom wall. That slide showed the victim's name, the date of the crime, as well as the city where it occurred. After he had familiarized the jury as to the murder charges, he went on to the next slide, which was a map pinpointing each of the locations where the victims' bodies were found. By glancing at that graphic, the jury could see why the case had been named the '60 Freeway Slayer,' since all the locations were on either side of the 60 Freeway, which starts in downtown Los Angeles and runs east all way to the desert near Palm Springs.

On the following graphics page are the charges in the '60 Freeway Slayer' case as well as a map showing where all the victims' bodies were found.

GRAPHICS 27

This slide gave a summary of the various facts of each murder.

PEOPLE v. IVAN J. HILL KA064034					
Ct.	**Charge**	**Date**	**Victim**	**Location**	**Cause/Death**
1	Murder	11/01/93	Betty Harris	Diamond Bar	Manual Strangled
2	Murder	11/05/93	Roxanne Bates	Chino	Ligature Strangulation
3	Murder	11/14/93	Helen Hill	Walnut	Ligature Strangulation
4	Murder	11/16/93	Donna Goldsmith	Pomona	Ligature Strangulation
5	Murder	12/30/93	Cheryl Sayers	Pomona	Ligature Strangulation
6	Murder	01/12/94	Debra Brown	Ontario	Ligature Strangulation
SPECIAL CIRCUMSTANCES: Multiple Murder – PC 190.2(a)(3);					

This was a map used to show the various locations of the murders.

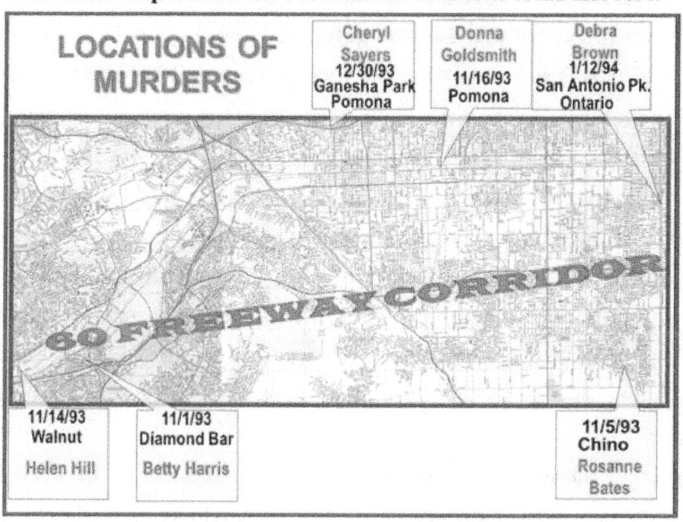

After giving them the big picture, he started to fill in the details to each of the six murders. He explained that Betty Harris's body was discovered in Diamond Bar shortly before 5:00 a.m. on November 1, 1993. The night before, Harris had brought the youngest of her four children to her sister's home in Pomona for a visit. She told two girlfriends that she would be back in an hour and left on foot for the store. She was never seen alive again. Harris had grown up in Pomona and attended Chaffey College in nearby Upland. John went on to say that she had been beaten and had sustained head injuries. However, the cause of death was manual strangulation, in which the killer had pressed his hands around her neck to prevent blood to flow to her brain and to stop her from breathing. This type of death requires considerable premeditation and deliberation. He showed the jury various photos of Harris' body lying in a parking lot between two large warehouses.

As John was finishing up with the first victim, there was a slight interruption as there was a gasp coming from the spectator section. Two women started crying and sobbing to the point that everyone was looking at them. Both got up from the hard-wooden benches and turned toward the exit. One of the women was clutching a handkerchief covering her face. The other woman continued to cry as she placed her hands over her ears in an attempt to block from hearing what had happened to her loved one. Both made it to the door and left the courtroom. John had warned the victims' family members that he was going to show photos of their loved ones. He explained that it was necessary for the jury to see what the defendant had done to their family member. Even with such warnings, the relatives thought they could handle it, but when they saw their sister or daughter with a ligature around their necks they were overcome by emotions.

Without missing a beat from the distraction, John moved on to the next victim as he clicked on the next slide of his presentation. This victim was Roxanne Bates (31). Her body was found on November 5, 1993, lying lifelessly on the shoulder area of a roadway in an agricultural area near a dairy farm in Chino. He supplied some basic facts about her life and then explained that her cause of death was ligature strangulation.

Moving right along the prosecutor said that count three involved the death of Helen Hill (35) (No relationship to the defendant), whose partially clothed body was found about 10:00 a.m. on November 14, 1993, in the parking lot of an industrial complex in the City of Walnut, which borders the City of Industry. She had been partying at the Elks Lodge in Pomona. Her cause of death was from two ligatures. One was made of cloth and the other made with a twine material. Her face appeared to be covered with duct tape and her hands were tied behind her back, also with duct tape.

The fourth count involved Donna Goldsmith (35) who was found dead on November 16, 1993, in a parking lot of a Pomona industrial complex. She had been married for 20 years and raised three children while working as a medical technician. Cause of death was ligature strangulation, and there were multiple ligatures. Some duct tape was found that had lipstick on it that came from her. Some wadded-up duct tape was found in a nearby trash dumpster. Her hands also were tied behind her back.

It all seemed so repetitive for the jury, as John started speaking about Cheryl Sayers (35), whose body was discovered in Pomona's Ganesha Park on December 30, 1993. Her body was found in the middle of a grassy area of the park by an elderly man looking for bottles and cans. Likewise, her cause of death was ligature strangulation.

After hearing about and seeing pictures of five women found dead in industrial parks and now a park, the jury seemed numb and unemotional. Some may have been reflecting on lofty ideals they had always held. Others had a blank stare as though their minds were in wonderment thinking, "This sounds like a ***Jack the Ripper*** case. I thought they never caught him?" John must have felt that the jurors had enough and didn't want to hear any more.

John knew he had to tell them about one more, so he clicked on his next slide and the name Debora Brown came up, showing it as another woman's body in a park. In order to prevent the jurors from zoning out, John quickly went over the facts that her body was found in the San Antonio Park in neighboring Ontario. Again, her cause of death was ligature strangulation. He related that there was glue on her face from the duct tape. He talked about the killer calling from a pay phone and some duct tape found on the ground under the phone.

On the following graphics page, shows photos where the victims' were found. Also shown is the pay phone with duct tape below it.

GRAPHICS 28

John was glad the slide presentation was completed and most likely the jurors were even more relieved that they didn't have to look at any more dead bodies. John wanted the jurors to understand that all of these deaths were deliberate and premeditated, since killing by strangulation takes considerable time to complete. The killer has plenty of time to reflect on what he is doing, compared to pulling a trigger of a gun, which takes less than a nanosecond to kill someone.

The prosecutor reiterated that the defendant, Ivan Hill, was connected to all of the murders by the fact that vaginal swabs and in some cases, panties had been analyzed and found to contain his DNA. John went over the DNA procedure to show how reliable it is. Then he finished up by talking about the corroborating evidence to support the DNA findings.

By the time the prosecutor had ended his Opening Statement, the jurors were sitting back in their chairs and some had their arms folded in front of them. They didn't seem to be looking with a sympathetic eye toward the defendant. If looks could kill, Ivan Hill would have been on a gurney at the coroner's office awaiting an autopsy to see if there was any HEART in his body.

When the Defense attorney stood up at counsel table and walked to the lectern that was the first time the jurors got a good look at the defendant, who sat motionless in his chair, staring straight ahead. The Defense attorney started out in her Opening Statement by saying that her client had in fact killed those women, BUT it wasn't as the way the prosecutor had described.

Some of the jurors had a surprised look on their faces, like, "Did I hear that right?" The attorney went on to say that her client was in a downward spiral of drug addiction at the time of the crimes, which she characterized as 'compulsive' rather than carefully thought out behavior. She went on and said, "Without deliberation, it is not a first-degree murder."

As if she was trying to gain some sympathy, she said, "Mr. Hill had lost 50 pounds and spent $3,000 on drugs in only a few weeks." This was an interesting strategy that the Defense was using. She was gambling that the jury would find the defendant guilty of six second-degree murders, thereby eliminating the Special Circumstances allegation that makes it a Death Penalty case. The legal wording of the Multi-murder Special Circumstances requires that at least one of the murders has to be found to be first degree.

Since the Statute of Limitation for rape had run, the prosecution could not rely on the felony murder rule to elevate these murders to the level of first degree. That was why the prosecutor spent so much of his Opening Statement explaining to the jurors that the act of strangulation takes so long that the killer has more than enough time to reflect on what he is doing. The prosecution had to rely on Deliberation and Premeditation in order to prove the murders were of the first degree.

After the Opening Statements by both sides, the prosecution started calling his witnesses. Proving up each of the murders required a number of witnesses. The prosecutor spent considerable time laying the foundation for the DNA collection by the coroner; the transportation of the samples to the labs; running the tests; obtaining a result; the meaning of the result; and the likely probability it is the same as the DNA of the defendant.

This becomes a tedious procedure. John wanted to simplify it, and he used several visuals he showed the witnesses. One was a photo of the **Sexual Assault Kit** showing the various vaginal swabs and that everything was connected by a designated number. The other exhibit was the **Table of DNA Analysis Results**, which showed the test numbers from the vaginal swabs and the one of the defendant. The jurors could see that all the numbers were consistent. At the bottom of the exhibit was the **Frequency of Occurrence Estimates**. In the Betty Harris killing, the jurors could see that a similar person having the same DNA would be 1 out of 604 trillion. Since Ivan Hill is black, the statistic for blacks is used. With that number being so high, it would be safe to say there was nobody else in the world with that same DNA.

The following graphics page shows the exhibits that were used to show the DNA results.

GRAPHICS 29

This was an exhibit showing the items in one of the Kits.

SEXUAL ASSAULT KIT

Sexual Assault Kit No.: 1174

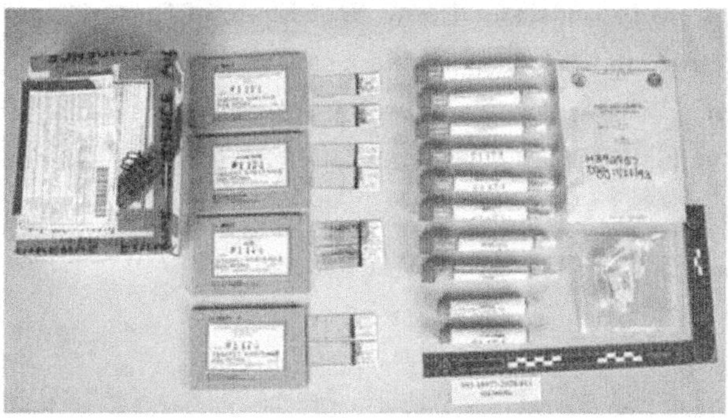

This illustrated the DNA results from the vaginal swab of one of the victims.

TABLE OF DNA ANALYSIS RESULTS

Count 1: Victim Betty Harris

SAMPLE ID	D3S1358	VWA	FGA	AMEL	D8S1179	D21S11	D18S51	D5S818	D13S317	D7S820	D16S539	TH01	TPOX	CSF1PO
006-302-C1/M Vaginal/Male	15, 16	16, 17	24	XY	14	30, 31	12, 17	11,12	11,13	11, 12	11	6, 8	8	10, 12
006-302-C1/E Vaginal/Male	15, 17	15	19, 23 (24)	X	9, 12 (14)	30, 32 (31)	12, 19 (17)	11, 12	12, 13	9, 11	9, 10 (11)	7, 9.3	6, 11 (8)	10, 11
006-302-C2/M Ext. gen. Male	15, 16	16, 17	24	XY	14	30, 31	12, 17	11, 12	11, 13	11, 12	11	6, 8	8	10, 12
006-302-C2/E Ext. gen Epithelial	15, 16 (17)	16, 17 (15)	24 (19)	X>Y	14 (9)(12)	30, 31 (32)	12, 17 (19)	11, 12	11, 13, (12)	11, 12 (9)	11 (9)	6, 8 (7)(9.3)	8 (6)(11)	10, 12 (11)
006-302-C Harris Reference	15, 17	15	19, 23	X	9, 12	30, 32	12, 19	11, 12	12, 13	9, 11	9, 10	7, 9.3	6, 11	10, 11
006-302-101 Hill Reference	15, 16	16, 17	24	XY	14	30, 31	12, 17	11, 12	11, 13	11, 12	11	6, 8	8	10, 12

FREQUENCY OF OCCURRENCE ESTIMATES

SAMPLE	CAUCASIAN	HISPANIC	BLACK
006-302-C1/M (Male fraction from vaginal sample) **1 out of**	300 Trillion	55 Trillion	604 Trillion

Once the prosecutor was certain that the jurors understood the DNA evidence, he went on to discuss the corroborating evidence that the defendant was familiar with the areas where the bodies were found. Witnesses indicated that the defendant worked as a warehouseman in the area where some of the bodies were found. Generally, he worked as a forklift operator for one business or another. But the evidence that connected him most was what was found in his wallet when he was arrested. There were numerous business cards of businesses near where the bodies were found.

In order for the jurors to understand how close some of these businesses were, John had visuals prepared showing each business card and the location of the bodies. Although this evidence wasn't too damning, it provided just another piece of corroboration that Ivan Hill was aware of the vicinity where the bodies were recovered.

On the following graphics page are maps showing that Hill had connections with the various crime sites.

GRAPHICS 30

This visual showed that the defendant was familiar with the area where each body was found.

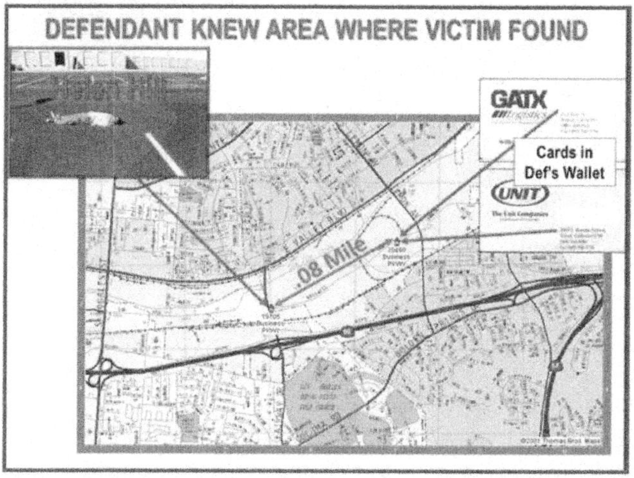

This visual showed that the defendant was familiar with the area where each body was found.

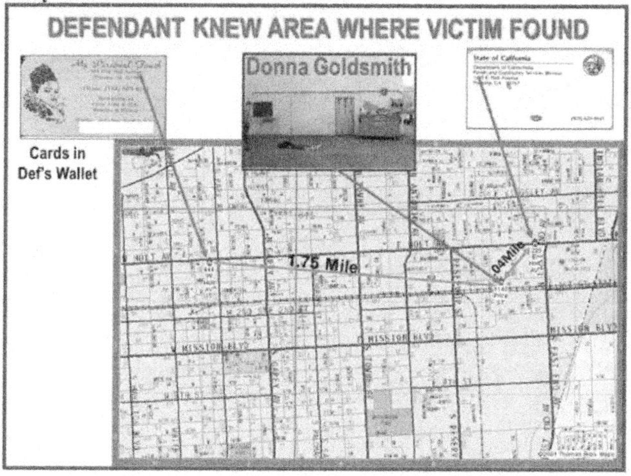

CHAPTER 20 HILL—OTHER EVIDENCE

The last '60 Freeway Slayer' murder occurred in January 1994. The following month, Ivan Hill was involved in a number of robberies in which law enforcement was able to convict him and send him back to state prison. While spending a decade in prison, he wrote a number of letters to his cousin from state prison. After a DNA sample was taken from him to be added to the state DNA database, he became concerned whether it would be somehow connected to the killings of these victims.

In one of those letters, he wrote to his cousin Tim on September 21, 2003, the following:

That was Debbie that worked with us at Siemens, not Diane. And yes, she was fine and still is. I ran into her in '83. We kicked it for a minute. But she was different from before. She was looking for someone to take care of her... So I kicked her to the curb. And went back to player status. That's when all hell broke loose which put my black ass where I am today. "Stuck like a Truck."

Another letter he wrote to his cousin Tim on September 29, 2003, stated the following:

As bad as my situation is, I'm still trying to keep my head up. Because all I can do now is handle it. I knew this day may come when they came with the DNA samples.

Granted, these letters weren't an outright admission, but they provided some corroboration showing his concern about the DNA samples.

The following graphics page shows portions of the letters he wrote his cousin.

GRAPHICS 31

This exhibit showed parts of the letter the defendant wrote to his cousin.

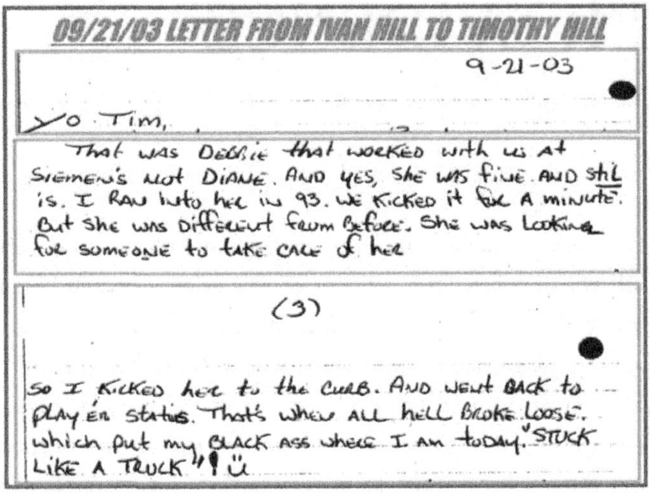

09/21/03 LETTER FROM IVAN HILL TO TIMOTHY HILL

9-21-03

Yo Tim,

That was Debbie that worked with us at Siemen's not Diane. And yes, she was fine and stil is. I ran into her in 93. We kicked it for a minute. But she was different from before. She was looking for someone to take care of her

(3)

So I kicked her to the curb. And went back to play'en status. That's when all hell broke loose. which put my black ass where I am today. "Stuck like a truck"! ☺

This is another letter that the defendant wrote to his cousin.

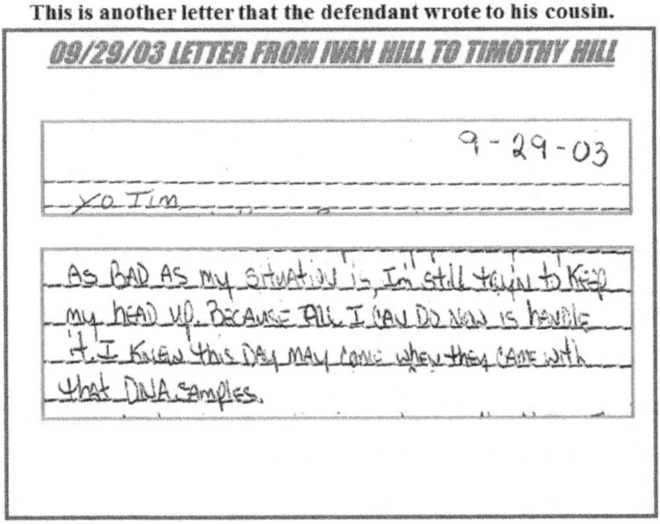

09/29/03 LETTER FROM IVAN HILL TO TIMOTHY HILL

9-29-03

Yo Tim,

As bad as my situation is, I'm still tryin to keep my head up. Because all I can do now is handle it. I knew this day may come when they came with that DNA samples.

The dispatcher's audio tape of the killer calling the Pomona Police regarding Debra Brown was the closest thing to a smoking gun. However, the problem with this evidence of corroboration was the fact that it was now ten years later that someone was trying to identify the voice on the tape to be that of Ivan Hill. When the detectives were going through the business cards in his wallet, they contacted the people listed on these business cards. The detectives asked these friends and acquaintances whether they thought they could identify his voice if they heard it again. The only two people that the detectives were able to track down were a girlfriend who lived with him in 1993, and a friend who knew him in 1993. *The following graphics page shows how Hill's voice was identified.*

The other form of corroboration that the prosecution showed the jury involved the type of knots that were found on the ligatures. John used several visuals in which an expert indicated that the knots around the victims' necks were all of the same type. Although this didn't connect the defendant to the crimes, at least it showed that all the victims were most likely killed by the same person. *The following graphics page shows the various strangle knots found around the victims' necks*

GRAPHICS 32

This was a visual showing who was able to identify defendant's voice.

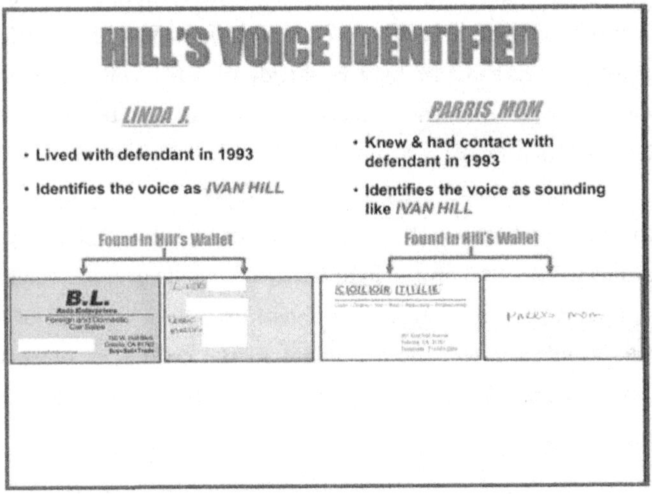

This was a visual that attempted to show the similarity of the ligatures knots.

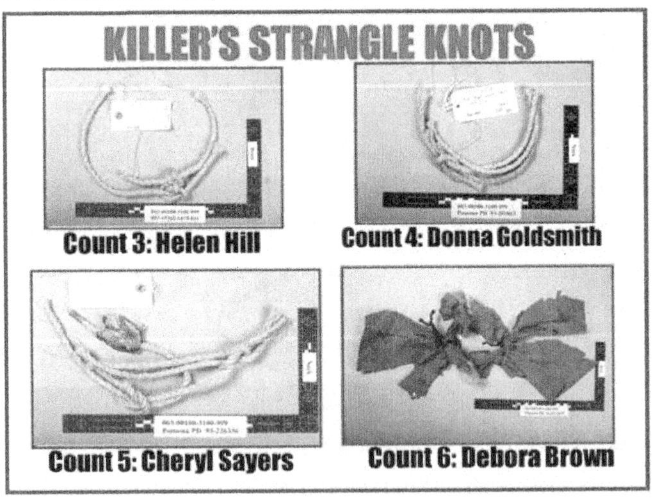

When the prosecution was finished presenting its evidence as to proving the crimes and that this defendant was connected to the killings, the proceedings were turned over to the Defense attorney. The Defense presented evidence that the defendant was heavily using drugs and wasn't in the right frame of mind to be able to form the necessary Deliberation or Premeditation. They used the fact that he was committing all sorts of robberies to obtain the necessary money for the drugs as well as the prostitutes.

Since both sides had presented their evidence, it was time for the Argument phase of the trial. John was a master of knowing how to pull all the evidence together so the jury would convict. First, he walked the jurors through the charges so they knew exactly what they had to decide. He went over the Special Circumstances of multiple murders and Prior serious felony convictions. If the jurors didn't find one of Special Circumstances was true, then there would be no Death Penalty phase. So it was imperative that the prosecution makes sure that jury at least found the Special Circumstance to be true.

Once John had gone through the housekeeping tasks, he moved on to the legal concepts. Many of the jurors had indicated that they had served as jurors on other criminal cases. John still wanted to take some time to explain what Reasonable Doubt was and what it wasn't. When he got them nodding that they understood that Reasonable Doubt wasn't the same as Beyond any Doubt, he realized he had made his point.

After discussing the concept of Doubt, John explained that an impartial comparison and consideration of all the evidence received in this trial showed without any doubt that Ivan Hill murdered each of the victims based on the DNA evidence; phone calls to Pomona Police after Debora Brown was murdered; and all the crime scene locations that Hill was familiar with.

The prosecutor started discussing DNA results in each murder. As to victim one, Betty Harris, he said, "The DNA profile obtained from male fraction of vaginal sample matches the DNA profile of Ivan Hill. The frequency of occurrence estimates is one in 604 trillion for Black subjects." Behind John on the large courtroom screen was the data that supported that statement. John repeated this five more times as to each victim.

After covering the DNA evidence, John moved on to HILL'S CALLS TO POLICE. John flashed on the big screen the exact dialogue between the killer and dispatcher. John reminded the jurors that they had heard from several friends and associates who said that was the voice of Ivan Hill. John wanted the jurors to fully comprehend the wording, "What's this, number five or six, I forget, but she's out there." Then he mentioned the second call was even more telling, when Hill said, "Y'all better catch me before I kill again." Those eerie words undoubtedly had to make some type of impression on each one of the jurors. It was almost like the killer was taunting the police in some type of 'cat and mouse game.'

Next the prosecutor went over the facts of each killing, starting with Betty Harris. On the courtroom screen could be seen a faded image of each murder victim. As John related the facts, they appeared on the screen over the victim's body. He said, "Betty Harris was last seen alive at the Mission Motel between 9 p.m. and 11:00 p.m. when she asked Felicia to watch her young son. She had explained she needed to make some money and would be gone for a couple of hours, but never returned. It was early the next morning she was found 'dumped' in a parking lot on Penarth Street some 15 miles from the Mission Motel."

John looked at the big screen and clicked for the next slide, showing Roxanne Bates' body dumped near a dairy farm in Chino. Then he went on to the next victim and said, "Helen Hill was last seen alive at the Zodiac Elks Lodge between 8 p.m. and 9:00 p.m., when she told her friend Lisha, she was 'going to go make some money.' The next morning Helen was found dumped in the parking lot at Business Parkway some seven miles from the Elks Lodge. Then he clicked the control to the projector and two of the defendant's cards appeared on the screen showing addresses near where the body was found.

Although it seemed to be tedious, John needed the jurors to remember the separate facts that went with the finding of each victim. He then went over the facts of Donna Goldsmith's crime scene on Price Street in Pomona. Then John followed that with, "Cheryl Sayers was last seen alive on Holt Boulevard in Pomona at 22:00 p.m. when she told Leroy she 'was going to go make some money,' and it was the next morning that her body was found lying on the grass in Ganesha Park.

The prosecutor finished talking about Debora Brown in the San Antonio Park in Ontario. However, he didn't need to say much about her, because the jurors had heard so much about this incident since this was the one in which the killer had called the Pomona PD dispatcher.

John divided his Argument into separate segments in order to keep the jury engaged in what he was saying. He felt comfortable that the jurors had a grasp of the facts of each of the murders, but he knew that the Defense was going to claim that he hadn't proven that Ivan Hill had committed all six murders with Deliberation and Premeditation. He knew from experience that some jurors have a misunderstanding of what constitutes Deliberation and Premeditation. Many believe that it is something that a person has contemplated for a long time, such as months or years.

John likes to go over the jury instructions and dissect every word of the definition. He said that the law states that DELIBERATELY means *carefully weighed the considerations for and against killing and knowing the consequences, decided to kill,* while PREMEDITATION means *decided to kill before committing the act that caused death.*

He stressed that it isn't the length of time spent considering whether to kill. He explained that a cold calculated decision to kill can be quickly reached. In other words, the TEST IS THE EXTENT OF REFLECTION, NOT THE LENGTH OF TIME. John then indicated that there were three ways he could prove that these murders were deliberate with premeditation. The factors to consider were:

1. Do the events before the murder indicate PLANNING?
2. Is the method Ivan Hill used to kill particular and exacting, therefore showing a PRECONCEIVED PLAN TO KILL?
3. The extent of Ivan Hill's REFLECTION when he strangled each victim to Death?

Then John started enumerating the defendant's actions that showed planning such as:

He had to choose his victim

Able to approach the victims without arousing suspicion

Able to convince the victims to go with him

Took victims to secluded areas

Scoped out locations as to where to take the victims wouldn't be seen or caught

Obtained and brought rope for strangling

Obtained and brought duct tape

Obtained and brought knife to cut rope and tape

Then John spoke about each victim and discussed what factors should be considered to show that the murders were Deliberate and Premeditated. Starting with the first murder of Betty Harris, the prosecutor said there was a long distance from the Mission Motel to where her body was found. The reasonable inference was that he drove around with the victim in his car after he murdered her. Next John talked about how long it took to manually strangle Ms. Harris. The defendant had considerable time to reflect on what he was doing as he sustained pressure on her neck for several minutes.

John continued to go through each victim's situation, and he showed how much Deliberation and Premeditation was exhibited in each killing. Finally, he got to the last murder of Debora Brown, and he stated that Hill had already murdered Betty Harris by manually strangling her, and murdered all the other victims by ligature strangulation; therefore he knew what happens when one strangles someone. But knowing all that, the defendant went ahead and did it again.

John went on to the final Argument slide, in which he reminded the jurors of the Extent of the Reflection that Ivan Hill had as he strangled Debora Brown, since he continually made a cold, calculated decision to take her life each second that he kept the ligatures wrapped around her throat.

On the following graphic page are copies of the two slides the prosecutor used to show the Deliberation and Premeditation exhibited by the defendant.

GRAPHICS 33

This slide spelled out the amount of deliberation & premeditation that existed.

THE MURDER OF **DEBORAH BROWN** WILLFUL, DELIBERATE & PREMEDITATED

Factors To Consider:

- Had Already Murdered Betty Harris By Manually Strangling Her To Death, Murdered Roxanne Bates By Ligature Strangulation, Murdered Helen Hill By Ligature Strangulation, Murdered Donna Goldsmith By Ligature Strangulation & Murdered Cheryl Sayers By Ligature Strangulation;
  - Knew What Happens When Strangle Someone But Went Ahead & Did It Again;
- Evidence Consistent With Act of Sexual Intercourse;
- Ligature Strangulation:
  - Sustained Pressure;
  - What Ivan Hill Thinking As Applying Sustained Pressure;
  - Deborah Brown's Life Literally In Ivan Hill's Hands;
- Waited To Murder Deborah Brown – Shows Control;

This slide spelled out the extent of the reflection the defendant had.

THE MURDER OF **DEBORAH BROWN** WILLFUL, DELIBERATE & PREMEDITATED

Factors To Consider:

Extent Of Reflection:

Clearly Shows The Murder Of Debora Brown

Willful, Deliberate & Premeditated.

Remember:

A Cold Calculated Decision Can Be Quickly Reached.

As Ivan Hill Strangled Deborah Brown He Continually Made A Cold Calculated Decision To Take Her Life Each Second that He Kept The Ligatures Wrapped Around Her Throat.

John's presentation was well prepared and presented. If John hadn't decided to be an attorney, he would have been an outstanding teacher. He understood what he wanted to communicate to his audience; in this case, it was a jury. Then he broke the information into bite-size categories and with the help of a visual slide show presented the material in a knowledgeable and convincing manner. When he finished his Argument, the jurors had received his communication and understood it. If all professors could learn how to effectively communicate, the college experience could be more enjoyable.

The Defense attorney in her Argument conceded that her client did kill the women but it wasn't first degree murder. She claimed that the strangling of his victims was acts of cocaine-fueled compulsion that were beyond his control. Although it seemed strange, the Defense attorney asked the jury to find her client guilty of MURDER. Her argument was that Hill wasn't capable of premeditating, so the Murders were only of the Second Degree.

After three days of deliberations, the jury returned to court to render six verdicts of GUILTY of first degree murder and finding the Special Circumstances to be true of multiple murders and having a prior murder conviction. That all meant the jurors would have to return to court in several days to hear evidence during the penalty phase of the trial.

The prosecution had considerable evidence to present to the jury to show Aggravation. Generally, a major part of the prosecution's evidence in the penalty phase is made up of the family members coming in to say how much they missed the victim. Since many of the victims were prostitutes or druggies, the prosecution didn't know how much weight the jurors would give to the families' testimony. John took a different approach by concentrating on all the previous crimes Hill had been convicted of. The prosecution showed the jury how Hill had been convicted of a robbery of a Glendora Liquor store where the store clerk was shot and killed. Also, he presented evidence of the various robberies in 1994 which landed Hill in prison for a second time.

John understood that the killing of six so-called prostitutes over a three-month period wasn't going to create a burning desire in the hearts of the jurors to impose the Death Penalty. He knew that the jurors would believe that they had done their job in convicting the defendant. He needed something that would grab the jurors' attention in believing that this time the defendant had gone too far.

The crime lab had more recently been able to connect Ivan Hill to more murders that occurred in 1986 and 1987. John therefore used the fact that he had been connected to two more homicides as the ultimate Aggravating factor. Those jurors who might have been leaning toward Life would have thought that he has to get something greater than Life. When the jurors heard about these two additional murders that may have been the preverbal straw that 'broke the camel's back.'

The Defense attorney's main objective was to prevent Ivan Hill receiving a Death sentence. She called Hill's mother, who testified that her son, while growing up, was savagely beaten by his father. At the age of ten, he became the man of the house. She said, "I don't want to see him die, because he is my son." While his mother testified, the Defense attorney projected on the large courtroom screen photos of Ivan as a child. His mother explained that he was the eldest son of five children and he received the harshest punishment. The abuse started when he was an infant, and his father would place a pillow over his face to silence Ivan's crying. When he was older, he received severe spanking.

When Ivan was seven, he watched as his father shot his mother in the face. Although she refused to press charges, the dysfunctional family continued on until the parents separated. The Defense called psychological experts to testify how his miserable family life had affected his life with women.

Then came the final moment of the Hill case, when it was time for the Argument for or against the Death Penalty. The prosecutor explained the procedure, which was determining whether the Aggravating circumstances are so substantial in comparison with the Mitigating circumstance that they warrant death instead of life without parole. First John said that they, the jurors, could consider the Circumstance of the Crimes of the present case. Although it seemed repetitive, he went over each killing, explaining how Aggravating the conduct of the defendant was. He finished up with the killing of Debora Brown, which could only be described as Aggravating.

John indicated that just the manner of killing of all these women was enough to show that the Aggravating far outweighed the Mitigating. Then he added all the prior crimes of violence that Hill had been involved in. He used a slide that showed ten of Hill's prior convictions, all involving violence. To top this off, John talked about the two additional murders that he had proved up during this Penalty Phase of the case.

The following graphics are copies of the two slides the prosecutor used to show the evidence that could be considered for the present case and the other was the various past criminal acts of violence that could be considered by the jury.

GRAPHICS 34

This slide was used in the Penalty phase to show what jurors could consider as Aggravating evidence.

a) CIRCUMSTANCES OF CRIME CONVICTED OF IN PRESENT CASE & ANY SPECIAL CIRCUMSTANCES FOUND TO BE TRUE

You Can Consider All The Evidence From The Guilt Phase

- Circumstances of Betty Harris' Murder
- Circumstances of Roxanne Bates' Murder
- Circumstances of Helen Hill's Murder
- Circumstances of Donna Goldsmith's Murder
- Circumstances of Cheryl Sayers' Murder

This slide listed other acts of violence committed by this defendant.

b) PRESENCE OR ABSENCE OF CRIMINAL ACTIVITY INVOLVING VIOLENCE

	Date	Crime	Location
1	09/25/76	ROBBERY	SHADY GROVE
2	01/07/79	ROBBERY	EL RANCH SECO
3	01/24/79	MURDER-ROBBERY & ATTEMPT MURDER	B&J LIQUOR STORE
4	05/11/89	ROBBERY	AVENUE PHARMACY
5	01/05/94	ROBBERY	MONTCLAIR FLORIST
6	02/17/94	ROBBERY	MOVIE BUSTERS
7	02/18/94	ROBBERY	MUSIC PLUS
8	02/21/94	ROBBERY	MUSIC PLUS
9	02/22/94	ROBBERY	MUSIC PLUS
10	02/11/86	MURDER	LORNA REED
11	01/25/87	MURDER	RHONDA JACKSON

John slowly went over the facts of the killing of Loren Reed and her body being found in Bonelli Park in San Dimas with a thick rope tied around her neck. By this time, the jurors were seated deep in their chairs with a stern look on their faces. Then the prosecutor said, "And there is more." He flashed on the courtroom screen photos of Rhonda Jackson's body lying in the bottom of a trash dumpster. Hill had used a sheet tied in knots around her neck.

When those two murders were added to all the other prior crimes of violence, the Aggravating evidence was substantial. Then it was time for Hill's Defense attorney to explain why the defendant shouldn't receive the Death Penalty. She emphasized that the defendant grew up in an abusive home where he regularly received savage beatings from his father. His attorney said that Life in Prison without Parole was more than sufficient punishment.

The judge gave the jury the final jury instruction and sent them out to deliberate. After several days of discussions, the jury reached a unanimous verdict of DEATH as the appropriate penalty. The matter was put over for sentencing, and that was when several of the victims' families addressed the court. The daughter of one of the victims said to the defendant, "I can never forgive you and I will never forget. I hate you. I hope you rot in hell. ... You look as if there's no hurt in you."

The Defense attorney asked Judge Fidler to reduce the sentence to Life Without the Possibly of Parole. She said, "I acknowledge the gravity of these crimes. I acknowledge the number of these crimes. However, my client was shaped by abuse he suffered as a child." Then the DA stated, "These were well thought out acts by Mr. Hill. We may not ever understand why he did what he did. But we do know the result of what he did."

After the victims' families and the attorneys from both sides made their statements regarding sentencing, the judge asked the defendant if he had anything to add, to which he slowly shook his head and uttered, "No, your Honor." Then the judge finished the sentencing hearing by saying, "I recognize the abuse, but it was not enough of a mitigating circumstance to save Mr. Hill's life." The judge recited the defendant's long criminal history of robbery and assault with deadly weapon and announced that the sentence would be DEATH by execution.

After that announcement, everyone thought the Ivan Hill case was over. The question was what to do about the two additional murders. How do you tidy up all the loose ends? Lorna Reed's (35) body was found in Bonelli Park in San Dimas in 1986. (Your author lives adjacent to this Park where the body was found.) Also, one year later in 1987, Rhonda Jackson (23) body was found in Ganesha Park in Pomona. Was it worth it for the DA's Office to bring murder charges against Ivan Hill for those two murders even though he had already received six Death Penalty sentences and was housed on Death Row?

The victims' relatives felt that these victims deserved to have their case adjudicated. John knew if the case had to be tried as a Death Penalty trial it would cost hundreds of thousands of dollars in court time. The idea was floated that if the defendant was willing to plead guilty to both these additional murders, he would be given Life Without the Possibility of Parole. Ultimately, that was how it was all worked out, and Ivan Hill now had a body count of nine when factoring in his first murder, his six '60 Freeway Slayer' murders, and the two added murders. Maybe Ivan Hill will gain some respect on Death Row as being a serial murderer of Nine.

For those who believe in enforcing the law, John Monaghan did a remarkable job in presenting the evidence to a jury and left it up to them to decide the appropriate punishment. For those who oppose the Death Penalty on moral grounds, you may feel more comfortable with a different result. However, John believes that those black prostitutes are human beings worthy of protection. He fought with his whole heart to see that justice was done no matter what status the victims held in society. Thank God for the 'John Monaghan types' of the world who do their job without any fanfare or any financial reward.

(Just an aside bit of trivia—January 6, 1994, was the significant date in this Ivan Hill case because that was the date of his last murder and his eventual incarceration, after which women were safer. However, that date of January 6, 1994, is better remembered as the date that Lorena Bobbitt was found not guilty due to insanity when she had an irresistible impulse to cut off her husband, John Wayne Bobbitt's, penis while he was sleeping in bed. Strange how that date has different meaning to different women.)

CHAPTER 21 DIXON—COLLEGE LIFE IN THE SUMMER

Thank God it's Friday' was the cry as the evening drew near on August 17, 2001. Once Friday hits, every college student has to deal with the question, what am I going to do tonight? August in Southern California can be a time of scorching heat waves, so most people spend their free time at the beach, by the pool, or inside in the air-conditioned building. The Cal Poly Pomona University is the perfect location for any young student who lives on the eastside of Los Angeles. It is truly centrally located. This appeared to be the case for Christina Burmeister. It was approximately 30 miles from her family home, allowing her to still live at home with her family with whom she was very close.

At the young age of 20 this tall attractive young lady was embarking upon her senior year at the college where she was majoring in Apparel Merchandizing and Management. She had a passion for writing which might explain why she excelled in communications. She even contemplated going into journalism upon graduation. She was an active member of Chi Omega Sorority where she had developed many close sisterhood bonds throughout her years. Christina was also Vice President of the Panhellenic Council that oversaw the Greek community. She had strong ties to the Greek community on campus which was large part of her social life.

At Cal Poly Pomona the sororities do not have their own houses for living and socializing however some of the fraternities had houses off-campus. Those fraternity houses consisted of old homes in downtown Pomona area where the group converts the upstairs bedrooms into dorm style rooms where some of the members live. Unfortunately, many of the frat houses are located in less desirable areas and safety is always an issue. However, the students don't dwell on criminal element in the area since they feel immune to any possible harm. For those into the Greek life style the frat houses are where they all congregate after classes and on weekends.

As a matter of fact, Christina was so well liked that she became one of the 'little sisters' of the Sigma Nu fraternity. She was very active with the Greek system and had been elected as vice president of the Panhellenic Council.

To her friends and the Cal Poly student body, Christina could be described as an outgoing, fun-loving personality whom everyone liked. The sorority girls were impressed with her 'happy go lucky' approach to school and her positive attitude toward life. The fraternity guys admired her because she was easy to talk to and concerned about the well-being of all those around her. Her sense of humor was infectious and she could be the life of the party. Over the years while enrolled at Cal Poly, she developed many close friendships with people who respected her.

On this sweltering Friday afternoon, she had been out shopping with her mother. By dinner time the family had congregated together for a sit-down meal. Christina's family would be defined as a tight-knit clan. She often spent time with her mother and sister and truly enjoyed their company. After washing the dishes, she and the rest of the family would watch television together. In the summertime, the TV programs were reduced to reruns. *America's Funniest Home Videos* was on; however, their reruns could be less than funny, especially if you remembered seeing it before. As it got closer to 10:00 p.m., Christina's and sister's options had narrowed to watching either ***20/20*** or ***48 Hours*** with the family.

Prior to making such a decision, Christina's cell phone rang. Quickly she answered it and heard her good friend asking her if she was going to attend the Sigma Nu house party. Since it was the end of summer, the fraternity was starting to plan for 'fall rush' which would begin the kick off for recruiting new members. Being that she was the life of any party and strongly tied to Sigma Nu fraternity, they were looking forward to her being there. Christina decided she had enough TV for the night and got ready to go out to the party. What was ironic was that ***Law & Order: Special Victims Unit*** was coming on at 10:00 p.m. If she had stayed home and watched it, she would be alive today, but by deciding to go to the frat party, she would end up as a real victim as depicted on the Special Victim Unit program.

Christina mentioned to her mom that she was going to drive over to the frat party. Her mom looked at her watch and said that it was too late to go that far. A typical mother-daughter discussion ensued in which the parent took the negative approach that bad things happened to people who go out late. Christina loved her mom but thought that she was just being overly protective. Like in any family negotiation, she promised her mother she would be back in two hours. At that point, her mother relented, and in an effort to build trust in their relationship, Christina promised her mother that she would 'be careful.'

With Mom's consent, Christina wasted no time in changing clothes and grabbed her cell phone and wallet heading out the door. To prove to her mom she wouldn't stay long, she left her light on in her room. She climbed into her new Chevy pickup truck and backed out of the driveway. She drove to the 91 Freeway onramp. Anyone who knew Christina knew about her new truck, which was a reflection of who she was. It was one of Chevy's S-10 Extended Cab models with a slightly lowered body. The sleek turquoise paint job finished off with classy decorative alloy rims was an eye catcher. Some might think this type of pickup should be a 'guy vehicle.' But for Christina, this was the perfect vehicle that allowed her to do anything without having to rely on others.

The so-called Generation X in 2001 craved Independence. They believed that they could take care of themselves and needn't rely on others. Christina was no exception in that she wanted to prove to all those around her that she wasn't a dependent soul. As much as she liked guys, she didn't want to be obligated to them for rides. She truly wanted to say to and show the world that she made it all on her own. She was going to pay for her pickup out of the money she earned from a new job after graduation. The truck made her feel indomitable, showing others that she could stand on her own two feet.

She embodied the spirit of one of the top songs of 2001, which was ***Independent Women Part I*** by the group Destiny's Child. The lyrics of that song really spelled out Christina's philosophy of life:

Question: tell me how you feel about this
Try to control me boy, you get dismissed
Pay my own fun, oh and I pay my own bills
Always 50/50 in relationship
The shoes on my feet
I've bought it
The clothes I'm wearing
I've bought it...
Cause I depend on me
The car I'm driving
I've bought it
I depend on me

That song so epitomized Christina, the 'Independent Woman' who felt she was unstoppable. She was so proud of the fact that she wasn't beholden to anyone, even her boyfriend. That attitude gave her confidence, and she could handle anything that came her way. To many Christina had the attributes of being a leader and definitely a role model for many others.

After turning off the 91 Freeway, she maneuvered over to the 57 Freeway and whizzed through the light traffic headed for Pomona. The new-car smell still permeated the cab of the truck. She loved the upgraded sound system that permitted her to crank up the audio and made the cab of the truck vibrate. As she sped along, she must have thought to herself that being a 'commuter' college student wasn't so bad and as a matter of fact it had its perks.

By 11:00 p.m. she was exiting the freeway and only minutes away from the fraternity house. As she reached the driveway, she glanced to see if there were any parking spaces and, seeing none, continued eastbound on Holt Boulevard, looking for some closed business that had room for parking. She noticed the 'Smoke Shop' on the corner and had ample parking spaces. She pulled in and parked. She decided to go into the shop to buy a couple of packs of cigarettes. She got out of her shiny new truck without plates and was pleased with herself since she had made the commute in record-breaking time.

The parking area was dark, so she couldn't see exactly who was in the area. She noticed several people but didn't pay any attention to them since her mind was focused on buying some cigarettes and then heading over to the fraternity house. From that moment in time on, no one knows for certain what happened to Christina Burmeister.

What we do know is that two men and one woman attempted to rob Christina in that 'Smoke Shop' parking lot. We know that at least one of the men had a large knife that he threatened Christina with. Possibly Christina didn't have any cash on her and the only thing of value was her ATM card to withdraw money from her bank. The robbers knew that the debit card was worthless to them without the correct PIN (Password Number). The robbers knew that they could threaten someone to get a PIN. However, robbers aren't necessarily trusting people. If a victim gives a fake PIN, then the robber can't obtain money from the ATM and thereby ends up with nothing.

These robbers thought the safest way to verify whether they were given the correct PIN number was to take the victim with them to the ATM or bank. By looking at the debit card, the robbers knew that it could be used at a Washington Mutual Bank. What happened next was that they forced Christina back in her truck and made her kneel on the floorboard with her head down as they proceeded to find a bank. They drove several miles to the adjacent City of Montclair, where they pulled in near the ATM machines on the outside of the bank building.

Throughout this entire ordeal, Christina was squeezed down on the floorboard in a cramped position. The robbers were demanding that she give them the correct PIN and undoubtedly threatened to do her harm if she lied to them. The male robbers decided to have the female robber go over to one of the three ATM machines to try to make a withdrawal. She pulled a hoody down over her head, covering most of her face. She inserted Christina's debit card in the machine and then the screen asked for the PIN. At that point, she punched in the numbers Christina had given them. When it asked for the amount of the withdrawal, she put in $200.

It was now almost midnight as the male robbers waited in the truck with Christina, wondering if they had the right PIN. Instantaneously, the female robber came back waving ten twenty-dollar bills. Everyone must have felt relief. The robbers had been successful and Christina must have thought that the robbery nightmare would soon be over. Greed began to take over and it was suggested why not do it again for the amount of $100. The female robber went back to the machine and withdrew another $100. Since no one knew exactly what the limit was, they tried it a third time, getting another $100.

The robbers had to think this was better than playing the slot machines at the local Indian casino. Now they had $400 in cash and didn't have the headache of taking stolen property to a receiver (fence) to get some dough. The robbers now could afford to buy some drugs and alcohol to get themselves bombed out of their minds. They must of thought what a great Friday night it had become. However, the celebrating was short-lived. They had to decide what to do with the young woman they had lying face down on the floorboards. She had been cooperative with them and had in fact been honest with them in regard to the PIN. While waiting in the truck, the guys threw a CD in a plastic case that belonged to Christina in the shrubs in the parking lot.

All the robbers had been in close contact with Christina, and she had had numerous chances to look at their faces. In other words, she could identify them at a later date. One thing for certain was that James Dixon, one of the robbers, had spent many years in state prison, and he had no desire to return. Could he threaten Christina sufficiently to get her to agree not to identify him? This would be wishful thinking, since Dixon knew he had no way to keep her quiet. Dixon didn't want to take any chances, so his mind was made up that she needed to be disposed of.

The next question for them was how do you kill someone and not get caught? Dixon had grown up as a gang member in Monrovia. This was a community ten miles west of where they were in the City of Montclair. Dixon remembered as a gang member that when they wanted to get rid of a rival gang member, they would take them up to the San Gabriel Canyon. This area was above Monrovia in the Angeles National Forest.

Highway 39 is a winding, rugged highway that becomes very congested on weekends. During the summer months, many families try to escape the sweltering heat of the city by traveling up into the mountains, where they can picnic or just hike. However, at other times of the year it can be an isolated place where all sorts of nefarious activities take place. The highway has many turnouts as it climbs the mountainside. In the middle of the night, gang members drive up the mountain road looking for turnouts they can pull into. With no one around for miles, dead bodies are tossed over the edge of the road and tumble-down hundreds of feet. Wherever the corpse lands, it becomes a feeding ground for the wildlife that roam the forest at night.

Law enforcement has no idea and can't even estimate how many bodies have been disposed of in the Angeles Forest. Your author has handled numerous cases where bodies have been tossed or buried along the sides of the highway. These corpses are discovered when some hiker stumbles over the remains of a body. But most of the time the bodies are not recovered. The San Gabriel Canyon is a part of the Angeles Forest, which you the reader may remember when we were discussing the Rademaker case. However, the San Gabriel Canyon is several miles east of the Angeles Forest Highway.

Dixon most likely had a flashback to his gangbanging days, when bodies were uniformly dumped in the canyon. The two male robbers drove in Christina's pickup all the way from the bank in Montclair to the City of Azusa, which is at the mouth of the San Gabriel Canyon. The male robbers had the female robber follow them in the robbers' car. It is unclear as to what time the two cars proceeded up the Canyon. At the far end of Highway 39 is Crystal Lake, which has a campground that would be popular during this time of the year. However, the majority of the visitors would have gotten to the campground early, set up their campsite, and gone to bed.

It definitely was after midnight that Christina's pickup started up the steep canyon. They would not have encountered any traffic, and most likely drove by numerous turnouts to find one that met their needs. One of the robbers, Mr. Singer, did the driving of the truck while Dixon positioned himself in the cramped space of the Extended Cab. It would have taken a little less than an hour to drive from the bank to the turnout in the mountains.

What was Christina thinking as they were driving along? Did she believe that they were going to release her somewhere in the mountains so she couldn't immediately report the robbery? Or did she know that she was doomed? Christina was a bright, savvy individual who undoubtedly kept thinking about what she could do to save her life. Eventually, they pulled into a wide-open turnout with no one around. The car driven by the female robber pulled in behind the truck. From this point on there is only the account given by Singer and the female robber as to what happened. Singer claimed he got out of the car as Dixon remained squeezed in the back area of the cab.

At that point Christina was seated in the passenger seat of her pickup. Singer and the female claimed they remained back by their car. They were waiting to see what was about to happen.

Singer recounted that he noticed that Dixon reached into the area of the passenger seat where Christina was seated and he made a motion with his arm. He could observe the pickup was rocking slightly side to side. They didn't hear any screaming or loud noise. Shortly thereafter, they saw Dixon get out of the driver's side door. When Dixon approached them, they noticed that he had blood on his clothing and on his hands. They knew that Dixon had a large knife in his possession. They all walked back to their car and got in. As they pulled out of the turnout, the headlights shined one last time on the sleek turquoise Chevy pickup, illuminating the faint outline of a young woman slumped in a reclining position. The three robbers headed down the mountain road most likely thinking that it was all in a Night's Work and they had made $400 in cash for all their efforts.

On the following graphic page is a map used to show where all crucial events occurred as well as a diagram where the victim was kidnapped.

GRAPHICS 35

This was a map depicting where the various events occurred.

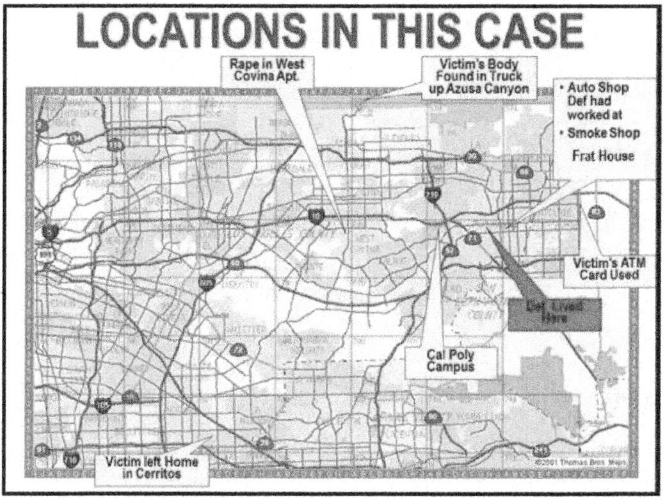

This was a diagram of the area of the frat house & where she was kidnapped.

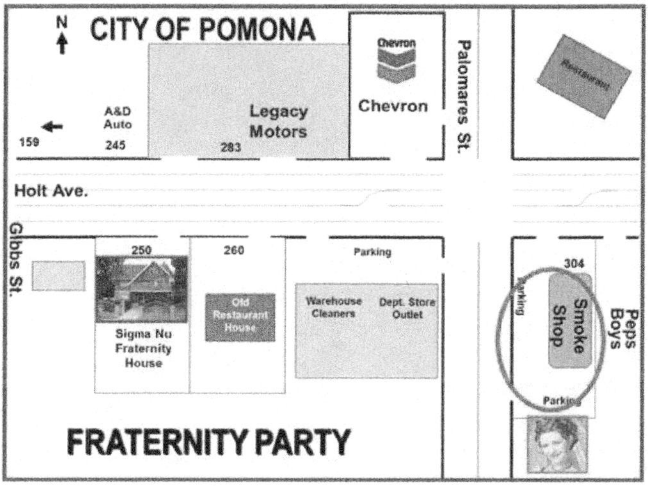

CHAPTER 22 DIXON—SHOCKING DISCOVERY

It is part of the Sheriff's Department jurisdiction to patrol the entire San Gabriel Canyon road, which stretches all the way to the Crystal Lake campground. This can be one of the most monotonous patrols, especially during the early morning hours. However, on August 18, 2001, Deputy Tack drew the 'short straw' and was given the tedious assignment of making the loop up and back. As he approached the 20-mile marker on Highway 39, he came around one of many hairpin turns and caught a glimpse of something that looked like a vehicle at one of the large turnouts. This created a curiosity for him so he headed that way.

He slowed down and could see what looked like a Chevy S-10 pickup parked near the edge of the turnout. Since this was too early for the usual weekend crowd, he decided to pull in and check it out. The most he could make out was someone reclining in the passenger seat. This seemed strange to him because he didn't see any other person in the driver seat. Deputy Tack exited his vehicle. He had turned up the police radio so he could hear it outside the car. As he approached the car, he could hear the dispatcher calling out a radio call of 211 at the 7-Eleven. Deputy Tack thought to himself, why do all the other deputies receive the exciting radio calls and he ends up with a parked vehicle in a mountain turnout?

By this time, he was adjacent to the driver's door and could see no one in the driver's seat. He had to lean down to look into the lowered Chevy S-10 when his eyes locked in on the most gruesome sight anyone could ever image coming across.

There before his eyes was a young woman whose throat had been slit, exposing her larynx and esophagus, with a sea of red blood that had streamed down her blouse.

The deputy had seen traffic accidents with bloody victims, but nothing like this. Near her throat, the blood had congealed and was giving off a dark tint, meaning that the body had been there for some time. Even though it was still morning, the bees and flies were darting in and out of the cab of the truck. Should he try to check for a pulse? As he looked at this woman's neck, he concluded that this woman was truly dead. At this stage, no paramedic was needed since only the services of the Coroner's Office would be necessary.

At that moment, Deputy Tack realized that he needed to notify the dispatcher of what he had discovered. The Homicide detectives had to be called to take charge of the investigation. This deputy would long remember this fateful Saturday morning when he was the first person to view the horrendous demise of the vivacious life of Christina Burmeister.

On the following graphic page is an exhibit of where the truck was found in the mountains as well as a photo of the victim dead in her truck.

GRAPHICS 36

This shows the turn-out where the victim and her truck were found.

The victim's body was found in the passenger seat with her throat slit.

While the Sheriff's Department was responding to a horrific crime, the Burmeister family was completely unaware of what had been uncovered up in the San Gabriel Canyon. Christina's sister, Elizabeth, was leaving the house when she glanced up the driveway and noticed that Christina's truck wasn't there. Elizabeth darted back into the house and went by Christina's room and popped her head in and observed that the bed was undisturbed and her sister was nowhere around. She hesitated for a moment, wondering whether she should say anything to their mother. Being a tattletale on her sister was not who she was. She and her sister had covered for each other on more than one occasion when one of them came home late.

However, this time seemed different and she felt compelled to tell her mother, Rosalia. She then woke up her mom, who within minutes had a dire premonition that something was wrong. The two of them tried to explore scenarios that might explain Christina's absence. Like an overprotective mother, she went into action. She grabbed her phone and dialed in Christina's cell phone number and got no answer. She repeated this by calling Christina's pager and waited to see if there was any response. Getting nothing, she continued to think of what to do next.

Rosalia thought of one of her daughter's closest friends who was going to the fraternity party. She called her and eventually got through to her. Christina's friend was half-asleep when she answered her phone, and Rosalia started interrogating her as to Christina's whereabouts. From the questioning, the friend could tell that Christina was going to be in plenty of trouble with her mother. Her first reaction was to wonder whether she should cover for Christina, or should she be honest and tell her that she never showed up.

The friend was in a quandary as to what to say. She really didn't want to get Christina in trouble with her mother. When she was asked point blank whether she saw Christina at the frat house, she reluctantly answered that she never saw Christina at the party. She indicated that she was there most of the evening and Christina was a No Show. This wasn't the answer that Rosalia wanted to hear, but she thanked the friend and asked her to call her if she later heard from Christina.

What should the mother and sister do next? Her mother could have been an apprentice of Sherlock Holmes. It occurred to her that she and Christina had a joint credit card at Washington Mutual Bank, which was Christina's main source of funds. Her mother called the bank number to learn about any activity on her credit card. If

Christina used it, there would be a paper trail of where she used it, like at a restaurant or an ATM machine to get cash.

Within seconds, Rosalia was being told that this credit card had been used just seconds before midnight at the ATM machine at the Montclair branch of the Washington Mutual Bank. This was reassuring to Rosalia in that Christina must be okay, since she was actively getting some cash. However, what was disconcerting was the fact that she withdrew $200 and only a minute later she withdrew another $100, followed by yet another such withdrawal.

These additional withdrawals were giant red flags waving in the wind. She couldn't think of any reason why Christina would make additional withdrawals. Like a mother cat, Rosalia knew something was wrong with one of her little kittens. First she called her husband at work and told him what she had discovered. He concurred something was wrong, but no one could figure out what it all meant.

Christina's mom took the next step no parent wants to make, and that was to call the police to file a Missing Person's Report. Since the Burmeister family lived in Cerritos, they would have to contact the Los Angeles Sheriff's Department Cerritos station that handles all the policing duties for their city. Whenever a parent has to make such a Report there are mixed emotions. Rosalia wanted to believe nothing was wrong and that possibly there was a slight misunderstanding as to where her daughter had gone and who she was with. The police are all too aware that most Missing Person's Reports turn out to be a misunderstanding or just a rebellious child wanting to wander away from an overly protective parent.

This beautiful sunny Saturday morning was forming several ominous clouds over the Los Angeles basin. The Sheriff's Homicide detectives were barreling up the San Gabriel Canyon road to the 20-mile marker turnout. They wanted to beat the weekend crowd that would clog the two-lane road to a snail's pace by noon. The information the detectives had was that a female body with a slit throat was found seated in a new pickup truck in one of the turnouts up the canyon. Was it a gangland homicide or was it a dope deal gone bad? These homicide detectives had been called up the canyon many times, but generally the victim was shot to death and the body is rolled down the hill. But the slitting of a woman's throat was a new one for these seasoned detectives.

As they pulled into the turnout, which was now filled with black-and-white units, they could see this classy turquoise pickup with the passenger's door wide open. They got out of the detective car and were met by the patrol sergeant who would explain to them the basic facts. The two detectives walked over to the open door and glanced inside. These were hardened homicide detectives who had seen it all. When they looked at the victim, all they could see was a young lady whose throat had been slit from ear to ear.

The detectives recognized that the cause of death wasn't going to be the issue in this case. It was going to be a Whodunit and Why type of case. They wanted to know who was the owner of the truck and who was the victim. The forensic team had been notified and were on their way. They wanted to get the crime scene photographed before a wave of tourists took over the canyon. In the meantime, they searched the surrounding area of the turnout looking for anything that might shed some light on who was present and who had done this to this young woman.

After the forensic photographer had finished up, the detectives started to look through the interior of the truck for clues and possible evidence. One of the detectives noticed a Tiparillo mouthpiece on the floor mat just behind the driver's seat. With a latex glove, he picked it up and placed it in an evidence envelope. This was an unusual find, since Tiparillos are small cigars made in Dothan, Alabama, with a homogenized sheet wrapper and binder which contained a blend of filler tobaccos. The height of their popularity was in the 1960s and 70s.

The detectives weren't so interested in who smoked Tiparillos but in the possibility that there might have been enough saliva to get a DNA match. This would be a long shot, but the detectives were impressed with results they had gotten in the past from cigarette butts, especially the filtered type. The detectives tagged the truck to be searched thoroughly for evidence once it was transported to a secure police garage. They wanted to see if there were any blood spatter patterns that could determine where the suspect was located when he sliced the victim's throat.

All the other items inside the interior of the truck were checked out and they were determined to belong to the victim. *On the following graphic page is a visual of where the Tiparillo was found.*

While the detectives were doing their tedious work of looking for evidence, the Burmeister family was at the same time checking out the ATM at the Washington Mutual Bank in Montclair. At this point, the right hand and the left hand were off doing their own thing without knowing what the other was doing. Elizabeth, the victim's sister, knew that withdrawals had been made at the Montclair branch, so she and two of her uncles drove out to the bank. They looked all over the bank's parking lot hoping to see something that would point them as to where Christina could be.

While walking around, Elizabeth looked in the shrubbery behind the ATM parking area and noticed a CD and a unique CD case that looked like Christina's. When she got closer, Elizabeth was certain that she had seen this in Christiana's truck. Christina's sister and uncles were now certain that Christina had been there in that parking lot. They were like bloodhounds who were excited they had tracked down her scent. However, the big question was what did this all mean.

Once the Burmeister family and the detectives joined forces, they realized they were on to something. The detectives got a search warrant for the bank video footage to see who was the person who made the three withdrawals. When the detectives got the videos all they could see was some person with a gray hoody over their face who made the withdrawals. They couldn't tell whether it was a woman or a man since the video was of such a poor quality.

As time marched on, the bank videos weren't yielding any useable evidence. The Tiparillo did reveal a DNA profile, but as the detectives searched the various databases, there was no match made. By the end of 2001, the Christina Burmeister case was ready to be placed in the quiet cold case files.

The following graphic page shows where the suspects used the victim's ATM card.

GRAPHICS 37

This was the back area of the truck's cab where the butt of the Tip-o-rillo was found.

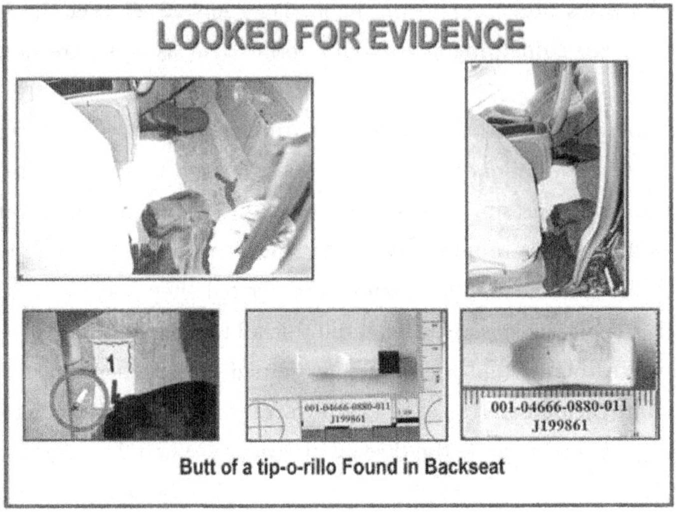

This was the ATM in Montclair where the victim's money was withdrawn.

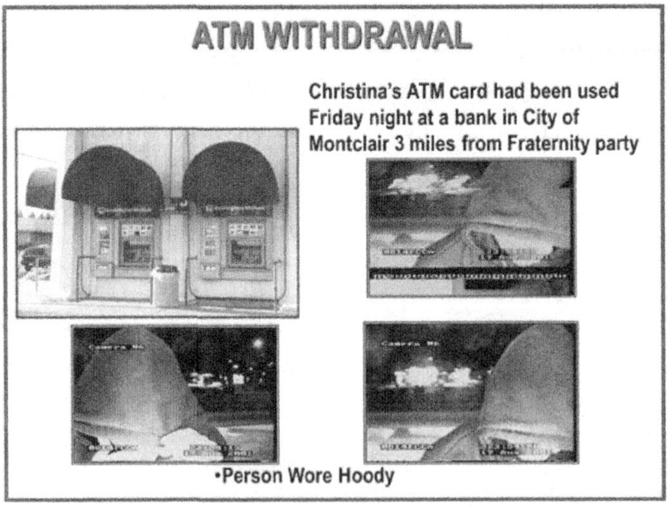

CHAPTER 23 DIXON— WHO CAN YOU TRUST?

The date of 9/11/2001 has forever been etched deep in everyone's psyche. The USA didn't know how to respond. From all the successes from World War II, the country had grown accustomed to the idea that 'Might Makes Right.' If only we could attack those who wanted to kill us and destroy Western Civilization, we could eventually be victorious. One of the side consequences of 9/11was a general paranoia that swept over the country.

In a strange way, that also applied to the Burmeister case. Since months went by without finding the killer, community paranoia developed. Everyone was looking at others wondering if they could be the murderer who slit Christina's throat. Could it be someone in the fraternity who went rogue? Could it be one of those foreign exchange students who came from countries where knives were common in settling disputes?

The Cal Poly administrators wanted to calm suspicions, since they knew that many parents would be leery of sending their daughters to a school where a female student was butchered by some unknown person. There were the non-Greeks who felt that the mysterious Greek system bred all sorts of mysterious customs.

The detectives tried to put the fears of the campus and administrators at ease. Then there were some even who thought that the detectives had purposely put the case on a 'back burner.' There were rallies on campus and in the student community encouraging people to cooperate with the investigation. Even reward money was offered for any kind of information on the case that would help move it along.

The detectives had meetings with the public in which they explained exactly where they were in the investigation. Their biggest question was trying to figure out what was the MOTIVE was for the killing. The withdrawal of money from the bank made it look like a robbery. Since Christina's wallet and other credit cards weren't recovered, it had the earmark of a robbery. However, what negated the robbery theory was the fact of the 'overkill' of the victim. The detectives couldn't recall when they had ever seen a robber slit a victim's throat.

The rage the killer demonstrated was more indicative of an ex-boyfriend or rejected suitor who wanted to strike out and inflict pain like the victim had caused them. However, Christina's boyfriend was quickly eliminated as a person of interest since he had never demonstrated violent like behavior towards her or anyone in general. What continued to stymie the detectives was the fact that no sophisticated criminal or even a neophyte criminal would slit a person's throat. The reason is that the victim's body sprays blood all over the place. In other words, such a killer would inadvertently end up with some of the victim's blood on them. With DNA testing, the killer could easily be caught.

On the following graphic page is a visual showing the Cal Poly Campus and the fraternity, which was off campus.

GRAPHICS 38

This shows the college campus & the Sigma Nu fraternity house.

This visual was a summary of the evidence for the rape cases and murder case.

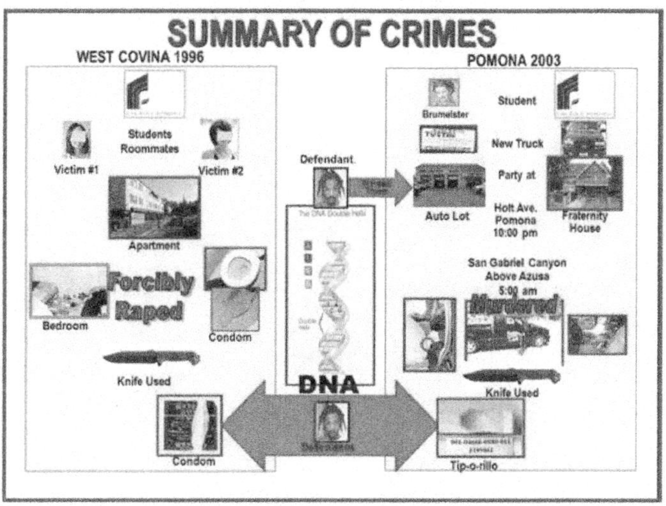

The months went by and even years went by without any break in the case. However, the way the Burmeister case was solved is directly tied into a double rape case that had taken place five years earlier in the neighboring city of West Covina. In order to sort it all out, we need to go back in time to 1996. Remember, that was the year that brought us the movies like *The English Patient*, *Fargo*, *Jerry Maguire*, as well as *People vs. Larry Flynt.* However, many would say the most important story for 1996 was the fact that a scientific team cloned the world's first sheep from adult cells and the baby lamb was named Dolly.

CHAPTER 24 DIXON—AN OLD RAPE CASE

July 19, 1996, was a terrible day for a group of four Cal Poly students who were sharing an apartment in West Covina. This was a convenient place for the students to live, since Cal Poly was known as being a commuter school and there was limited housing for students. The apartment complex was within feet of the Grand Avenue onramp to the I-10 Freeway, which one takes to get to the campus. Besides being convenient to Cal Poly, the apartment was in a safe neighborhood, and in addition to that it was enclosed by a security fence requiring residents to use a key to gain access.

James Wong (a pseudonym) could be considered a lucky guy since he shared the apartment with three young women students. They all got along as well as four strangers could, considering they had to share a kitchen and bathrooms. Since everyone was immersed in their field of studies, the main purpose of the apartment was merely a place to sleep.

During the early morning hours of this Friday, July 19, everyone was deep in sleep. James was alone in his bedroom and was awakened by a bright light shining in his face. Since he was still half-asleep, he tried to grasp what was going on. Even though it was dark in the room, this light revealed two black men kneeling over him.

Both men held handguns, and one pointed the gun at James' head. He didn't recognize who they were and wondered what they were doing in his room.

Then one of the men told him, "Don't say a word or you will die." James realized this was a life or death situation so he complied. Next, they asked him where the phones were and he told them in the kitchen. One of the men then went into the kitchen and ripped the phone off the wall. They then duct taped his mouth and tied his hands and feet with some type of cord. James then clearly realized that he was about to be the victim of a home invasion robbery.

The robbers forced him to walk to the next bedroom, where two of the women were sleeping. Since they had tied his feet, James couldn't easily shuffle to the other room. The robbers grabbed him and dragged him into the girl's room and threw him onto the floor. One of the robbers went over to the bed where Lillie (a pseudonym) was sleeping and nudged her shoulder. It was either that contact or all the commotion that startled her awake. Next thing she noticed was a gun placed against her head as the man told her to be quiet and ordered her to turn over on her stomach.

Lillie sensed something terrible was about to happen to her. She felt alone and helpless. The man started removing her underwear and rubbing his hand down her back. Next, she felt his frigid hand rub her buttocks, then suddenly his fingers inserted deep into her vagina. In a terrified voice, she pleaded with him to stop. All her protesting caused him to bind her arms above her head with a telephone cord. Then he took her ankles and wrapped them with duct tape.

Lillie now felt totally vulnerable as he took a razor-sharp knife and cut her shirt off, exposing her breasts. Then the man asked where she kept her valuables. She didn't know what to say as he went in search for loot. Shortly, he returned and again he demanded to know where the money and jewelry were. She thought to herself that she was just a poor student and what would be the chances of her having expensive jewelry.

She was entirely truthful and told him she didn't have anything. The robber didn't like her response and told her, "We will have to take something else." Afterward she heard the strangest sound of the robber tearing open what sounded like a condom package. He grabbed her like a piece of meat and turned her over on her back. Then he took his knife to cut the duct tape binding her ankles, thereby sliding her legs apart. The next thing she knew was that the robber was on top of her inserting his condomed penis in her vagina.

This had to be the worst day of her life as the robber continued to rape her. Lillie didn't know what to say or do. With all the intense emotional and physical pain, all she could do was beg him to stop. Her plea was met by the robber/rapist taking his knife and sticking it to her neck and telling her, "Be quiet or I will slit your throat."

Lillie was petrified. All she could hear in the room was the sound of her roommate Gina (Pseudonym) crying and pleading the other robber to stop raping her. As dreadful as what Lilly was experiencing, Gina didn't fare any better. She had been sound asleep when she was awakened by a light shining in her eyes. All Gina could see was the figure of a black man with a bandanna around his face standing over her pointing a knife to her head. The man told her to be quiet and turn over on her stomach, to which she complied. At that point, all she could hear was the noise of dressers and closet doors being opened and closed. It sounded like someone was ransacking their apartment.

Then the commotion ended and the robber with the bandanna came back over to her bed and started to wrap her wrists and face with duct tape. He abruptly ordered her to turn over onto her back, at which time he pulled off her clothing. She heard what sounded like the tearing open of a condom pack and the next thing she knew was that he was sliding on top of her, placing his penis between her legs and eventually inserting it into her private part.

He continued to rape her as she pleaded for him to stop. All she could remember was that her roommate was on the other bed being raped by another black man. Gina wondered when was this hell on earth going to end. After a lengthy time, he pulled his penis out of her vagina without any condom. Although she had duct tape partially over her eyes, she was still able to glance over at the robber/rapist, who had a panicked look on his face. He leaned his head down and peered between her legs trying to find the condom, which had somehow disappeared.

When both of the robber/rapists tired out, they left the bedroom and were heard going into the bathroom. Next came the sound of the toilet flushing, and then there was a dead silence in the apartment. James had been tied up on the floor throughout this ordeal, and he struggled to get free. Both Gina and Lillie were frozen with fright and no one knew what to do. Was it safe to try to tear the duct tape loose? Were the robbers/rapists truly gone or just rummaging through the apartment looking for items to steal?

The three of them had one thing in common, and that was to find a way to escape without being caught by the crooks. Gina was able to wiggle off the duct tape on her hands, at which time she pulled off the tape covering her eyes. She could see Lillie on the other bed and went over to her to remove the tape and cord binding her. Then they pulled a blanket off James and cut him free. The three of them were elated to be alive, but all had shared with each other the one worst experience any human being could be subjected to.

They paused for a moment, realizing that the phone had been yanked off the wall, and they decided to go to one of the neighboring apartments to seek help. It took several minutes to get someone to wake up and open their doors to these traumatized victims. The police were called and responded in force.

A detective was called in and he examined the apartment for evidence. He was able to determine that some rings were taken as well as a gold bracelet. Also missing were a Swiss Army Knife, a boom box, and a mag light; all items taken were of limited value. What was more surprising to the detective was there were four condom wrappers on the floor, and they found a used condom floating in the toilet bowl. Apparently, the one robber/rapist thought he had flushed the full condom down the toilet. Somehow through fate, the condom wasn't disposed of but became a key piece of evidence.

The police took Lillie and Gina to Queen of the Valley Hospital, where a rape kit was used to collect evidence. When the doctor was examining Gina, he noticed a condom was wedged to the side in her vagina. He fished it out, and it was placed in an evidence envelope. When the doctor removed that condom he had no idea that ten years later it would be the key to solving the Cold Case of Christina Burmeister.

On the following graphic page are copies of the two slides the prosecutor used to show the apartment where the two rapes occurred. Also below are the photos of the apartment bathroom where the condom was found in the toilet.

GRAPHICS 39

These are photos of the apartment house where the rapes occurred.

These are photos of the condoms used in the rape cases.

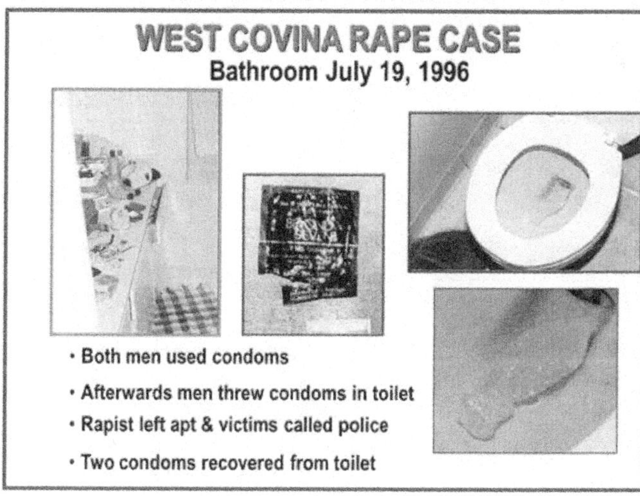

CHAPTER 25—DIXON—THANK GOD FOR DNA

The West Covina Police Department tried their best to solve the 1996 rape cases of Lillie and Gina. The detective submitted the DNA profile that was obtained from the two used condoms. Unfortunately, the database that existed back in 1996 was very limited. It wasn't until the passage of Proposition 69 in 2004, that the database received a large number of submissions of DNA profiles that had been collected from prisoners in the state prison.

During the late 1990s, James Dixon was in and out of state prison. Before he was released from prison, a DNA sample was taken. His DNA profile was placed in the database in after the passage of Proposition 69. It wasn't until January 5, 2005, that the West Covina Police and Sheriff's Department were notified that a single-source male DNA profile obtained from the condom recovered from Gina matched the DNA profile of a James Dixon.

Needless to say, the West Covina detective was ecstatic with this good news. Sometimes good news travels fast through law enforcement. The Sheriff's detectives on the Burmeister case heard the good news on this old rape case in West Covina and thought about the Tiparillo saliva DNA profile. They asked the crime lab to compare the condom's profile with the Tiparillo profile. Was this going to be a waste of time, comparing the two profiles? It was worth a try, since nothing was coming together with this very Cold Case.

Remarkably, there was a match. The detectives got a court order to take a new DNA sample from James Dixon, which they did and immediately had it analyzed. In short order, the word came back that the Tiparillo saliva DNA was from James Dixon. What a godsend for the Sheriff's detectives, Christina's family, the Greek community and the entire Cal Poly campus. Now the hard part began, which was to build a 'bullet proof' case against James Dixon.

For years, John Monaghan had worked with the Sheriff's detectives to find the suspect and develop the evidence that would be needed to obtain a conviction and earn the killer of Christina Burmeister a new home on Death Row. Since John had been working with other Sheriff's detectives on the serial killer in the Hill case, John understood all the hoops and hurdles that the prosecutor had to go through in order to have the DNA admitted into evidence in court.

One of John's concerns with DNA cases had always been the need to be able to corroborate the DNA match. The question was whether combining the two rape cases with Christina's murder case would supply sufficient corroboration. The problem was when the detectives showed Gina, Lillie, and James a six-pack photo lineup with Dixon's photo in it, none of them were able to identify him as one of the suspects. It had been nine long years since the rapes occurred, so it was no wonder they weren't able to identify Dixon as one of the rapists.

The only form of identification that the detectives were able to extract from the victims was the fact that they did remember that the suspects had tattoos on their chest and arms. The detective followed up with the possibility that the victims could identify Dixon's tattoos. John obtained a search warrant from a judge to require Dixon to allow photos to be taken of his various tattoos. All over his body he proudly displayed tats of his gang's name: 'Du Roc Crips" or 'DRC.' Numerous photos of tattoos were shown to the victims to see if they could recognize Dixon's tats. As hard as the victims tried, they couldn't pick them out.

By February 8, 2005, law enforcement arrested Dixon at his home in Pomona. He must have been surprised to be arrested for a nine-year-old rape and a three-and-a-half-year-old murder. Also arrested at the same time were Henry Singer (29) as well as Martha Dixon (26) (Pseudonym), who was the wife of defendant James Dixon. When the detectives interrogated both Henry and Martha about Christina's murder, they were willing to admit they were present but that they didn't do the killing.

By using the aiding and abetting legal theory, the prosecutors would be able to prosecute both of them for Christina's murder. Their Defense attorneys knew that the DA was definitely going to seek the Death Penalty in the Burmeister murder, since it was so egregious. Over the next two years, both Singer and Dixon's wife had plenty of time to think about their future. Neither wanted to receive the Death Penalty, nor did Life Without the Possibility of Parole really look that desirable. The big issue was, could they talk the DA into a straight Life sentence that meant they could be out in a little over a dozen years?

After extensive negotiation, John was able to get the DA administration to agree to Life for both of them. Since he wanted some corroboration for the Burmeister case, he hammered out a case settlement in which the wife could plead guilty to first degree murder and receive a straight Life sentence. However, he needed Henry Singer to help him convict his fellow gang member Dixon. The agreement was fashioned for Singer to basically 'Sing' in court by testifying to the truth of what really happened the night of the murder, which would result in a Life sentence. On the other hand, if Singer didn't testify truthfully then he would be sentenced to Life Without the Possibility of Parole (LWOP).

John agonized over the plea bargain, but he knew that he needed strong corroboration to get the Death Penalty for Dixon. On November 7, 2007, Singer and Dixon's wife entered their pleas of guilty. The wife immediately received her Life sentence. Singer's sentencing was put over until after he had testified in Dixon's trial.

John Monaghan was now ready for trial, and it was just a matter of time for the Defense to make their decisions to be ready. During this time, the DA's Office was reassessing how prosecutors should be assigned to the cases handled by the Major Crimes Division. The case of the ***People vs. Robert Blake*** was tried by a single prosecutor from Major Crimes Division, and the outcome was a Not Guilty Verdict. The District Attorney at the time was Steve Cooley, who responded to the jury's not guilty verdict by saying that "jurors were stupid." Many legal scholars believed the DA could have more eloquently expressed his displeasure.

Some of the DA administrators believed that having two prosecutors on the big publicity cases would reduce the chances of Not Guilty Verdicts. The concept of two prosecutors has some merit since it better divides the workload, especially in the trials that take months to try. It can be extremely stressful to have to be in court every day and prepared for every contingency. However, the two-prosecutor policy can run into problems, since top-level litigators sometimes have giant egos that don't take kindly to being told by someone else what to do and how to do it.

John Monaghan was the quintessence of the best of the best and had proven time and again he was more than capable of handling the biggest cases in the DA's Office all by himself. However, John's boss had to follow the DA's Office new two-prosecutor policy. The question was, who should be selected to be John Monaghan's co-prosecutor? Cathryn Brougham was working her way up in the Major Crimes Division and had successfully handled some challenging cases. She didn't have John's experience level, but she was eager to learn and willing to take on any type of case.

The DA administrators decided that they would pair John up with Cathryn on the Burmeister case. Although this wasn't going to be the perfect marriage of co-prosecutors, there were some perks for John. Over the years that John was preparing the Burmeister case, he was constantly getting resistance from the two rape victims. Both Gina and Lillie had been traumatized by what they had gone through when they were viciously raped. By now, ten years had gone by, and both women had tried hard to forget all the fear they had lived through. Neither woman wanted to testify in this case. They didn't want to have to relive the worst moments of their lives. The mere fact of having to come face to face in the courtroom with the defendant Dixon was such a repulsive thought to them. All they wanted to do was go on with their new lives.

John understood the dilemma that Gina and Lillie were going through. He couldn't blame them for their strong feelings. John knew that without the rape victims, Dixon would be getting away with these terrible rapes because he had traumatized his victims. As good a prosecutor as John was, he was having witness problems that couldn't be resolved.

What was noteworthy was the fact that Cathryn Brougham had come out of the Family Violence Division. There she had to deal with women who were so traumatized that they didn't want to testify. What Cathryn had learned was that sometimes she had to talk 'woman to woman' with these witnesses to develop a rapport. Sometimes trying to be logical in an emotional situation just doesn't work.

Perhaps just placing a hand on the witness's shoulder and saying that you understand their feelings can develop the trust and empathy that is needed to get the witness to come to court to testify.

John soon recognized that Cathryn could be a giant asset with the two rape victims. Thus, the dynamic duo of John and Cathryn was formed. Who was Cathryn Brougham? When anyone met Cathryn, they were struck by her imposing appearance. What can't go unnoticed is the fact that she is a tall slender woman who is physically fit. Her lofty physique allows her to tower over others, especially when wearing her high heels.

Since John had worked on the Burmeister case for several years, he was firmly aware of every facet of the case. However, Cathryn was a fast learner, and soon she was up to speed on the facts and evidence in the case. Then the day came when they both agreed that they were ready for trial.

CHAPTER 26 DIXON—TIME FOR TRIAL

March 3, 2008, it was time for the Opening Statement to begin. John slowly arose out of his chair and took three paces over to the lectern. He arranged his notes on the lectern and then he tilted his head back so his eyes were focused on each juror. The jurors were filled with anticipation, wondering what this case was really about. John wasn't about to disappoint them as he quickly described the sordid facts of the murder. He related that Christina Burmeister, who was 20 years old, left her house in Cerritos to travel to Pomona to attend a fraternity party but never made it there. The next morning, she was found dead in her pickup on a mountain road up in the San Gabriel Canyon.

He told the jury that the evidence would show that Christina was abducted somewhere near the fraternity house. Her kidnappers drove her in her pickup to the Washington Mutual Bank in the City of Montclair, where Dixon's wife withdrew $400 from Christina's join account that she had with her mother. From there they drove her up Highway 39 into the San Gabriel Canyon. Part way up, they pulled into a turnout and a Mr. Singer got out, leaving Mr. Dixon in the rear portion of the Extended Cab of the pickup while the victim sat in the passenger seat. Then the witness will testify that at that point Mr. Dixon slit her throat and killed her.

While talking to the jury, the prosecutor showed various photos of the truck and several photos of the victim reclined in the passenger seat with her neck slit open and blood saturating her clothing. At that point, some of the jurors winced in their seats. Their facial expressions changed dramatically as several of them crossed their hands and leaned back in their chairs.

Then John transitioned from the facts of the crime to who did it, explaining, "No suspect was found for about three years until detectives matched Dixon's DNA to the tip of a tiparillo recovered from the floorboard of the victim's truck." John went on to say that they would hear how the DNA came about. Furthermore, at least one of Dixon's accomplices would testify to an inside view of what really happened and who had done what.

Then the prosecutor moved on to the rape cases that happened five years before the murder. At that point, some of the jurors' faces took on a perplexed look as to what the 'rape cases' had to do with the murder case. John told the jurors, "In addition to the murder, Mr. Dixon is accused of breaking into a West Covina apartment in 1996 with another man, tying up one male resident, and raping two young women." Then he explained that as a result, two condoms were recovered and one contained ejaculation fluid that matched Mr. Dixon's DNA. When that match was discovered, the detectives in the Burmeister case submitted their DNA profile from the Tiparillo mouthpiece to the crime lab for a comparison. That resulted in a match to the defendant, Dixon.

At the end of his Opening Statement, John wanted to make sure that the jurors didn't get too confused by two totally separate crimes with the only nexus being the fact that both involved the defendant's DNA. He said, "Based on the evidence we will present, we will ask you to convict Mr. Dixon of the rapes and of the murder."

In order to prepare the jurors for the order of the testimony they were about to hear, John clarified that he would first be calling the witnesses in the rape cases and later call the witnesses pertaining to the murder. It was unclear whether John's Opening Statement was so convincing that the Defense attorney decided not to give a Defense Opening Statement. She indicated to the court that she reserved her Opening until the prosecution had put on all their witnesses and evidence. This may have been a wise strategy for the Defense, because no one knew for sure if the accomplices to the murder or the victims of the rapes would actually testify. And if they did testify, would they retract what they had told the police?

Then it was time to call the first witnesses. Prosecutor Cathryn immediately called witnesses regarding the rape case. In order to protect the identity of the rape victims, Lillie was given the fictional name of Jane Doe #1 and Gina was known as Jane Doe #2. Both took the witness stand with trepidation and told the jury the horrific story of how these two black men came into their apartment room demanding valuables. These robbers threatened them with guns and knives while they were tied up with duct tape and phone wire. Then Lillie told the jurors that the one robber asked her again where the money and jewelry were and she honestly replied she had nothing, he said to her, "If you don't have anything for us to take then we will take something else." At that point, he took the knife and cut the duct tape on her ankles. Then he pried her legs apart so he could savagely engage in multiple acts of forcible rape.

Back in the courtroom, the prosecutor stood near the victim on the witness stand so it was as if she was having a conversation with the prosecutor. It was obvious to everyone in the courtroom that the witness was terrified to look at the defendant. Even though Lillie was now in her 30s, she still didn't feel comfortable talking about the details of the rape in front of all the people in the courtroom. In her Asian cultural background, the terms penis and vagina were never discussed in public. From the pained look on some of the female jurors' faces, one wondered what they were thinking. Were these jurors thinking how they would feel if they had to describe the worst event that ever happened in their life in front of a bunch of strangers?

It was then Gina's turn to testify. Telling her story again made her relive in her mind thoughts and fears that she had desperately tried to suppress for the last ten years. From the tears in her eyes and her choked up voice she managed to permit the defendant his Constitutional Right of Confrontation of Witnesses. To some, it seems quite inhuman to require rape victims to have to appear in front of the rapist and testify as to all the cruel and heinous acts he maliciously did to her. One wonders whether the founding fathers meant to be that callous to rape victims. However, that was the Law of the Land and the victims had to comply with this unpleasant situation.

The Defense attorney had the right to 'Cross Exam' both Lilly and Gina. When both were asked if they could identify the defendant as one of the rapists both victims replied NO. That led to the next group of prosecution witnesses, who testified to finding the condoms that were collected and analyzed for DNA profiles. A

DNA expert came into court and explained the scientific process and the conclusion that the defendant's DNA profile matched the DNA in one of the condoms. The frequency of a repeat of the defendant's profile was one in 394 Quintillion. That meant it was highly unlikely that anyone on earth had the same DNA profile.

It was time for the prosecutor to transition to the murder of Christina Burmeister. In order to commence that part of the trial, Christina's mother Rosalia was called to the witness stand. She was asked what happened on the night of August 17, 2001. She explained to the jurors that her daughter around 10:00 p.m. asked her if she could go to a frat party in Pomona. She told her that it was unwise for a 20-year-old woman to venture into the Pomona neighborhood alone in her new pickup truck. However, Christina's retort was to promise her mother that she wouldn't stay that long and would be back in a couple of hours.

Rosalia relented, and that was the last time she ever saw her daughter alive. The next morning, her older daughter, Elizabeth, woke her up to inform her that Christina had not come home. She thought something bad had happened so she tried to call and page her but received no response. Then she called the bank where she shared an account with her daughter. She learned that there had been three withdrawals from the account. This fact troubled her, and she told the jury that she then knew something was terribly wrong. As a result, she called her husband and they agreed to contact the Sheriff's Department.

The final question was for her to look at a photo of her daughter to identify the shirt she had on when she left the house. Mrs. Burmeister glanced at the photo and choked back tears and said, "That was what she was wearing, although it appears to be a different color due to the blood that had soaked her blouse."

The next witness was Christina's sister, Elizabeth, who testified to going to the Montclair bank with her uncles and finding one of her sister's CD cases in the shrubs in the parking lot. After her testimony, there followed a stream of witnesses, including the friend who called Christina to invite her to the party; Deputy Tack, who was the one who discovered Christina dead in her truck parked in a turnout up in the San Gabriel Canyon; the detective who found the Tiparillo butt in the rear portion of Christina's truck; the sheriff's criminalist who tested the Tiparillo butt for DNA; and the DNA expert who explained the match to the defendant.

The prosecution's star witness was Dixon's accomplice, Henry Singer, who described how the victim was kidnapped. He then explained how they took her to the bank to withdraw money from her account. Later Singer told how he drove the truck up Highway 39 into San Gabriel Canyon, where he pulled into a large turnout. He got out of the truck, leaving Dixon in the back area while the victim was seated in the passenger seat. He related to the jury that as he stood behind the truck, he watched the defendant's arm holding a knife while slitting the victim's throat. At that point in his testimony, he looked directly at the jurors and with his right-hand wiped tears from his eyes. In a muffled voice, he uttered that he now wished that he had done something to help that woman.

The prosecutor asked him if he had pleaded guilty to the murder of Christina Burmeister, to which he admitted that he had. The prosecutor went on to ask him if he was to receive a sentence of Life in prison upon him testifying truthfully at this trial. Again, he said that was his understanding. Upon cross-examination, the Defense attorney tried to imply that this witness was testifying against the defendant in order to avoid the Death Penalty. For almost two days, the accomplice Henry Singer was grilled by the Defense attorney to make him look like he was the real killer and not the defendant.

The prosecutor knew that the Defense attorney was trying to place Singer in the driver's seat at the time of the killing. In order to disprove that, John called another criminalist, who testified that he had examined the interior of the truck. His opinion was that the blood spatter inside the cab of the truck suggested that nobody was sitting in the driver's seat when the victim's throat was slashed. This testimony totally corroborated the accomplice's version of the events.

John asked the judge to hold a hearing out of the presence of the jury regarding the testimony of Dixon's wife. At that hearing, the bailiff escorted Mrs. Dixon into the courtroom. She was asked if she was willing to testify against her husband, James Dixon, to which she replied that she wished to invoke her legal right not to testify against her husband. Her plea bargain didn't require her to testify in order to receive a sentence of Life instead of Life Without the Possibility of Parole (LWOP).

Undoubtedly, this was a disappointment for the prosecution, but John knew that when you roll the dice in Hell sometimes it comes up snake eyes. Thankfully the accomplice, Henry Singer, did come through and he sang loud and clear, although it would have been nice if the wife would have testified to corroborate Singer's testimony.

After the prosecution was finished putting on witnesses, the Defense called a few witnesses, but they were pleased that they had dodged a bullet by the defendant's wife's refusal to testify. As the Defense came to a close, it was time for a crucial decision—whether the defendant Dixon would testify on his own behalf. The defendant could take the witness stand and try to convince the jury that he was not guilty. Or the defendant could remain silent and rely on the argument that the prosecution hadn't proved its case. Everyone in the courtroom waited to see what the defendant would do.

Then the Defense attorney leaned over and, in a whisper, asked the defendant one last time if he wanted to testify. With a slight shaking of his head, he gave his attorney his answer. The Defense attorney in slow motion stood up and announced, "The Defense wishes to Rest its case." At that point, the judge asked the defendant if he wished to testify, to which he replied that he did not. The judge took a waiver from the defendant as to his right to testify, and the testimony portion of the trial was over.

That meant that it was time for both sides to argue their case. Since it was the prosecution that had called most of the 30 witnesses during this lengthy trial, the jury had gotten to know the prosecutors, especially John Monaghan. He had given them a clear and concise Opening Statement of what he was going to prove. By now, the jurors realized that he had kept his word and proved up everything he said he would. Albeit he did tell them in his Opening that there were two accomplices and at least one of them would testify and provide an inside view of the murder. Although he wasn't able to get the wife to testify, he did at least get one of the accomplices to testify.

This was the time that the prosecution had to convince the 12 jurors of the strength of their case. John stood before this jury and there was a hush throughout the courtroom. Standing tall at the lectern, he projected an aura of strength and knowledge. He was thoroughly familiar with every aspect of his case. When he was challenged by Defense counsel, he could cite the pages in the transcript that refutes the claim. This case was easy for him to argue, since years earlier he laid a solid foundation by persuading the rape victims, Lillie and Gina, to testify and negotiation with Henry Singer to testify against his longtime buddy had paid off. John was careful in talking to the jurors about the DNA evidence. He realized that most jurors have no understanding how DNA works. He wanted them to understand that if a certain procedure is followed, one gets valid results. This is very much like not understanding how a clock works but accepting that it can accurately tell time.

After he summarized the evidence for the jury, he shifted his Argument to the more tedious part of the jurors' job, which was navigating their way through all the verdict forms. John knew from experience that there were severe consequences if the jury foreperson or even the jurors themselves don't properly fill out the Special Circumstance forms. The prosecution could be prevented from moving forward to the Penalty phase if certain boxes aren't marked correctly. John stressed the importance of the findings that Christina was KIDNAPPED as she was driven from the Smoke Shop to the bank in Montclair, as well as when she was transported up the San Gabriel Canyon. Also, he needed the jury to understand that the taking of her ATM card constituted a ROBBERY.

When John felt he had maximized the jurors' interest span, he ended his Argument and the Defense took over. The Defense zeroed in on the vulnerable part of the prosecution's case. She first addressed the rape victims' testimony. She concentrated on the fact that neither victim could identify the defendant as one of the rapists. But she saved her main attack for the accomplice's testimony. She didn't contest that her client was involved, since his DNA was on the Tiparillo. She conceded that the defendant may have been in the back of the cab of the truck, but stated that didn't prove he was the murderer. The only evidence that the defendant was the person who killed the victim was the testimony of the accomplice, Henry Singer.

Then she went over his testimony, in which Singer stated that he drove the truck up to the mountains. She emphasized that Singer was in a much better position to kill the victim than her client, who was tucked in the rear of the Extended Cab. She reiterated that Singer would say anything in order to save his life. She emphasized that by Singer implicating her client the DA was promising him a sentence of Life instead of LWOP.

After the Defense had finished her Argument, the prosecution had a chance to rebut what she had said. That was when John asked the jurors to remember how one of the criminalists had testified that in his expert opinion the blood spatter on the driver's side of the truck indicated that no one was seated in the driver's seat when the victim's throat was slit. His reasoning was that when her artery was severed on the left side of her neck it spewed a mist of blood on the driver's seat and driver's door panel.

John said that the blood spatter totally corroborated what Mr. Singer testified to, which was that he had exited the driver's side of the truck before the killing took place. At that point, the Prosecutor sat down and the judge read the final jury instructions. At the conclusion of the instructions from the judge, the jury went out to start their deliberation. The very next day, the jury came back with a verdict of guilty of First-Degree Murder with the Special Circumstance of Robbery and of Kidnap to be true. They also convicted the defendant on both rape charges. The jury then was excused for several days, after which they would return to start the Penalty phase of the trial.

On the designated day, all the jurors were back in Judge Genesta's courtroom in their jurors' chairs. Needless to say, since a person's life was at stake the mood of the courtroom was very intense. When the judge asked if the prosecution wished to make an Opening Statement, John acknowledged that he did. Slowly, he stood up from the counsel table and walked over toward the jury box. He looked at all the jurors and in a gloomy voice he said, "Good Afternoon." With those words, he gave a forced smile that instantly disappeared as his voice expressed a serious demeanor that compelled the jurors to listen attentively.

John explained to the jury that their duty in the Penalty phase of the trial was to consider whether the Aggravating evidence presented to them substantially outweighed the Mitigating evidence, and if so the verdict would be for DEATH. The prosecution would be presenting to them information about the defendant's prior acts of violence. John said that besides the defendant's prior criminal record they could consider the facts of the present case as to determine whether they were of an aggravating nature. In addition to that, the prosecution could present Victim Impact evidence regarding how the loss of Christina had impacted the lives of her family and friends.

With that said, the prosecutor sat down and Defense counsel got up and asked the jurors to withhold their judgment until they heard and considered all the evidence.

The actual presentation of evidence during the Penalty phase didn't take long, since it was mainly introducing court documents showing all of the defendant's convictions and prison records. These included the defendant's resume in chronological order, which included the following: in 1987, while the defendant was in high school, he chased another student into a church with a knife; in 1992 and 1993, he was convicted of possession for sale of drugs; in 1995 and 1997, he was convicted of possession of a gun by a felon; and in February 1996, he sodomized an inmate while in prison. When he was released from prison that next year, he raped the two women in their West Covina apartment, and later that year he pulled a gun on a policeman in an Ontario park.

The Defense put on some evidence indicating he had mental challenges in his life as well as an abusive childhood. After the Defense finished with their evidence, it was time for both sides to argue their case. John approached the jury and stood there and took a deep breath. John told the jurors that it wasn't an easy task to come back recommending Death. However, he said in this case the manner in which Christina was killed was in and of itself aggravating. On top of that, the defendant's criminal record was definitely aggravating. He said that there was only one punishment that would be appropriate in this case, and that was DEATH. He went on to say, "Mr. Dixon, through his actions, has earned the penalty of death and a one-way ticket to Death Row real soon."

The prosecutor then slowly went over the facts of the case by saying, "Can you image the last hour of Christina's life? She was kidnapped outside a Pomona fraternity party. Her hands were bound behind her back, possibly by her pantyhose, and she was driven face down in her new truck to a Montclair bank, where they withdrew $400 from her account."

At that point, John stepped back and took a long breath. Then, with his stern East Coast accent, he slowly pronounced the word "I-M-A-G-I-N-E" defendant could have walked away at that point, but instead he drove Christina up Highway 39 above Azusa to a turnout where he cut her throat and left her to die." The tone of his voice was contemptuous as he said, "The last thing Christina saw on this earth was Dixon's face and a knife." John extended his hand outward and pointed to the defendant, who was seated at counsel table partially blocked by his attorney.

John finished with his description of the crime scene by adding, "Christina would have instinctively put her hands to her throat when it was cut. The blood would have gushed through her fingers. Say she lost consciousness in 10 seconds." Then with a grim voice John started to slowly count, "One, two, three, four" up to ten. Then he said, "Imagine what those 10 seconds were like to her. IMAGINE THE TERROR she must have felt." Then John slowly turned around and walked back to the counsel table.

The Defense attorney stood up and tried to preserve her credibility by admitting that the defendant may have been involved but he may not have been the killer. She harped on the fact that the accomplice, Singer, had gotten such a deal from the DA. She asked the jurors to consider the possibility that Singer had assigned Dixon more than his fair share of blame in the killing in order to win a reduced sentence for himself. She stressed, "He doesn't tell the truth. He is an outright liar." She finished by saying the only fair thing to do was to give them all a Life sentence.

The Defense concluded her Argument, and the judge read the final jury instruction. The jurors were sent out to deliberate whether they should recommend Death or LWOP. The jury consisted of seven women and five men. They were out for only two hours and came back with a recommendation for DEATH.

After the case was over, a reporter asked Christina's mother her reaction to the jury's verdict, and she said, "We are relieved that the jury recognized the brutality of the killing and held the defendant responsible for it. Christina's life should not have been lost at that age or any age; a life should not be lost in that manner. Justice was served today." The Defense attorney told the reporter, "It's very tough in a case like this to spare somebody's life who committed a heinous murder."

Finally, a reporter cornered John Monaghan. He seldom if ever talked to the news media. However, because of the extreme aggravation of this case, John made an exception when he said, "Most of the people who were his victims were completely and totally innocent. He is nothing but a FULL-BLOWN PREDATOR."

John's assessment of the defendant, James Winslow Dixon, most likely was a fair and accurate description of a human being that may have no HUMAN EMOTION. This was one case that John and I, the author, discussed for years. My daughter was also a student at Cal Poly when Christina was viciously murdered, I remembered many nights driving over to campus and picking up my daughter when her night classes let out. We all lived in fear for years not knowing who the killer was. During that period, everyone was a potential suspect. Was it another co-ed? Was it a staff member? Was it a member of the sports team?

Fortunately, John continued to work with the Sheriff's Homicide detectives to solve this albatross case hanging around the community's neck. I was more than aware how difficult this case would be to prosecute. Thank God for John's tenaciousness in that he stayed with this case to the bitter end. Although the public has no way of knowing how John Monaghan was able to get this PREDATOR off the streets, he and other members of the Major Crimes Division quietly without any fanfare take on some of the most challenging criminal cases. One of the purposes of this book is to shine the spotlight on this elite group of prosecutors who make our community safer and allow us to live our lives without fear.

CHAPTER 27 ALVAREZ CASE—GLENDALE METROLINK TRAIN CRASH

The morning of Thursday, January 27, 2005, was just like any other workday. Many of the suburbanites woke up early to get themselves ready for the long commute to the City of Angels. These business commuters enjoyed living far and away from the hustle and bustle of the mammoth metropolis. These workers are willing to pay the price of two long commutes each day. Throughout most of the world, people like to live in the center of a city, but Southern Californians like the freedom of having large-lot houses made accessible by their sporty cars.

Years ago, the ribbon of freeways made it easy to commute to downtown; however, over time these motorways became giant parking lots better called 'gridlock.' It took years for the 'city fathers' to develop some type of mass transportation system. The answer for the Simi Valley and the northern part of the San Fernando Valley was the building of the Metrolink line from Moorpark to Union Station in downtown LA. (Now called the East Ventura Line) The travel time by using this commuter train has been cut in half, thereby giving the people at least another hour to enjoy being at home.

These 'Metro linkers' over time became used to rushing to the various rail stations, parking their car, and jumping on the trains precisely at the same time each day. Once on board, these commuters took on various roles. They knew for the next hour they could transition into possibly the most peaceful time of their day. They didn't have to worry about traffic or be concerned about finding a place to park. Each commuter was free to do whatever they wanted. The older crowd might take out a paperback books and flip to their bookmark to continue their reading adventure. Some might try to discreetly read a newspaper without encroaching on their fellow passengers' private space.

There are the unwritten commuter rules that are strictly adhered to. First, you don't talk to other commuters unless they have somehow indicated a willingness to talk to you. When the portable radio was invented, this caused all sorts of problems for bus and train commuters. Not until they came up with earphones were radio devices permissible to be used by commuters. One of the commuters' pet peeves is the younger commuters who listen to their 'hard metal' music with their earphones on but the other commuters can still feel the drum beat three seats away.

However, the greatest inconvenience to pleasant commuting occurred with the introduction of the cell phone. What drives commuters crazy is the passenger who continually talks on their cell phone. It's not uncommon for some people to talk during their entire commute. The other passengers become so frustrated to have to overhear what someone had for lunch or how they enjoyed their yoga class. All the other passengers patiently wait for someone to be brave enough to say something to the rude cell phone user, but seldom does anyone speak up.

However, this Moorpark Train #100 was made up of hardcore passengers who seemed like more of a large family. Most of the commuters knew each other and would greet each other every morning. Each one seemed to have their assigned seat, even though there was non-assigned seating. It is strange how the commuters are 'creatures of habit.' Generally, the 'talkers' gathered in one part of the train car and the 'readers' and 'sleepers' migrated to other corners where they wouldn't be disturbed.

This Thursday morning was just a replay of any other day. A group of deputy Sheriffs were up front, talking about law enforcement issues. Deputy James Tutino told his fellow deputies he had to go in early because they were having a morning meeting at his job at Central County Jail. He said he had planned to drive his old Mustang that morning but his left leg was hurting him. Since he had a stick shift, he didn't feel up to doing all the clutching with his sore leg. His colleagues made fun of him, claiming that he was getting too old to drive his classic Mustang.

Henry Kilinski lived in the City of Orange, and on this morning was taking the northbound train to his job in Burbank. He usually commuted by car, but his family encouraged him to take the train on this rainy morning since they felt it was safer for him. He was a happy-go-lucky guy who had aspired to go into firefighting. He and his wife had been a couple for years, and it was only recently they decided to get married. His life was now complete with his wife and stepdaughter. Family meant everything to him, including his parents and sister.

Another commuter was William Parent, age 53, who lived in Canoga Park and commuted every workday to downtown, where he worked for the Los Angeles Unified School District. Although he wasn't married and didn't have children, he was very close to his siblings.

Thomas Ormiston had worked for Amtrak for years but got an offer from Metrolink to work for them as a conductor. For him, this was an easy way to glide into his retirement in several months.

The Metrolink Southbound train #100 was an enjoyable way of life for most of these 250 passengers. The train operated like clockwork and was one of those things in life that everyone took for granted. The train cars were the double-decker types made of sturdy steel, which guaranteed a smooth ride as it glided along the tracks. The locomotion for the train came from the diesel car to the rear. The Metrolink authority had decided years earlier to use push-pull trains. Therefore, the trains didn't have to waste time turning around at the end of the line to re-position the locomotive in the front of the train.

What that all meant was saving time and money for the fast-moving Metrolink trains. The passengers never noticed a difference; in the morning the front car (called cab-car) was like a regular train car, except it had a small area for the engineer to sit and operate the locomotive, which was at the rear of the three-car train. However, in the afternoon it would be the locomotive that would be in front, and the engineer would be seated at the front of the locomotive. For the Metrolink passengers, it all seemed transparent whether the front car was a locomotive or a cab car.

However, there were those passengers who seemed to get a thrill riding up front in the cab car train. Those seated in the front seats could look forward and get the same view the engineer had of the tracks in front. When the train was speeding over 70 miles per hour down the rails, it was better than the old 'E' Ride at Disneyland (or, for the younger readers, the Fast and Furious ride at Universal Studios).

When riding the commuter train, there is always the feeling of invincibility. That morning, the #100 Metrolink pulled out of the Burbank station, heading for its next stop at Glendale station. Those on board could feel the exhilaration as the well-built metal cars slowly picked up speed. The amazing part was how quickly the passengers felt the surge of power from the locomotive propelling them like a missile down the straight railroad tracks. Whenever the train came near a traffic crossing, the engineer sounded the shrill of the horn.

At 6:03 a.m., train #100 was on time and was approaching the Chevy Chase (this has nothing to do with the comedian from Saturday Night Live fame) traffic crossing, and the engineer blew the horn announcing to those who lived nearby that if they hadn't awakened it was time to get up. Since it was still dark outside, the train's high beam headlight pierced the gloomy skies ahead of it. The rain was more in the drizzle mode, giving the landscape a wet and dreary look. The deputy sheriffs were up next to the engineer in the front cab car, just talking cop-talk. All of a sudden, the engineer seemed to freeze with fright. Were his eyes playing tricks on him? What could this object be that seemed to be dead center on the tracks? Should he sound the horn again, or should he hit the emergency brakes? The ominous decision of a possible disaster was in his hands.

Hitting the emergency brakes meant dozens of his passengers would be hurled like rag dolls through the steel train and would be seriously injured. There was no time for reflection. Every nanosecond, the object on the tracks was growing larger. His eyes told him that it was a car on the tracks, which isn't an uncommon occurrence on this set of tracks. Occasionally depressed people will commit suicide by parking their cars on the tracks. Other times it is people in a hurry to get to work and they go around the crossing barriers and get stuck. Since it was around 6:00 a.m., it was most likely someone playing the 'late to work' scenario.

But as the train barreled closer, that theory didn't make sense because the car wasn't even near the street crossing. The engineer must have thought to himself, 'What the hell is this SUV doing on my tracks?'

Juan Manuel Alvarez was a human being who was afflicted with many emotional and mental issues. He had a craving for Methamphetamines, which was disrupting his family life. He was married and had two young children. Like any father, he wanted to be with his children as they grew up. He tried to hold down a job that would provide for his family, and he worked off and on in the Compton area. However, his drug use may have caused him to lose his jobs or he may have been the victim of a changing economy. Finding a new job didn't seem to be a high priority for him.

The bottom line for Juan Alvarez was he didn't have a job, and as a result, he was not able to provide for his family. He became depressed because of his situation. Was it the drug use that was creating his problems, or was the drug use his way of dealing with his problems? It didn't matter; the end result was that he was continually under the influence of the Methamphetamines. When he was high as a kite or when he crashed into withdrawals, he was far from a role model for his children.

Eventually, his wife had had enough of his dysfunctional behavior, so she filed for divorce and obtained a restraining order keeping him away from the children and herself. This meant he no longer could live with the family in Compton, so he began to wander from place to place. Juan Alvarez met a lady in the Atwater community of Los Angeles who had gotten to know him through his Aztec dancing. At one time, he was involved in a dance troupe that promoted the ancient world dancing. He seemed most comfortable when on a dance floor with his Aztec brothers. He enjoyed wearing the various feather headdresses and wearing a loincloth. With the repetitive beat of the drum, he seemed to enter into a trance of another world where he felt at home.

This lady had a rental unit near her home and offered it as a place for him to stay. With his sleeping bag and a beat-up cardboard box full of personal items, he called this one-bedroom unit his new home. The downside of this new location was that he didn't have any friends in this neighborhood. So it was understandable that he spent his free time getting high on Meth. He was angry that his wife had obtained a

Restraining Order that prevented him from coming by to visit with his kids. Although the Restraining Order was meant to be a positive thing, it was turning out to be a negative force that was pushing Juan deeper into his depression.

During the early morning hours, Juan had time to think about his wretched situation. How could he get his wife back? What did he have to do to convince her that he was willing to turn his life around? In the past, he had promised her that he was finished wasting his life on drugs. She had seen and heard him beg her to give him another chance. She had continually heard his sincere pleas that the next time it would be different. Unfortunately, his wife had heard every pathetic story from him, and with two children to raise she had run out of patience.

Juan loved and missed his wife and the children so much that he had to find a way to convince his wife he was sincere in changing his ways. How could he impress his wife? Maybe if something bad were to happen to him she might become sympathetic toward him. His mind kept reflecting on what could he do to cause his wife to feel sorry for him.

He had considered committing suicide, since his wife would feel some guilt for pushing him over the edge. However, he really didn't want to kill himself but only get sympathy from his wife. So what action could he take? He could cut his wrist and appear to be bleeding to death, which was one way to get her attention. Juan was squeamish about seeing blood, so his mind tried to conjure up a less painful way to appear to be committing suicide.

He remembered how the media liked to play up stories about people committing suicide by parking their cars on the railroad tracks. These crashes made for good media coverage and instantly the poor soul was on the front page of the newspaper. He liked the concept but wasn't keen on the idea of having to patiently wait for the train to arrive to cause a big impact.

Somehow, he got the idea that he wanted to create a giant fire that would consume the car. In order to carry out his momentous destruction plan, he needed to get some gasoline for the gigantic explosion. At one time, he had a bunch of gas cans that he could get filled. But after his wife had kicked him out of their house, he somehow lost track of where he had placed those cans. So he found two large plastic containers that he could fill with gasoline. Years earlier, a law had been passed which prohibited anyone from using ordinary plastic containers to transport gasoline. Even though that was the law, Juan had no difficulty pulling into a self-service gas station and filling up two plastic containers and placed them in his Jeep Cherokee.

Juan obtained the gasoline. It was hard to comprehend how he was going to use all this gasoline to win back his wife. Next, he had to find a place where it would make sense to park a car on the railroad tracks. Obviously, he couldn't just stop his car on the track at a railroad crossing. If he did that, someone would come from behind and honk their horn. Somehow, he needed to find a way to drive parallel down the tracks and at a certain point pull over onto the tracks.

After driving away from the gas station, Juan came across the Chevy Chase Drive traffic crossing of the tracks used by Metrolink. This was a busy crossing that involved two tracks for both the northbound and southbound trains that were also used by Union Pacific as one of their main freight lines. In other words, he was selecting a busy set of tracks that would soon see rail traffic.

As Juan drove parallel to the tracks, he kept looking for a place he could turn to the left to be able to drive onto the tracks. Although it was now after 6:00 a.m., it was the perfect place for him to jerk the steering wheel of his Cherokee to the left, and he accelerated. The tires squealed as the wheels spun in the railroad gravel into the air behind the Cherokee. As the front tires hit the steel track, the Cherokee lurched back and the smell of burnt tire rubber filled the morning air.

The Cherokee seemed to have a mind of its own. It didn't seem willing to be blown to smithereens within minutes. Juan was intent on making sure that his vehicle was directly on the path of the next train on that track. With a little more nudging, the Cherokee was straddling both rails. Juan stopped the SUV and turned off the ignition. Swiftly, Juan jumped out of the driver's seat and opened the back door. There he lifted one of the plastic gas cans out and placed it on the ground while he grabbed the other gas can.

In an almost methodical manner, Juan took the cap off the plastic container and started pouring the gasoline all over the hood and dousing the roof as he walked around his car. When he was finished with the container, he just tossed it to the side and picked up the other container and poured the gasoline all over the seats and interior of the cab. By then the Cherokee reeked of gasoline and no one in their right mind would then get inside it and sit down in the driver's seat.

One of the fortuitous events was that two individuals saw Juan do all this dousing of the car. They were some distance away and couldn't see what liquid was poured from the containers. Only later, when the plastic containers were recovered, could it be proven that they had contained gasoline.

All that could be proved with certainty was that Juan Alvarez parked his Jeep Cherokee on the tracks and poured gasoline on his vehicle. Juan was seen getting back in the car. What we don't know with any degree of certainty was what was going through Juan Alvarez' mind. Was he intent on committing suicide and the gasoline was a way to guarantee that he wouldn't survive? Or was he hoping that the car would be so badly burned that the Coroner's investigators couldn't say with certainty whether there had been any human being killed in the vehicle?

As Juan was sitting in his car, his mind had to be racing a hundred miles an hour. The pungent odor of the gasoline from the interior of the Cherokee had to be so strong that no one could possibly think clearly. All of a sudden, this Meth head who wanted to kill himself was having second thoughts. We know that the engineer was frantically blowing the train's horn. Was it the noise from the horn that startled Juan to his senses? No one knows for certain what caused Juan to spring like a hunted deer from the Jeep and run to the side of the tracks as Train #100 barreled directly toward his car.

On the following page is a map showing where Juan Alvarez lived in relation to the train crash. Also there are exhibits showing photos of the railroad track and the placement of the Jeep on the railroad tracks..

GRAPHICS 40

Trains crashed on the border of cities of Los Angeles & Glendale.

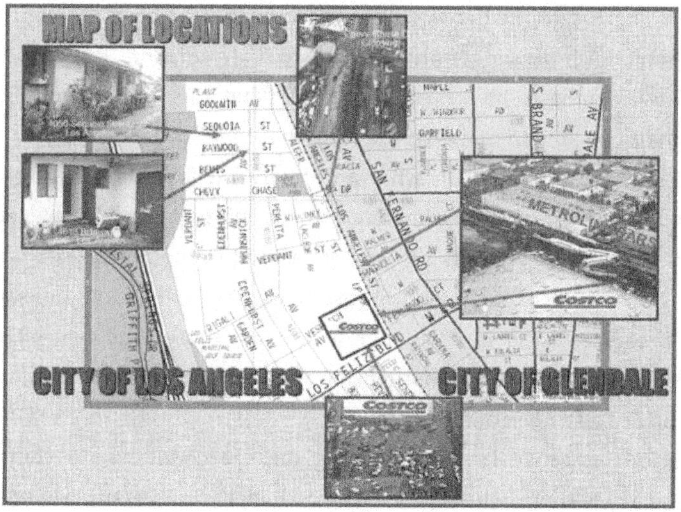

Aerial view of train cars that crashed.

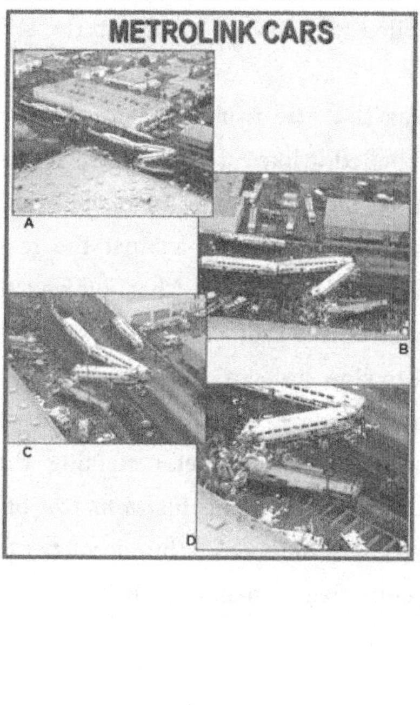

This shows how Jeep was driven on tracks.

At that moment in time, hundreds of lives would be shattered forever. Cher's song ***If I Could Turn Back Time*** would have been appropriate. But it was only a song and no one could turn back time. Nothing could change the fate that was about to occur. The initial reaction was that the passengers noticed that the regular brakes were being activated. Then there was a feeling of a thud of Train #100 hitting an automobile. These seasoned commuters most likely had been through this drill on prior occasions. Each passenger on #100 had to feel, 'Oh, Shit. I'm going to be late to work.' This was going to be a mere delay and what was going through their minds was, 'How will I be able to make up the time that I will be late?'

The initial reaction was, 'Oh what an inconvenience this all will be.' Then the next moment was something completely different from anything ever mentioned about train wrecks. Somehow the front car seemed to momentarily go airborne, and then there was the noise of the bottom of the carriages dragging and scraping along gravel. The noise was so intense that it startled those who had dozed off for a peaceful slumber before facing another day at work. At that exact moment, there was a strong whiff of an indescribable smell.

The passengers froze in place waiting for the conductor to come on the PA system to instruct them what to do. Others had their 'seventh sense' of 'fight or flight' response kick in and they automatically lifted their feet and pressed them against the seat in front of them. They coiled their bodies to absorb the shock they were anticipating.

What had happened to Train #100 was that the front car had struck the jeep Cherokee and for several hundred feet propelled it like a rocket. However, as the car was disintegrating in front of the cab car, its steel body and drive shaft got wedged in one of the rail switches. The amount of force striking against the rail was so intense that it broke a three-foot section of the steel rail. That allowed the front wheels of the front cab car to derail, which meant that Train #100 was now a free speeding object with nothing in front of it to slow it down.

At that point, there was nothing to slow down the hurtling train cars. The passengers could hear the intense grinding noise of metal striking the gravel railroad bed. The passengers must have thought that it was just a matter of seconds before the train cars would come to a stop. Then there was a thunderous crash as the front car of Train #100 struck a freight locomotive on a side track. The front car was no match for this 100-ton freight locomotive. The impact crushed the front car like an accordion.

Since it struck on the right side the entire front car, the kinetic force spun the rear of the car to the left. As fate would have it on that dreary morning, the Northbound #9100 was speeding north on the parallel track. It had left Glendale station and was picking up speed with its 30 or 40 passengers, most of whom were heading home from working a midnight shift in LA. If it had left five seconds earlier, so many lives would have been saved.

What happened was that the rear of the front car of Southbound Train #100 spun with great force to the left, striking the Northbound Train #9100 second passenger car and cutting a gash in the metal shell of the car. The force was transferred to the rear car of this northbound train, knocking it off the tracks onto its side. All though this rear car wasn't packed with passengers, those on board were totally surprised, since their mindset was that they would be getting home in a few minutes. These passengers had no chance to brace themselves. In an instant, their world was topsy-turvy. Many of them went from pleasantly reading a book or magazine to flying through the air and landing on other passengers and backpacks. Since the lights had gone out and it was totally dark outside, their eyes couldn't be of much help reorienting them to what was happening. Their ears could make out sounds of glass breaking and steel striking steel. The most they could surmise was that they seemed to be in a train car on its side that continued to glide over gravel before it came to an abrupt stop.

After the rear car had detached, the remainder of the Northbound Train #9100 continued to wobble, trying not to lose any more cars. As #9100 struggled to stay on the tracks, its second train car swayed to its side so much that it struck a metal signal tower. By that time, the engineer was able to get the train stopped. Meanwhile, the metal tower bobbed in the air and finally toppled onto the second car.

CHAPTER 28 ALVAREZ—TIME FOR SEARCH AND RESCUE

By 6:08 a.m., the Metrolink tracks between Chevy Chase Drive to Los Feliz Boulevard had gone down in history as the site of the second-deadliest train disaster in America. The question was what to do next. The so-called first responders were the passengers who had survived. What should their role be? Should they go to the aid of their fellow passengers, or was their first priority to get themselves away from this mess? Some of the walking passengers thought of picking up their personal belongings, such as purses, laptops, backpacks, and even their lunch bags. The magnitude of what they were going through had not sunk in. How could anyone think about saving a sandwich bag when they had just been spared their lives?

The heavy-duty freight train on the siding had been completely knocked over and diesel fuel was leaking from its fuel tanks. The diesel oil smell was scary for most of the passengers, who thought it was likely to explode at any moment. (Generally, diesel fuel on its own will not ignite) It was still dark, but there was the flicker of flames from the car parts that were burning. The initial reaction of many of the passengers was to get as far away as they could before any inferno would occur. (Most people believe that diesel fuel is as explosive as gasoline.)

However, a tug-a-war of emotions was coming over the survivors as they tried to find their way out of the wreckage. They could hear the faint sound of moaning and the occasional cry for help. Many of the passengers didn't want to leave their fellow passengers so there were many heroic acts during those early morning hours that never rose to the attention of the media. Some of these acts involved removing debris or pulling seats off trapped passengers and pulling them to safety.

However, this left emotional scars on some of those who tried to help. Many had to make life-and-death split-second decisions as to who was helpable and those who were beyond help. To the average person, this was an agonizing decision. As the time and years move on, they will reflect on whether they made the right decision to pass over a person who was moaning for help as their body lay trapped, spraying blood all over the surroundings. There would be moments of regret in the future, but at that moment in time life and death decisions had to be painfully made without reflecting on the consequences.

No one had to make tougher decisions than the employees at the local Los Feliz Costco Discount store. One of their forklift operators was unloading a stack of merchandise in the store. As he pulled out into the Costco parking lot, a loud crash caught his attention. It seemed to be coming from the railroad tracks that ran along the backside of the big-box store. To his surprise, he saw some type of train car strike a freight locomotive parked on a siding.

He couldn't believe what he was seeing. This gigantic locomotive was knocked over onto its side and starting to skid into the Costco parking lot, making a loud grinding noise. He watched in disbelief as the locomotive came to rest mere feet from his forklift. What should he do next? He had never experienced a train crashing into the parking lot. His response was typical of many. He yelled at one of the Costco clerks to call 911 to report the train wreck. He could see flames coming from several of the train cars. He jumped down off his forklift, ran into the warehouse, and grabbed a fire extinguisher. He yelled at other employees to find more fire extinguishers and bring them outside to the parking lot.

Without thinking, the forklift operator and his volunteer fire brigade had to take several large steps to maneuver over the crashed chain link fence. Once they were on the train tracks, they rushed to the first fire and started spraying with their handheld extinguishers. It didn't take long before their extinguishers ran dry and someone ran back and got more extinguishers. As they stood there, they could smell the diesel fuel leaking from the locomotive fuel tanks. At that moment, these volunteers first responders may have re-thought the wisdom of their heroic acts.

Shortly thereafter, these Costco employees went into rescue mode as they could hear the sighs for help from the injured and dying.

The location of this disaster became the next problem. Where did this train crash occur? The answer to this question can't be easily answered. The Metrolink tracks rested within several feet of the City of Glendale, which has its own fire and police department. However, on the other side (the west side) of the tracks was the City of Los Angeles, which has one of the largest fire departments in the country.

The area where Juan drove his car onto the tracks was in the City of Los Angeles. Also, the freight locomotive came to rest in the Costco parking lot, which was in the City of LA. After the crash, the phone lines lit up at both dispatch centers for the two cities. These dispatchers had to make a split-second decision whether to send units. The City of Glendale knew they had to respond because they had jurisdiction of the Metrolink tracks. On the other hand, Los Angeles Fire Department realized that they were clearly responsible for any fire caused by the freight locomotive.

The dispatchers from both agencies sent first responders. As soon as they arrived, they knew they both were being confronted by something that was bigger than anything they had trained for. No one knew that this incident was going to result in 11 deceased and 200 injured. Between the two cities, who was going to be in charge? During the first moments, the first responders went into a rescue mode as well as extinguishing the fires. Where this got tricky was that Glendale Fire decided to set up a triage center on the east side of the tracks. They used their large saws to cut down a chain link fence and placed a green tarp on the ground for a place for the paramedics to examine the injured to determine who needed immediate help and who could wait for attention.

By this time, it was daylight, and a drizzle of rain showered the makeshift triage area. As much as administrators wanted rescue operations to go smoothly, there were all sorts of obstacles that prevented them from going like clockwork. Many of the injured had walked or been moved to the west side of the tracks to get away from the flames of the sporadic fires. They were far from the triage area where the assessment team was located. Also, ambulances were having difficulty responding to the triage area, which was tucked between several buildings that didn't have easy street access.

The first responders were trying to work out the logistics of how to run such a large disaster site between two large city agencies; however, there were still dozens of passengers who were trapped in the twisted metal of four of the train cars. The professional first responders were ready to take on the role that they had trained for throughout their careers. They spread out, taking on the various train cars. With axes and pry bars they tried to find ways to enter the damaged cars. Some areas were totally blocked, and they tried various doors or windows to smash open in order to gain entry.

The responders were encountering the Costco volunteer brigade, who were shouting out where the pinned and wounded could be found. Often uninjured passengers were holding bloody hands or cradling the gashed heads of their fellow passengers, and they would beg the professionals to stop and provide attention to the injured. However, the professional rescuers would acknowledge the injured but would merely say they would send help for them as they continued to penetrate deeper into the maze of twisted metal.

The professionals understood the reality of the situation, which was to locate the most seriously, injured and recognize those hopeless situations that could easily divert the limited resources that were available to save lives. These were the cold hard facts of being a professional first responder. If someone is hopelessly pinned in the wreckage and is bleeding out, they have to turn a blind eye and move ahead to expend their resources on those who are savable. The duty of the first responders is to assess the situation and direct resources where they are needed.

The initial responders have to ignore the begging for help and be strong enough to focus on the assessment stage. Once the scope of the situation is learned, then the secondary responders are assigned to rescue particular individuals. If mechanical equipment is needed, it is dispatched to those who require it. The 'jaws of life' became the most popular tool in this train crash situation. So many passengers were still pinned in the twisted metal. Pry bars and axes weren't strong enough to extricate those trapped passengers. There was a waiting game as to who could get the use of the 'jaws of life' to free those deeply trapped. When the mechanical tools were brought in and used there was the fear that a spark from them might ignite a fire that could consume everyone before they could be removed.

Accessibility to the crash site was much easier from the west side. Los Angeles Fire Department's response was overwhelming, and within minutes the Costco parking lot was packed with dozens of fire trucks and paramedic units. The emergency personnel were like an invading army inundating the crash site. Amazingly, the first responders didn't attempt to determine which side of the boundary line an injured person was on.

The best way to describe the first hour of the rescue operation was 'organized chaos.' Glendale had set up the triage center on the east side, while the Los Angeles personnel had better access for ambulances on the west side. In any disaster situation, the key is to have ONE CENTER OF COMMAND. In this way, there is kept a master list of the injured and deceased and where they have been taken. In this situation, there were 200 injured who had to be transported to hospitals. In order to save lives, the objective of the caregivers is to ship the injured to medical facilities as quickly as possible. During the early stages, every minute counts.

Within minutes of the train crash, there were numerous news helicopters buzzing overhead. Within 15 minutes, the entire Los Angeles neighborhood was being shown the images of the train wreck with plumes of smoke filling the air. The unintended consequence was that the passengers' families were making phone calls inquiring whether their loved ones were on that crashed train. Immediately, family members called their loved ones on their cell phones to inquire if they were okay.

Fortunately for many, they learned that their loved ones were fine because they were late and missed the train or that they had caught an earlier train. However, for some of the cell phones weren't being answered. What did that mean? Was the person not answering because something bad had happened to them? Were they killed or injured or taken to a hospital? The fact of not knowing the whereabouts and physical condition of people who were on the train caused great emotional anguish for the family members trying to obtain information.

Fortunately for some, the outcome was a happy ending. In some cases, the passengers had their cell phones in backpacks or briefcases which were lost somewhere in the debris of the train cars. Others had their cell phones crushed or damaged so they weren't working. However, for many families they entered the 'No Information Zone.' They initially called the police departments to encounter lengthy delays, and when someone answered the standard response was "At this time, we don't have a list of injured or survivors."

The calls were being referred to the local hospitals. This was where the family members quickly learned how many dozens of medical centers existed in the Los Angeles basin. Often the hospital receptionists indicated, because of privacy concerns, the hospital can't give out information about admitted patients. By this time, the family member became so stressed that the only other avenue of information was to call the Coroner's Office. One quickly learns that many of the unclaimed bodies are listed as John Doe or Jane Doe and that one is free to visit the Coroner's Office to check out those unknowns.

Most people think that pain and suffering of such a tragedy is experienced only by those who are directly involved; however, this doesn't take into account the unbelievable stress that family members go through trying to track down their loved ones. The torment of not knowing the condition of loved ones can seem to be an unending nightmare.

One of the luckier passengers was scrambling to get out alive when he heard a fellow passenger cry out for help. Within three more steps he would be able to jump free of the wreckage. Then the cry was "Please help me, I can't move." At that moment, a Good Samaritan was born. The one passenger leaned down to the voice and said, "Okay, we will get you out." He looked down at the injured man and could see he was bleeding profusely from multiple lacerations.

For some unexplained reason, the Good Samaritan said, "You are going to be okay, you're not going to die." For the next 15 minutes, the aider continued to hold the hand of the injured person and reassured him everything would be all right. Eventually, the responders came to the suffering man and tenderly placed him on a stretcher and four men lifted him out of the wreckage. The injured passenger kept saying, "Don't let me die." Throughout, the Good Samaritan held his hand and comforted the wounded person that he was going to be just fine. They carried him over to the triage area, where he was placed in a special section.

As the man lay on the stretcher, the aider was beside him offering encouragement. As time passed, the Good Samaritan noticed the man was no longer conversing with him. As other injured came to the triage area, they were carried off to awaiting ambulances. The Good Samaritan continued to hold the hand of his fellow passenger until one of the paramedics came over and checked for a pulse, and finding none took the sheet on the body and pulled it over the man's pale lifeless face.

The Good Samaritan looked aghast and wondered what he should do next. For over a half hour he had promised that he wouldn't let the man die. Now what should he do? He didn't know the injured man's name, and he had no idea how to contact his family. Not knowing what to do, the Good Samaritan gently placed the deceased hand under the sheet. The Good Samaritan gradually stood up. He stared down at the sheet and with a slightly guilty look on his face, the Good Samaritan faded into the madding crowd that had converged on the crash site.

By now the air was filled with the grinding whine of the firefighters' saws cutting through the twisted metal. There were still dozens of passengers pinned in the wreckage like trapped animals in cages. These passengers were in unbelievable pain and suffering with the angst of not knowing if they would be rescued before they succumbed to their injuries. Some of the stuck passengers were lucid enough to know the dire consequences they faced. John was a large frame individual who was trapped beneath debris with a metal train seat on top of him. As he moved his right hand, he reached up and touched his head. He could feel something damp. He brought his hand back down and looked at his wet fingers and could see what appeared to be blood.

His initial reaction was *That can't be good.* As he touched his head again, he could feel more blood oozing out of his scalp area. Should he panic? The smell of fuel was getting more overpowering, and he thought about what was going to be his demise. Was he going to burn to death or bleed to death? No one was making any noise as though they were on their way to save him. As time went by without any help, John's situation was a mood of hopelessness and he was feeling that he would not be one of the lucky survivors. His mind wandered in and out of consciousness. All he could think of was his family. He and his wife had a joyous life together and had two wonderful children.

John thought how he could convey to them how much they meant to him. He had no paper or pen to record his thoughts. All he had was a hand full of his blood. He glanced in front of him and saw the metal backing of the seat in front of him. Could he possibly handwrite something on the metal backing? At that moment, he stretched his hand to the back of his head and felt it as he rubbed it on his bloody head. He tried to lower his arm and reach out to touch the metal seat in front of him. He surprised himself as he started to finger-paint on the seat the words "I love (using the shape of heart) my kids." He reached back to his head and got more blood as he swung his hand to write, "I love (using a shape of a heart) Leslie."

As he tried to write his wife's name, he started to fade. From that point on, he lost consciousness and only had limited memory of his rescuers. They needed to bring in the 'jaws of life' to get the debris off him. When he was removed from the wreckage, all he could think about was how lucky he had been. What happened next was one of those situations that go viral. One of the Fire captains from Los Angeles looked at the train seat that had been lying on John. At first all he saw was a bloody mess on the back of the seat. Then his eyes focused on the bloody smear, which was really handwritten. He thought to himself, 'How could anyone who was dying be eloquent enough to write an 'I love you' note to his family?'

The captain had a camera on him, and he took several pictures of the bloody back of the seat. He showed it to someone, and the next thing he knew was history being made. The photo of I LOVE MY FAMILY went viral, and the entire world was talking about what a touching statement. Of course, John knew nothing about what he had created.

Since John was one of the last survivors to be rescued, his name didn't get on the survivors' list. For hours, his wife was in a panic trying to find where John may have been taken. A friend of his wife contacted her and asked her if she was the 'Leslie' in the photo that 'had gone viral.' She knew nothing about such a photo. This was frightening, since everyone thought whoever wrote the 'love message' must have died. Leslie kept searching for John and was overjoyed and relieved when she saw him in his hospital room. Eventually, she got around to mentioning whether he knew anything about a bloody message on the back of one of the train seats. John was taken aback since so much of the recovery was a blur in his mind. He replied that he must have done it when he thought he was going to die. John smiled at Leslie, indicating that he wrote it for her and the kids and never thought it would be shared with the world.

On the next graphic page is an exhibit of the bloody message on the back of the train seat.

As the rescuers worked at a fever pitch to get the injured removed from the scene, the dead were remaining in place. The police detectives needed to precisely determine where each deceased was located on the train. This wasn't going to be an easy task, since some of the dead had been removed from the train and taken to the triage area where they died. However, the detectives were able to locate most of the deceased and were able to take photos of where in the twisted metal they died. This without a doubt was one of the most horrific tasks anyone one would have to do.

The first responders couldn't help but notice that one of the dead lying on the gravel near the first car was wearing a deputy Sheriff's uniform. Seeing the body of a fellow law enforcement officer was extremely difficult for these first responders, and they placed a sheet over the dead deputy's body. Since the deputy had his uniform on, his nametag was in plain view with the name 'Tutino.' Somehow, the word got to the Sheriff's Department that Deputy Tutino was one of the victims. A large grouping of Sheriff's personnel assembled at the crash site. As soon as the word came down that the deceased could be removed, an informal honor guard was created and surrounded Deputy Tutino's body. The body was placed on a stretcher and dozens of uniformed officers stood at attention saluting their dead comrade. Most of them followed in formation to a waiting van, where he was transported from the crash site. The news media quickly took notice of this informal ceremony, and photos of it went viral.

What was interesting about Deputy Tutino was that he worked the gang activity in Men's Central Jail. There he came into contact with the members of the Mexican Mafia and all sorts of gangsters who had squandered their lives. The reason he liked working the jail detail was that working hours were such that he could go in early and get off early so he could coach the sports teams at Simi Valley High School. He was genuinely concerned about the youth of the community and wanted them to excel in sports, not drive-by shootings. His service to law enforcement and the community was recognized by the State Governor, who ordered that the state capitol flag be flown at half-staff in honor of Deputy Tutino.

Since the other deceased weren't wearing name tags, it was more difficult to determine their identity. In those cases, the detectives had to look for some form of identification so the next of kin could be properly notified. In some cases, it only required reaching into the deceased's pockets for a wallet or some type of identification card. However, others had their purses, backpacks, and briefcases separated from them.

On the next graphic page is the exhibit used to show the jurors where the victims were located in the train cars. Also shown is the bloody handwriting of I love my family.

GRAPHICS 41

These are the eleven passengers on the two trains who were killed and where they were located on the trains.

One of the trapped passengers thought he was going to die so he wrote in his blood a message on the seat in front, "I love my kids & my wife."

CHAPTER 29 ALVAREZ—TIME FOR AN INVESTIGATION

As the morning faded to noon, the crash site took on another aura. The rescue phase was transitioning into recovery stage just by the fact that all the train cars had a giant red 'X' designating that car had been thoroughly searched and all passengers dead or alive had been removed. Next came the investigators, especially from the Departments of Transportation who were responsible for the safety of the railroads. However, it didn't take long before the lookie loos descended on the crash scene. It was hard to determine who had a legitimate reason to survey the site.

By this time, the Glendale authorities were getting a confused picture of what had caused the crash. The engineers from both trains had survived and were talking about what they had seen. The engineer from Train #100 said he saw a vehicle on the train track when the train was traveling 79 mph. He put on the regular brakes and ran back through the front car yelling to the passengers to 'Hold on." Although he was injured, he was able to talk to investigators.

The engineer on #9100 said he saw the vehicle on the tracks and came to a stop as soon as the signal tower toppled on the end of his train. The word came in that there was a witness by the name of Douglass Ross who related that he had seen around 6:00 a. m. a blackened-out truck driving parallel to the tracks. Then, to his surprise, the vehicle stopped. The occupant got out and started pouring some type of liquid on the truck. When he was finished, he threw the white plastic bottle inside the vehicle. Then the driver drove further down the tracks and veered onto the tracks where he stopped the truck. The driver appeared to be a male Hispanic in his 20s, wearing a gray poncho with a hoody. Several minutes later, the witness heard a loud crash coming from the area where he had seen the truck on the tracks.

This was all surprising to the investigators and no one knew what to make of it. Then Edward Branch made contact with authorities and told a story that corroborated what Mr. Ross was saying. Mr. Branch said he was stopped at the crossing gates on Chevy Chase Drive when he glanced to his right and saw a truck-like vehicle on the tracks about 50 yards south of the street. The dome light in the vehicle was on, so he could make out the figure of a person who appeared to be on the passenger side "doing something." Then as the train was speeding through the crossing, he noticed the man wearing a poncho jump away from the truck seconds before the train hit the vehicle.

By this time, the police department and the fire department began to wonder what they were dealing with. Originally, the scenario was that some poor soul had their car stall on the train tracks and the train accidentally struck that vehicle. Now the authorities were hearing these stories that someone might have purposely placed the vehicle on the tracks. The statement that the one witness made that the driver was pouring what looked like gasoline on the vehicle caused the investigators to ask the question "Why?"

Nothing was adding up. Next, a call came in to a 911 operator in which there was a request for an ambulance in the area of Atwater Village in the City of Los Angeles. Something about a despondent man trying to kill himself. Paramedic John Roe responded to the location. There he started treating a Juan Alvarez for superficial wounds to his chest and forearm. This patient couldn't stop talking. He continually rambled on about something to the effect of, "It's my fault"... "What happened on the tracks" ... "I need to live to pay for all the things I've done."

This paramedic was well aware of the train collision and wondered if this guy had something to do with it. Since he worked for the City of Los Angeles, he didn't know what he should do with this information. Fortunately, the Glendale investigators received this information about Juan Alvarez and the beginning pieces of the puzzle started to fit together. The investigators realized they needed to scour the entire area where the train collision occurred.

They recognized the gigantic scope of the area that needed to be searched. It could take days to track down all the scattered debris along the tracks. At about the same time, the investigators were hearing the news from the Department of Transportation that they needed to clear the crash site to put in new rails since this set of tracks needed to be back in operation within two days.

The investigators didn't even know what they wanted to look for at this early stage of the investigation. What was remarkable was that the investigators didn't throw their hands in the air and complain, but instead selected a group of officers to be in charge of collecting everything that possibly could be relevant. Later they could decide what items they wanted to conduct forensic tests on.

The question was, how large an area to search? What was important? The information that they had was the vehicle was placed on the tracks just below Chevy Chase Drive. That seemed to be the northernmost point and Los Feliz Boulevard to the south. It wasn't a perfect crime scene, since rescuers and rail authority personnel were still in the so-called restricted area. What the Glendale detectives hastily learned was that they were going to have a narrow window of opportunity to search and document the area.

Next, the searching officers needed some idea as to what they should be looking for. Initially, anything pertaining to the vehicle should be examined and photographed. The next obvious question was what to do with the large pieces of the vehicle, such as the drivetrain and crushed body frame. Since the detectives were feeling the pressure from the rail authority to get this critical track back in operation, it was decided to remove the larger parts of the vehicle wreckage. In this way, those items would be preserved and later they could sort out the relevancy of it all.

After deciding how to handle the vehicle parts, the detectives then went on a search of the tracks to see if there was indentation of the gravel that would identify where the vehicle was placed on the track. When the detectives were about 100 yards down from the Chevy Chase crossing, they could see two indentations in the gravel next to the track. When they measured the two depressions, it was determined that it was the exact distance between the back wheels of an automobile. They could see some black marks on the gravel possibly indicating the spinning of rubber tires.

Another relevant point was the spot where the vehicle was located. There were gouge marks on the various railroad ties from that point all the way south on the tracks. About 50 yards further down the tracks there was a cross over of the track from the set of parallel tracks. There the detectives could see that a large chunk of the rail had been broken off, possibly by some part of the metal frame of the vehicle. The gravel to the right of the tracks seemed gouged out where the train had careened off the rails from that point on until it hit the freight locomotive.

As the detectives were making their assessment of the crime scene, the select group of officers who were working as a CSI team methodically looked for parts of a vehicle and then photographed what they found. Next, they picked them up with their latex gloves and with the smaller items placed them in various size bags, duly labeling where they were found. As they proceeded southbound, one of the officers came across a wallet, and when he looked inside it had the driver's license of a Juan Manuel Alvarez. A little further down the tracks, another officer found a smashed-up license plate. He radioed in the plate number and shortly thereafter the dispatcher announced that the registered owner of the Jeep Cherokee was a **Juan Manuel Alvarez** with an address in Compton, California.

As tedious as the evidence collection was, it proved to be invaluable. They were able to find two plastic containers that had an odor of gasoline. Later, both containers were forensically tested and they came back with a residue of gasoline.

The next graphic page is one of the exhibits used to show where the various items were found on the tracks.

GRAPHICS 42

The crime scene covered a long distance. Various diagrams were prepared to show where the items of evidence were found along the train tracks.

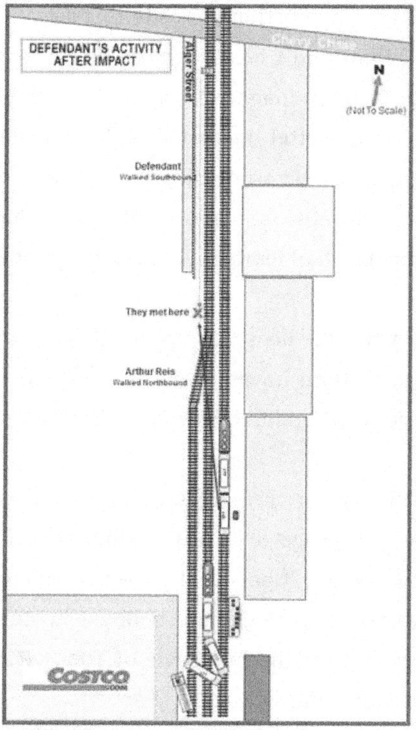

This diagram on the left was to show the jurors where the train cars came to rest.

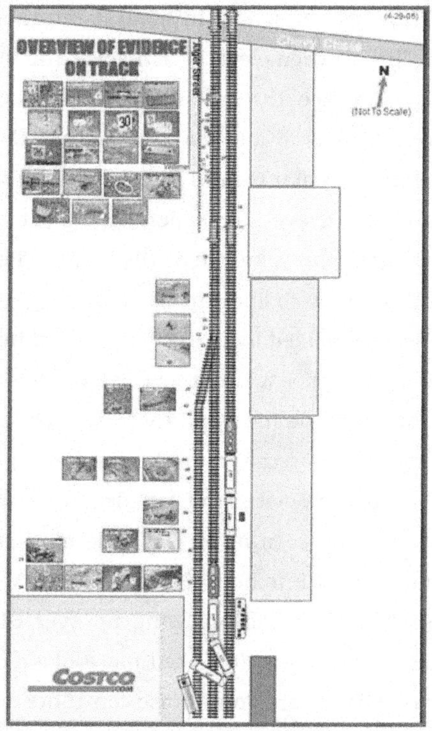

This diagram on the right was to illustrate where the items of the Jeep and the gasoline were found.

As for me, Thursday morning, January 29, 2008, was like any other day as I took the bus to my downtown DA's Office. By 7:45 a.m., I was walking into the Los Angeles Criminal Courts Building prior to the heavy traffic of cops, attorneys, and defendants. I checked in with my staff and found that all the major cases had been covered for the morning. I told the staff I was leaving to get my ice coffee at Starbucks and would be back to go over a Timeline that needed to be done for one of the homicides cases starting trial.

With my coffee cup in hand, I returned to the courthouse ready to take on the day. The crowded elevator arrived at the 17th floor and I headed to the Major Crimes Division to see the assistant head deputy, John Monaghan. I went by the head secretary's office and saw Cherkether Clemons, better known as Kiki. Whenever someone in Major Crimes Division was desperate to get something done, they would go to Kiki. Every large operation, be it a corporate or government entity, has a gatekeeper who is known as the 'Can Do Person.' I had learned years earlier that Kiki was the person to know in 'Majors.'

When I walked by her office, I asked her what the boss was up to. She gave me a look as though I was out of the loop. She said, "Ron haven't you heard?" The way she said it made me think that I was truly out of the know. She said, "Pat and Alan have left to go to the train wreck."

I asked, "What's the big deal? We never go to train crash sites." She said, "Haven't you seen it on TV?" She motioned me to go over to her small TV in the corner. I went into her office to see the TV and couldn't believe my eyes. A helicopter shot showed smoke billowing up over Glendale as the camera zoomed in on the wrecked train cars. It looked more like a scene from the hit movie of 2005, ***War of the Worlds***, where Tom Cruise confronts disaster after disaster.

The next day I saw Alan Jackson and asked him if they thought they would have enough evidence to file charges against the suspect who parked the car on the tracks. Alan smiled at me and said, "Ron, you wouldn't believe the mental issues involved in their case." He was off to a briefing on the Train Wreck case and said he would get back with me when he had received the photos and more information.

Several months later, Pat Dixon, the head deputy for the Major Crimes Division, asked me to be present for a meeting he was having in his office on the Glendale Metrolink case. At that meeting, Pat introduced me to the head investigator, Bob

Breckenridge, assigned to the case from the Glendale Police Department. I looked at him and smiled and stated that the last time I had heard that name 'Breckenridge' was when I was trying a rape case in Judge Paul Breckenridge's court.

I merely said it for casual conversation. This detective was quite tall, and he leaned over to shake my hand. As he firmly shook my hand he said, "Oh, Paul Breckenridge is my dad." This response caught me off-guard and I inarticulately said something stupid like, "Boy, your Dad was one tough judge." This most likely wasn't the best way to meet and greet someone. However, in my defense, I was merely saying what every prosecutor had thought for years when they were assigned to Judge Breckenridge's court for trial. His dad was a brilliant legal scholar and was in charge of writing the jury instructions that all judges used throughout the state.

When you had to try a case in his court, you had to be up on the law or he would castigate you for not being prepared. I couldn't imagine Judge Breckenridge having a son in the police department. His dad had been a long-time public defender whose job had been to get his clients acquitted. What was surprising about Judge Breckenridge was that as a public defender he had heard every contrived story from the defendants he had represented. As a judge, he showed no sympathy for lying defendants after they were convicted.

As I sat down at this Metrolink train crash meeting, I thought to myself that maybe I could have handled the Breckenridge introduction better. Pat immediately asked Investigator Breckenridge to bring everyone up to date on what they had uncovered in the Metrolink case. He explained that he had been in charge of documenting where all the deceased had been located. Following that, he went over the forensic results that had come back on the various parts of the Jeep Cherokee.

I was surprised that partway through his presentation he deferred the next part of the meeting to the Arson investigator, Mike Richardson, from the Glendale Fire Department. Prosecutors are used to working with police investigators who focus on a suspect just like the prosecutors do. However, Arson investigators tend to concentrate on 'Point of Origin' or what was the 'Accelerant.' An Arson investigator can go on for hours discussing those topics while the prosecutor wants to know "Can We Prove the Guy set the Fire?"

When the investigator started to talk, I thought he was going to dwell on burn patterns and the like. But within minutes I was impressed that he was concentrating on how to prove that suspect Alvarez had poured gasoline on the vehicle. He explained how they had analyzed numerous parts of the Jeep Cherokee and found the residue of gasoline. My first reaction was that all that gasoline obviously came from the Cherokee's gas tank. To my surprise, the next thing he showed were photos of the Cherokee's gas tank showing that it had not been ruptured. They were able to recover several gallons of gasoline that were still contained in the gas tank even after all the impact. Therefore, the vehicle's gas tank didn't contribute to the gasoline that was on all the various vehicle parts.

The more information I heard from the police and fire investigators, the more I was impressed that they truly knew what they were talking about. When the meeting ended, I asked them for various photos and reports, which they agreed to send me. Within several weeks, I had enough of the source materials to start preparing what the prosecutors needed to explain the case to the trier of facts (the jury).

In the beginning, I created the exhibits that would be used to orient the jury as to what happened and where it happened and who was involved. *Those orientation exhibits were shown on earlier graphic pages in the book.*

We wanted the jury to understand exactly where the defendant drove his Jeep onto the railroad tracks. The defendant gave various scenarios as to how the Jeep got onto the tracks. He later claimed he tried to get the Jeep off the tracks but was unable to back it off. An exhibit was created to show the indentations where the rear tires were. There were several rocks that had tire marks on them. These rocks were not in the indentations where the tires were stuck.

The next exhibit was three photos of a 1993 Jeep Cherokee that looked similar to the defendant's vehicle. Witnesses described the vehicle by using various terms such as car, truck, and SUV. This exhibit showed the jury that a Jeep Cherokee could fit any of the descriptions that the witnesses had given.

At one point, the defendant was claiming that he was diligently trying to get the Jeep off the tracks. I prepared an exhibit showing that the ignition of the Jeep when recovered was in the 'off' position. By placing photos of the defendant's Jeep's ignition next to photos of a similar Jeep's ignition in various positions, it showed that his Jeep was in the 'off' position and thereafter was not running.

In order for the jurors to understand the extent of force the train struck the Jeep, I took six photos of the remains of the Jeep and placed them on one exhibit. In this way, the jurors could see from all angles that there was not much left of the defendant's vehicle after the impact and the fact that it had been dragged down the train tracks.

The following graphic page shows various exhibits used to show the defendant's Jeep and the location where it was on the tracks.

GRAPHICS 43

This shows where the Jeep was driven on the tracks

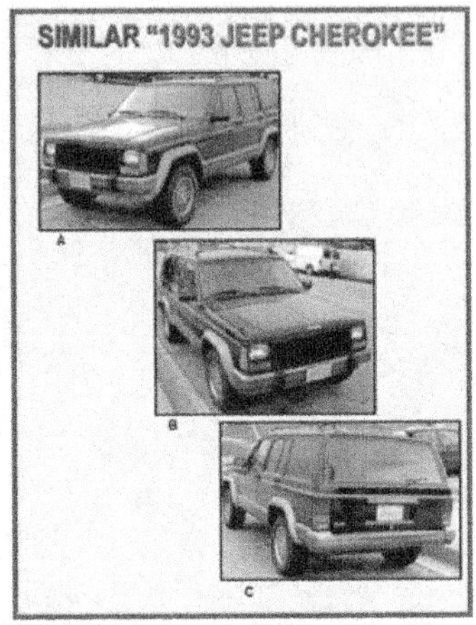

This is the type of Jeep placed on tracks.

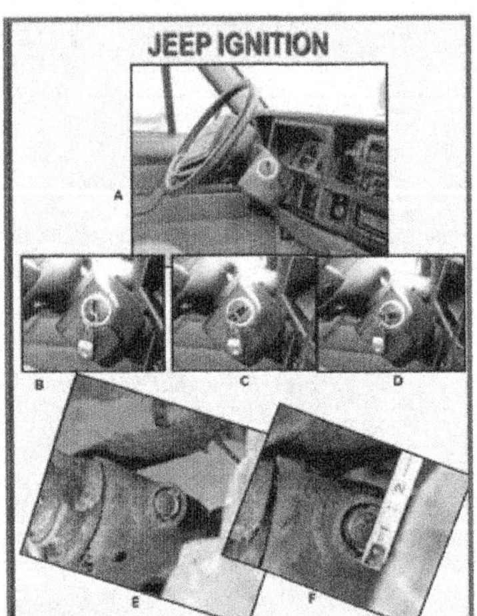

This was used to show that the ignition to the Jeep was in the off position.

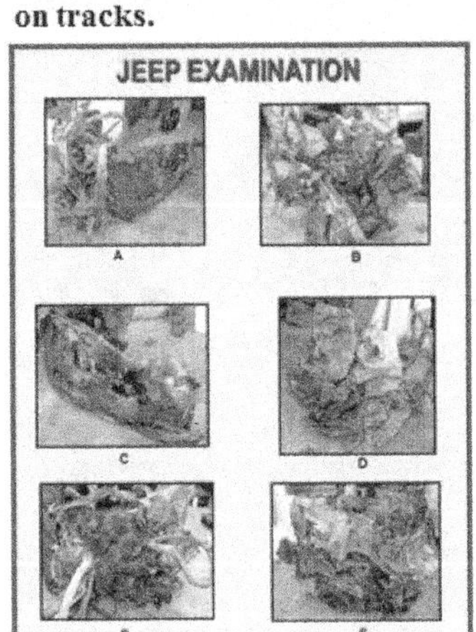

This group of photos showed what the Jeep looked like after the crash.

In the early stages of the case, it was unclear what the defendant was going to claim regarding the fire at the train crash site. The prosecution realized that one of the keys to the case was proving that the defendant in fact committed a felony—to wit, ARSON—for the felony murder rule to apply in order to elevate this killing to a first degree murder. This was necessary for the defendant to be eligible for the Death Penalty.

It was essential for the jury to understand that the defendant had poured gasoline on his car for the purpose of causing a fire, which was ignited by the train crashing into it. What had to be eliminated was that the fire was caused by the Jeep's gas tank rupturing from the crash, thereby resulting in a fire. Also, the jury needed to know that the diesel fuel from the freight locomotive didn't cause the fire.

That was why I created an exhibit called ORIGIN OF FIRE, which showed the plastic containers that had been used by the defendant to pour gasoline on his Jeep. On the bottom of that exhibit there were photos showing the locomotive's diesel tanks and the Jeep's gas tank, which had not ruptured and still contained gasoline. The prosecutors could use this one exhibit to illustrate to the jurors that there was an arson and that it was caused by the defendant pouring gasoline on his car.

Another exhibit was titled PLASTIC BOTTLES ON TRACKS, which showed photos of the railroad track pointing out where the plastic containers were found. There was also another exhibit titled SAMPLES ANALYZED FOR GASOLINE, which contained multiple photos of items from the Jeep, and next to them was a forensic tag indicating that gasoline was detected on them. Lastly, there was an exhibit showing photos of the lab technician opening the Jeep's gas tank and showing the amount of gasoline that was removed from it.

The following graphic page shows all four exhibits regarding the source and use of gasoline.

GRAPHICS 44

The prosecution used this exhibit to show that the fire came from the gasoline that defendant poured on the Jeep.

These were the plastic bottles use to carry the gasoline

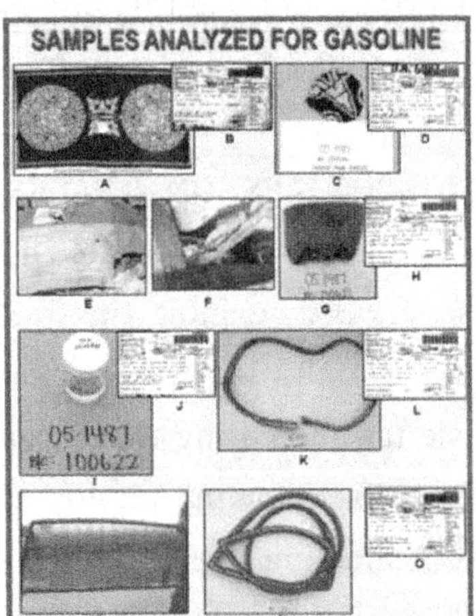

These were recovered items that contained gasoline.

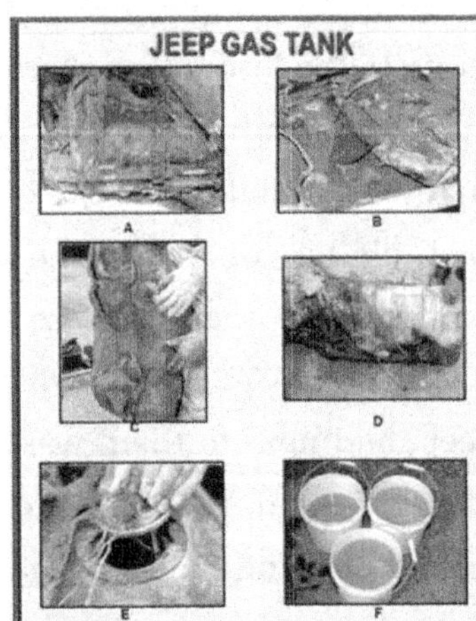

These photos showed that Jeep gas tank didn't cause the fire.

At first it was unknown whether the defendant was going to deny that he was present on the tracks and whether the Jeep Cherokee was owned and possessed by him. I created various exhibits that the prosecutors wanted to use during the trial. The first one was titled DEFENDANT'S WALLET & ID FOUND ON TRACKS, which was a collection of photos showing the wallet, which contained the defendant's identification. Another photo showed where it was found on the tracks. This tied the defendant to the crash site.

Another exhibit listed as EVIDENCE OF POSSESSION OF JEEP contained various photos showing the license plate that was found on the railroad tracks. The accompanying photos showed other items pertaining to who possessed the vehicle. The exhibit titled REGISTRATED OWNER OF JEEP showed the copy of documents from the DMV showing that Juan Alvarez had purchased the Jeep Cherokee from another party. One of the documents listed the defendant as the new owner of the Jeep. The last exhibit of this series was the one showing the DEFENDANT'S HOUSE. The purpose of that exhibit was to show where the defendant was living in the Atwater village area. *The following page shows the various items that proved that the defendant was at the crash site and that the Jeep belonged to the defendant.*

GRAPHICS 45

This exhibit shows where defendant's wallet was found & what was inside.

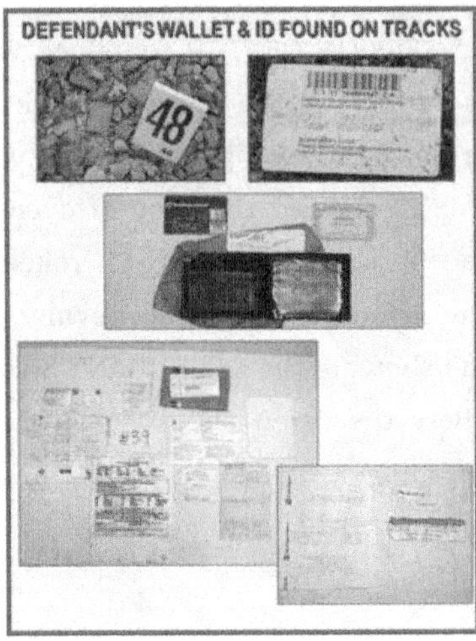

Items found along the tracked showed that Alvarez owned the Jeep

These are photos where Alvarez was living.

The Jeep was registered to Alvarez.

The prosecutors wanted some type of visual aid showing the defendant wasn't serious about committing suicide. I made two exhibits that consisted of photos of the cuts that the defendant said he had done to himself. Then, another exhibit titled AERIAL VIEW OF LOCATIONS was used to show the jurors how close the defendant lived to the crash site. The other exhibit involved the clothes that were removed from the defendant when he was arrested. These items were tested for gasoline, and next to them was the forensic tag that showed that gasoline was detected on all them.

The following graphic page shows the superficial injuries on the defendant, and the clothing that had traces of gasoline. Also is the exhibit that showed where the defendant lived in relationship to the train wreck.

GRAPHICS 46

Alvarez had injured himself by cutting himself on his chest and arms.

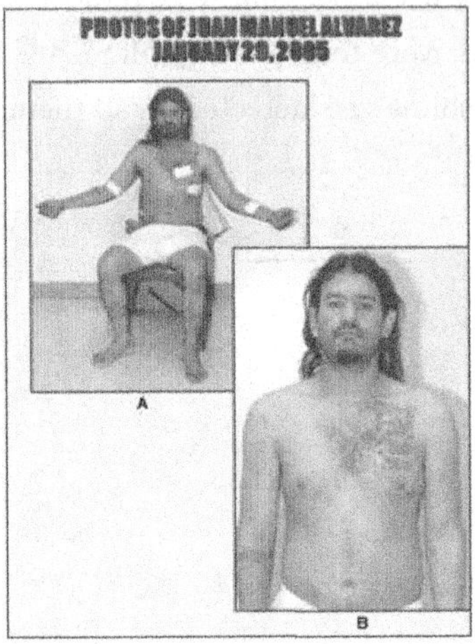

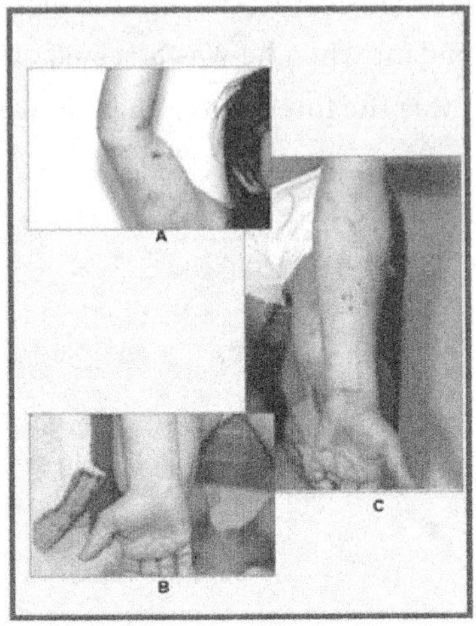

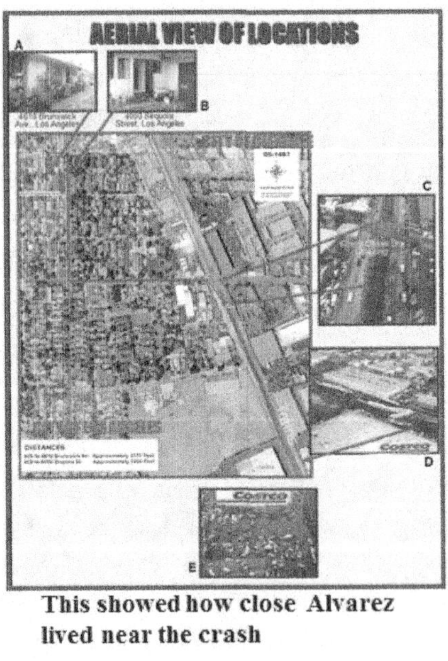

This showed how close Alvarez lived near the crash

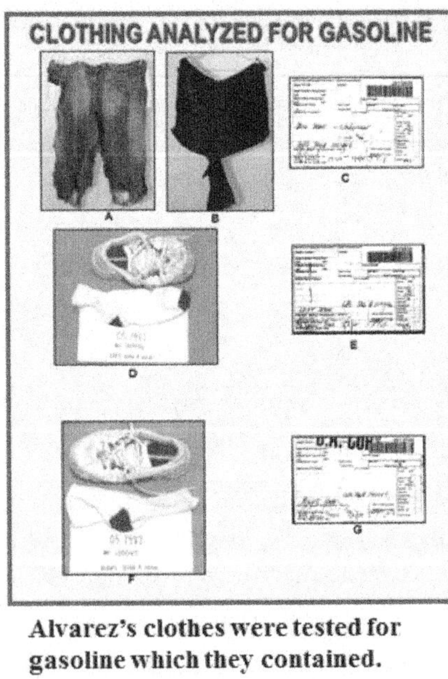

Alvarez's clothes were tested for gasoline which they contained.

CHAPTER 30 ALVAREZ—WHAT'S THE LAW?

After all of the above exhibits had been created and agreed upon, the next task was working on how best to explain all the critical legal issues. In a Murder case, the prosecution needs to prove there was a killing of a human being, the killing was unlawful, and the killing was done with malice aforethought. In this case, there was no Expressed Malice, since the defendant didn't say or do anything to indicate that he intended to kill the victims. However, there appeared to be Implied Malice, since the defendant did commit an intentional act, the natural consequences of the act were dangerous to human life, and the act was deliberately performed with knowledge of the danger to and conscious disregard for human life.

Initially, it would seem that the DA could make a case for MURDER against the defendant. However, that would be for SECOND DEGREE MURDER. The DA wanted to prove FIRST DEGREE MURDER. The easiest way to do that was by showing that the defendant committed the killing with DELIBERATION (formed or arrived at after careful thought, weighing of the considerations for and against) and PREMEDITATION (considered beforehand).

However, the big question for the DA was, how do you prove that Juan Alvarez did carefully consider before the driving of the vehicle onto the tracks, as a method to kill the victims? Since the DA wasn't going to be able to rely on Deliberation and Premeditation to prove FIRST DEGREE MURDER, what other way can the prosecution prove Murder One?

The answer was to use the legal concept of FELONY MURDER to supply the FIRST-DEGREE part. All that is required is that the killing was committed during the commission of a specified felony like ARSON, and that the defendant had the intention to commit that felony, such as ARSON. It doesn't matter if the killing was intentional or accidental.

The next question is whether the pouring of gasoline on his car would be considered ARSON. The elements of the crime of ARSON OF PERSONAL PROPERTY are that the defendant set a fire to burn his own personal property, the fire was set willfully and maliciously, and that the defendant engaging in this conduct causes injury to another. To prove this, the prosecutor had to rely on the witness who saw a person pouring some type of the liquid on the vehicle which later was proven to be gasoline.

There was another way the DA could prove FIRST DEGREE MURDER, and that was to show the defendant intended to commit the crime of TRAIN WRECKING. This is a seldom-charged offense, since factually it rarely occurs. Under this approach, the prosecutor has to prove that the defendant intended that his actions would result in a train wreck.

As you, the reader, have seen over the previous several pages, the explanation of the law in this case was convoluted and easily could cause the jurors to zone out with so much legalese. If the jurors didn't thoroughly understand the jury instructions as the judge read them, then the jurors wouldn't be able to apply the law during their deliberation. Later, simplified charts were prepared for the prosecutors to use when explaining the laws.

The following graphic page contains the various slides used to explain the law to the jurors.

GRAPHICS 47

This was used to explain the elements to murder using Implied Malice.

MURDER WITH MALICE AFORETHOUGHT
Penal Code § 187

1. The defendant committed an act that caused the death of another person, and
2. When the defendant acted he had a state of mind called malice aforethought.

IMPLIED MALICE

1. Defendant intentionally committed an act.
2. The natural consequences of the act were dangerous to human life.
3. The defendant knew the act was dangerous to human life, and
4. The defendant acted with conscious disregard for human life.

- *Hatred or ill will not required.*
- *Deliberation or the passage of any particular time not required.*

This visual was used to illustrate the Felony Murder concept..

FIRST DEGREE FELONY MURDER – DEFENDANT COMMITTED THE FATAL ACT
Penal Code §189

1. The defendant committed or attempted to commit a specified felony.
2. The defendant intended to commit that felony, and
3. While committing or attempting to commit that felony the defendant did an act that caused the death of another person.

- ***The defendant may be guilty of felony murder even if the killing was unintended, accidental, or negligent.***

This visual showed the elements for the crime of Arson.

ARSON
Penal Code § 451

1. The defendant set fire to or burned a structure, or property, and
2. The defendant acted willfully and maliciously.

"Willfully" means willingly or on purpose.

"Maliciously" means intentionally doing a wrongful act or acting with the intent to defraud, annoy or injure someone else.

The Preliminary Hearing was held in Judge William Pounder's court. At that time, the prosecutors were Pat Dixon and Alan Jackson. Since the two of them had been with the case from the beginning, they knew which witnesses to call to prove to the judge that there was sufficient evidence. The hearing went like clockwork, and the judge held Juan Manuel Alvarez to answer for 11 murders, arson, and train wrecking. Then it was a matter of time for the Defense to be ready for trial. Months went by, then years went by, and the Defense asked for more continuances. The victims' families had to wonder if the case would ever go to trial.

CHAPTER 31 ALVAREZ—TIME FOR TRIAL

In March 2008, Juan Alvarez's attorney told a group of reporters the theory of the Defense's case. He explained that his client was merely trying to commit suicide and at no time was he trying to harm anyone else. He went on to say that Alvarez would testify during his trial to describe why he poured gasoline on his car as his 'method of choice' for taking his own life. His attorney said, "Alvarez set in motion events or circumstances that led to this incident, but he didn't have malice, which is required in murder."

His attorney wasn't keeping secret what the Defense was going to be. He revealed that the witnesses on the train would testify that the initial crash of the train into the SUV didn't kill anyone. It was the second and third crashes into a parked locomotive and another passenger train that caused the deaths. All these tragic coincidences could not have been foreseen by the defendant. The attorney went on to say that Alvarez would testify that his vehicle's wheels became wedged on either side of the rails and tires spun in the gravel when he tried to move the SUV. Further his attorney said that the defendant tried putting rocks under the wheels, but the SUV remained stuck on the tracks.

The Defense attorney seemed to be trying the case on the courthouse steps. If there is no gag court order, the attorney can talk to the news media about his or her case. Often, Defense attorneys will make such statements favoring the defendant in hopes this will influence potential jurors who will be selected to serve on the case. Other times, the attorney is trying to gain favorable treatment from the news media that is eager to get any such prior information which helps them report more favorable stories.

While the Defense made numerous attempts to tell their side of the story, the prosecutors remained silent, not making any out-of-court statements. In order for the media to learn the prosecution's side of the case, the reporters reviewed the prosecutors' documents filed with the court and tried to extrapolate what their position would be. The news media stated, "The prosecutor in court papers have argued that the evidence in the case refutes Alvarez's claim of a suicide bid."

For years, there had been strained relations between the DA's Office and the news media. Immediately after the disastrous O.J. Simpson case, the DA's Office received considerably bad news coverage. The media liked to portray the Los Angeles DA's Office as being unable to win the big publicity trials. Then in 2005, the DA's Office found itself with another Not Guilty verdict in the Robert Blake case, which was tried by one prosecutor. From that point on, the administration decided not to assign only one prosecutor to the publicity cases but two top prosecutors. The feeling was that two prosecutors could better guarantee a good outcome to the big cases.

Near the fall of 2007, the DA's Major Crimes Division had a catastrophic dilemma. They had the Michael Goodwin case, involving the murder of Mickey and Trudy Thompson, ready for trial. It had been assigned to two of the top prosecutors, Pat Dixon and Alan Jackson. Both of them had been assigned the Phil Spector case. In other words, Dixon and Jackson were going to be tied up with the Goodman case and immediate after that they would both start the Phil Spector case. The Spector case started in March of 2007, and it was anticipated that it would be over by the time the Alvarez case was scheduled to begin in April 2008.

However, the moons, planets, and stars apparently were out of alignment, since on September 26, 2007, the Phil Spector case resulted in a hung jury. This hadn't been anticipated. Now both Pat Dixon and Alan Jackson had to be ready to retry the Phil Spector case. Since they had been slated to try the Alvarez case, the DA's Office now had to find two prosecutors who could step in at the last minute and try this highly complicated Alvarez case.

John Monaghan was between trials, and he could squeeze in the Alvarez trial starting in March of 2008. As stated earlier in the James Dixon case, the DA's administration had adopted a new policy that all publicity cases in the future would be tried by **two prosecutors**. For years, Monaghan had always tried his cases by himself. He was like the Iron Man, who could do it all by himself. He wasn't the type who liked to try a case by the 'committee approach.'

Obviously, Monaghan was more than capable to try the Alvarez case by himself, but the new DA policy requiring two prosecutors had to be followed. The administration had a delicate issue to resolve: who could they pair up with Monaghan? Since Cathryn Brougham had been paired with Monaghan in the Dixon case, the administration was pleased how well they worked together. This was a no-brainer for the DA's administration, so John and Cathryn found themselves teamed together to do the Alvarez case. It was felt that Catherine would be a good fit to work with Monaghan, since he had vast experience in Death Penalty cases and she had an insatiable willingness to learn anything to improve her litigation skills.

Cathryn had moved up to Major Crimes Division when they needed a replacement for Eleanor Hunter, who had been appointed as a judge. Cathryn Brougham had tried some major cases and received good reviews.

Cathryn was constantly compared to Amal Alamuddin, who is a barrister at Doughty Street Chambers in London and who is better known as **Mrs. George Clooney**. Since Cathryn had been an attorney/barrister longer than Amal, it could be said that Mrs. Clooney had copied Cathryn's style as to the way she walks and talks. When they are both dressed for court they could pass for twin sisters. They both project an image of a woman who is on a mission to fight for justice.

The other issue the administration had to deal with was the fact that the Alvarez case was definitely a high-publicity case. Although Monaghan tried the toughest cases, he stayed away from the publicity cases because he didn't like dealing with the news media. This dislike may have stemmed from being burned by the news media earlier in his career. Often reporters approach prosecutors claiming they only want background material and they promise not to quote the prosecutor as a source. However, several days later the prosecutor sees what he or she had said in confidence attributed to him or her in the news piece.

The bottom line was that John had an uneasy relationship with the news media. He might be considered curt when he ignored reporter's questions. As a rule, John didn't do interviews with the media, since he subscribed to the belief that a criminal case was to be tried in court and not on the courthouse steps. The DA's Office may have felt that Cathryn might be able to better handle the news media while John concentrated on the courtroom legal issues.

The replacement of prosecutors just before trial can be devastating for a case. Yet John and Cathryn's transition into this case was amazingly smooth and seamless to the news media. John was a quick learner, and within a short time he had command of the facts and how to utilize the witnesses to make the strongest case for the People. John gave Cathryn certain phases of the case while he retained an overview of the case, especially the issues pertaining to the Death Penalty.

From the beginning, the case had been assigned to Judge Pounder's court, which was a good place to try a Death Penalty case. Judge William Pounder was well versed in the law, since he had worked for the State Attorney General's Office before becoming a judge. There he became a master of the intricacies of the Death Penalty. The other benefit of trying a case in Judge Pounders court was the fact that he was a genuinely 'nice person.' He was understanding when there were logistic problems and didn't run his court like a tyrant. In other words, it was always a delight for both the DA and Defense to try a case in his court.

Jury selection can be the most critical time when a case can be won or lost. John knew how critical the jury selection would be in this case. The Defense had a strong argument that this defendant was not a killer but just a mentally disturbed individual who shouldn't receive the Death Penalty. Without a doubt, John Monaghan had the best insight as to how to pick a Death Penalty jury. For him, it was like having clairvoyance in identifying those potential jurors who didn't have 'the balls' to impose the Death Penalty even though they thought the defendant deserved it. John had an extrasensory perception when reading over the jury questionnaires. It might be the potential juror's answer or even something crossed out on the questionnaire that tipped off John how that person would vote when it came to the Death Penalty. After much questioning by both sides, and exercising preemptive challenges, a jury of three men and nine women was selected to decide the fate of defendant, Juan Alvarez.

After a three-year delay, the jury trial actually began on April 28, 2008. Judge Pounder asked if the prosecution wished to make an Opening Statement, and Cathryn Brougham announced that they did. Cathryn got up from counsel table and walked over to the lectern. Cathryn would be described as being pleasant on the eyes in the sense of having exquisitely coiffured auburn hair which surrounds her elongated face with prominent check bones. Her large hazel eyes are highlighted by her broad eyebrows perfectly accenting her eyes.

Being tall and slender, she made an imposing presence. Initially, Cathryn projected a Vogue model look that some might label as 'drop dead gorgeous,' but there was more to Cathryn than her enchanting appearance.

When she began talking about the case, the jurors seemed fixated on her and she had their complete attention. With her deep, clear-cut voice, she started her Opening Statement saying, "The defendant wanted to regain the affections of his estranged wife. He needed to do something big to get her attention. He was conducting a pretend suicide similar to several such acts he had allegedly committed in the past. He would use these pretend suicide attempts throughout his life in order to get attention, sympathy, and pity."

Cathryn continued to maintain eye contact with the jurors as she went on to describe what Alvarez did. "He was hooked on meth, suffered delusions, and kept accusing his wife of having an affair. Then he became increasingly obsessive and threatened to kill her. By October 2004, his wife had kicked him out. When he continued to hound her, she got a restraining order. The defendant chose the path of destruction, but instead of deciding to kill his wife, he decided to murder 11 strangers." To support the prosecutor's position, she mentioned he was able to win her back and the proof was that since his arrest his wife had canceled the Restraining Order and was now visiting him in jail.

Cathryn's part of the Opening Statement concentrated on the defendant's mental condition. When she was finished, she sat down and John Monaghan took over by discussing the facts of the case. He said, "Alvarez intentionally left his SUV on the tracks near Glendale, doused it with gasoline, and used the Metrolink as a match to light his vehicle on fire." Then John used a slide show presentation to illustrate how the defendant's actions affected the victims. First he flashed on the courtroom screen a photo of each victim as they appeared in life. Then he added to the slide additional photos of the victims' twisted mangled bodies after the crash.

Without a doubt, this had an impact on the jurors as well as the victims' family members who were seated in the audience area. Family members had been warned that such photos would be shown and told they could remain in the courtroom if they wished. Some family members stayed and covered their faces when their loved one was shown on the screen. As difficult as this was for everyone, it was necessary that the jurors realized the gravity of the defendant's actions.

After John had summarized the facts of the case, he sat down and next the Defense attorney got up and gave his Opening Statement. He described that all these deaths were an ACCIDENT. He went on to say, "My client never imagined his Jeep could cause a powerful train to derail or that anyone, other than himself, would die. Civil, moral responsibility does not equal criminal guilt." Alvarez's attorney wanted to paint a picture that his client was a victim of social injustice. He stated, "My client was born in East Los Angeles and spent his preteen years in Mexicali as a depressed psychotic with a history of suicide attempts beginning at the age of 8, when he tried to hang himself."

In order to create more sympathy for Alvarez, his attorney told the jury, "He was delusional about his wife having an affair and became so intense that he believed another man was in bed at night with the couple. His family tried but failed to get him help. He viewed the restraining order as a way to get him out of the way for his wife's lover."

When both sides had finished with their Opening Statements, it was time for the prosecutors to call their witnesses. Just like the in Preliminary Hearing, both engineers were called to give their view of the train crash. Next were the officers and CSI technicians who found the various parts of the Jeep Cherokee. These witnesses continued to tell the jury that they found the plastic gasoline containers and identification of the defendant along the tracks. The jurors were most interested in hearing the testimony of the two civilian witnesses who saw the defendant drive the Cherokee on the tracks, as well as the one who observed the defendant pouring a liquid onto the Jeep.

The arson investigator was then called to explain that traces of gasoline were found on many of the parts of the Jeep strewn along the railroad tracks. The plastic containers had residue of gasoline. He explained how the Jeep's gas tank was recovered and still had several gallons of liquid gasoline in it.

A paramedic also testified he responded to the call that a man was trying to kill himself. He indicated that man was the defendant and that he said the following:

"It's my fault what happened on the tracks. I need to live to pay for all the things I've done." Then Investigator Breckenridge testified to the exact locations where each victim was killed. This was followed by several medical examiners who explained to the jury that each of the 11 victims' Cause of Death was 'Blunt Force Trauma.'

Alvarez's wife ended up as one of the most crucial witnesses for the prosecution as well as the Defense. She testified that her husband had exhibited bizarre and delusional behavior for at least five years before causing the deadly Metrolink crash. She went on to say, "He also tried to kill himself three times. He was extremely possessive of me and often accused me of having affairs, even with my nephew. I had to be in the middle of the bed facing him. He had to be holding my hand, because he thought if I turned over, somebody else was there. He thought I had cameras on the mirrors in my closet. He would say, 'Why are you recording me?'"

Then the Defense attorney outright asked her, "As you sit here today, do you think there is something mentally wrong with Juan Alvarez." Her response was, "Yes, I do." The Defense was able to use the defendant's wife to paint a picture that the defendant didn't have the mental capacity to commit murder.

However, Prosecutor Cathryn Brougham asked the defendant's wife if he had ever attempted to receive help. She admitted that her husband never seemed committed to getting help for his drug habit or mental illness. The prosecutor went on to ask her how she reacted after his previous attempted suicides. She admitted that she would always show him affection and pity after his suicide attempts. As to the present situation of the train crash, she testified that she had withdrawn the Restraining Order she had against him and started to visit him in the jail because she felt guilt.

Both sides felt they had gotten what they wanted from the testimony of the defendant's wife. The prosecution witnesses had testified that they saw Alvarez pull his vehicle onto the tracks. So the Defense needed to call the defendant to the witness stand. This was a big gamble for the Defense, but they believed they had to call the defendant to explain his conduct.

When he was seated in the witness stand, everyone in the courtroom was focused on the defendant. What would he say? The first thing he did was apologize for killing 11 train passengers. "I feel terrible and I ask for forgiveness. I believe some of the family members are here today. I am sorry for what happened; I never meant to hurt any of your loved ones. That could have been my mom or dad."

The defendant went on to explain what happened that morning and what his thinking was. "That morning I woke up in a good mood. As I was driving to a service station to get gas, I thought of committing suicide. I guess I snapped. I thought I was hearing my wife and someone else in the back of the car. They were calling me 'stupid' since I couldn't see them. I started to get a little freaked out. My family was trying to put me in a mental home. I started thinking I'll never get my kids. At the service station, I filled two water bottles with gasoline and then drove to an alley near the railroad track in Glendale. There I doused my hair and car with gas. But as I sat in the car, my skin started to itch and I felt nauseous. I started thinking it was a bad idea to burn myself. It was going to be very, very painful."

Then Juan Alvarez went into why he changed his mind. "I looked around and saw the railroad tracks. That's when it came to my mind that it would be the fastest way for someone to die. That's when I moved my Jeep onto the tracks but soon changed my mind about dying. So I just thought this is pretty crazy...the whole suicide idea. Then I tried to move the Jeep off the tracks, but the wheels were stuck. So I jumped from the car just before the crash."

Then his attorney asked Alvarez, "How did you feel when you heard people had died because you put your Jeep on the tracks?" Alvarez answered with the one word, "Traumatic."

Then it was the prosecution's turn to cross-examine the defendant. John Monaghan had been sitting at counsel table just waiting to hear the words from Alvarez' Defense attorney, "No further question of the defendant, your Honor." John was known as one of the very best cross-examiners. He knew how to phrase probing questions in a way that the witness didn't know where he was going with this line of questioning. For John, every question was calculated to elicit a response that he would be able to use in constructing his Argument.

John doesn't permit the witness to wiggle out of the tough questions. He wanted to show that Alvarez's actions were willful and intended to cause death and destruction. Alvarez's response was that he never intended to harm others. He said, "It was an accident, just a stupid mistake." John fired off the next question, "You don't want to be convicted, do you?" Alvarez shot back "Nobody wants to." John's follow-up question was, "You don't want to take responsibility? You want to walk out of here don't you?" The defendant seemed stumped as to how to answer that question.

When John tried to pin the defendant down as to what crime he was guilty of, Alvarez snapped back saying that he was culpable of 'being stupid' and of trespassing. This answer made it sound like he was belittling the 11 lives that were lost. Then John tried to cast doubt on Alvarez's statements that he had doused himself with gas in an attempt to burn himself. He wanted to show that the true intention was to cause the train to catch fire to make for a big crash.

John kept questioning Alvarez and got him to admit that he often carried a knife and sometimes a machete. On one occasion, he pulled a knife on his cousin. He further admitted that he had thoughts about killing his wife at her job.

The Defense needed to convince the jury that Alvarez demonstrated the characteristics of a person who is prone to commit suicide. Therefore, the Defense called a psychologist who interviewed the defendant for two hours and concluded that Alvarez fit the profile of someone who was prone to paranoia, chronically distressed, and had impulsive suicidal tendencies. Then the psychologist testified that Alvarez's self-destructive thoughts were not consistent with someone who would premeditate acts of violence.

The big question was, how likely would the jurors be swayed by such testimony? Most studies have concluded that jurors as a whole are skeptical of psychological testimony in a criminal trial. Prosecutors don't always know how much cross-examination is necessary. In this Alvarez case, the prosecutor, Cathryn Brougham, was given the task of creating some doubt about the psychologist's testimony. She asked whether the defendant could have padded his answers to her, since he knew she was going to ask him about suicide. The psychologist had to acknowledge that a client could try to tailor his answers to appear more troubled than he really was.

Cathryn finished her cross-examination by asking the psychologist why she didn't take notes of the interview or even attempt to record it. The jurors had to wonder why a truly professional person wouldn't want to be more thorough. Cathryn had set up the psychologist, since the Defense undoubtedly told her not to keep notes or record the interview. The reason for that was if they had any such notes or recording, copies would have to be turned over to the prosecutors during pre-trail discovery.

Both sides had finished calling witnesses, and it was time for the Argument stage of the trial. Prosecutor Brougham started arguing by saying, "Don't forget these 11 victims. He sacrificed 11 lives." She used a slide show to display life and death pictures of the dead—smiling faces above images of bloody, mangled bodies buried in wreckage. She went on to argue to the jurors that, "Alvarez doused his Jeep Cherokee with gas and parked it on the tracks about half a mile south of the downtown Glendale, hoping to wreak havoc. He ran from the vehicle shortly before a southbound Metrolink commuter train slammed into it, causing the train to derail and strike a parked Union Pacific freight train and then collide with a northbound Metrolink train, causing 11 deaths and at least 180 people being injured."

CHAPTER 32 ALVAREZ—THE DEFENSE'S THEORY

The prosecutor summed up the evidence during this eight-week trial. Then it was the Defense's turn to argue. The Defense attorney was creative in presenting his Argument by speaking in the voice of his client. It was an attempt to personalize the Defense's position when most people would be skeptical of the defendant saying, 'I am sorry to the 11 separate families who are missing a loved one.' The Defense attorney stood up in front of the jury and said the following: "My name is Juan Alvarez, I caused an accident that killed a lot of people." The attorney went on to talk about Alvarez's difficult childhood of extreme abuse from a cruel father and his eventual involvement in drugs. Then he said in Alvarez's voice, "Drugs were like friends to me, like important members of my family."

Then the attorney explained how Alvarez's marriage was torn apart by his craving for drugs. "My wife asked me to choose between her and the drugs, and I couldn't do that. I would always go back to the drugs." The Defense attorney's approach may have seemed strange to many in the courtroom, but it was a desperate attempt to switch the focus from the dead victims to the defendant, a sad Meth head loser. The Defense attorney went on to say that the poor defendant had no intention to kill the people on the train or to cause the train to derail. His only intent was to kill himself.

The Defense attorney finished up by saying that his client was guilty of causing a terrible accident but not murder. The question he set up for the jury to consider was as follows: "Did Mr. Alvarez act in conscious disregard of human life? If the answer is no, then no matter how hard it is for you to decide this...you will have to agree that Mr. Alvarez caused a tragic, fatal accident.

Since the Defense had framed the issue of the defendant's conduct as not criminal, prosecutor Brougham took advantage of her Rebuttal Argument to explain that there are several other options for jurors to convict the defendant of lesser crimes if they do not find the intent to kill. She explained that the jurors could find the defendant guilty of felony murder in which a person who commits a crime, such as arson or train-wrecking, can be guilty of murder if the deaths occurred as a result of those actions. She said, "He was mad at the entire world, and he wanted to hurt somebody."

The judge read the final jury instructions and sent the jury out to deliberate. It only took little more than a day for the jury to come back with a guilty verdict for the 11 murders plus arson. Also, the Special Circumstance was found to be true, which required the jurors to come back in several days to start the Death Penalty phase of the case.

On July 7, 2008, the prosecution started calling the victims' relatives to the witness stand to testify to the impact the victims' deaths had on them and their families. For years, the high courts wouldn't permit the prosecution to present any evidence about how the loss of the victim had impacted the families' lives. Then the U.S. Supreme Court stepped in and made it abundantly clear that the impact of the death of a victim is a proper subject that jurors could hear about in determining the proper punishment. In the finding of the defendant's guilt or innocence the courts have always maintained that this should be decided only on whether the defendant committed the crime and not on to what extent the killing impacted the victim's family.

When that change in the law came about, the prosecutors started to have the victim's family testify in front of the jury during the Penalty phase of the trial. Except in gang and organized crime cases, the victim's family often makes up the best part of the prosecution evidence during the Penalty phase. The loss of a loved one in a tragic situation is sure to touch the most unsympathetic juror. Here in this Metrolink case, 11 victims' families had the opportunity to testify in front of the jurors. They told what the victim's loss had meant to them and how their loss had affected their lives. In this case, these victims were totally innocent and had done nothing to bring about their demise. On top of that, these victims were hard-working people whose only act was to leave early for work so they would be on time.

For over a day, the prosecution displayed one set of family witnesses after another telling the most heart-wrenching stories that couldn't help bring everyone to tears. Even the judge noticed the trail of tears. He told the attorneys that the jurors were "having a hard time." The judge said, "Almost all the jurors are crying." He turned to the nine women and three men jurors and said, "If you start to lose it, and you can't take it anymore for a while, let me know and we'll take an extra break."

Without a doubt, the prosecution's 'Victim Impact' evidence made a giant impact on the jury. After the last family member had testified, it was decided that it would be the appropriate time to have the jury field trip to visit the four mangled train cars. The court had the Sheriff's Department arrange the transportation and address the security concerns. The jurors were taken by Sheriff's vans from the downtown Criminal Courthouse by deputy Sheriffs to an empty industrial lot in Glendale. There, four of the train cars had been stored as evidence in an enclosure sealed by a tall fence with razor wire on top.

The jurors were given as much time as they needed to walk around the four train cars. They wandered around the rusty, sheared-off underside of the compartments. Some of the jurors walked in groups and tried to peer through the dirty train windows so they could see inside. Some windows had been broken out so it was easier for them to see the smashed walls and seats tossed about in a mess of bent metal. They could see that the two-level train cars had the upper level caved onto the lower level. Throughout the interior of the cars was gravel everywhere. Parts of the compartments had been churned up as the train skidded off its tracks. Curiously, the floors of the train cars still had newspapers from the date of the crash as well as Metrolink schedules scattered throughout.

What impact all this twisted metal was having on the jurors couldn't be deciphered from their somber expressions. Some had questions, and the judge indicated they would try to answer them when they returned to the courtroom. Was the jury viewing beneficial to the DA or the Defense? No one knows the answer, but it did provide the jurors with some context of what all the injured were talking about when they tried to describe how they were pinned under parts of the wreckage that required the 'Jaws of Life' to extricate them.

The next day after several questions about the field trip, it was time for the Defense to present any Mitigating evidence they thought would be helpful for the defendant. The Defense attorney called Alvarez's cousin, Beto, to testify to receiving a recorded phone message from Juan just after the train crash. This message was played for the jury so they could determine if the defendant felt any remorse for what he had done. On the recording could be heard the defendant sobbing as he said, "I didn't mean to do this, Beto. A lot of innocent people died. I don't deserve to live Beto...Please pray for me."

Another Defense witness called to testify was Alvarez's mother, who indicated that Juan's father had beat her for getting pregnant with Juan because he didn't want any more children. Even Juan's mother admitted that she had beaten Juan as he was growing up. She related that Juan once tried to hang himself with a clothesline. She described her son as follows: "He was a very serious, quiet boy. He never played with anyone."

Alvarez's wife testified what a 'good father' he was and that he loved his two children even though the daughter wasn't fathered by him. The wife finished her testimony by saying, "There's always going to be a place in my heart for him."

When all the witnesses had testified during the penalty phase, it was time for the Argument. Prosecutor Monaghan started out by saying, "He does not deserve your leniency for his deliberate, intentional acts. He does not deserve your mercy...In this case, Mr. Alvarez has forfeited his right to live." The prosecutor explained that the defendant's psychological health and troubled upbringing should not be used as an excuse or a crutch for his actions later in life. "People do terrible things. Mr. Alvarez did a terrible thing and now he must pay for that with his life."

After the prosecution had finished, the Defense attorney got up and approached the jury. He started out recognizing that he had to acknowledge the obvious, which was that what his client had done was terrible and was reprehensible. "There is nothing I could say, construct, put into words that could alleviate the tremendous pain and suffering and the prolonged loss of each of the families. I admit the survivors would suffer for the rest of their lives, but it is up to each juror to make a rational decision." His attorney described Alvarez as a self-acknowledged meth addict who survived a tortured childhood and had exhibited mental instability. He reminded jurors that Alvarez had written in his diary five weeks before the crash of his desire to commit suicide. The Defense attorney went on to say, "It was a confluence of unpredictable, almost unforeseeable triggers that led to this tragedy. He had a tortured upbringing in which he was beaten like a dog. His mother is useless, his father is a monster, and he has nowhere to go. This is the world this man was brought into and was raised in." With this depiction of the defendant, the Defense attorney ended by saying that the appropriate punishment in this situation was Life Without the Possibility of Parole (LWOP).

For over two months this jury had been hearing evidence about one of the most significant train tragedies in American history while at the same time hearing about the life of one of the saddest losers of all time. They had been filled with revulsion at what the defendant had done and sympathy for the pathetic life the defendant had been subjected to. The jury's job was to determine whether the Aggravating evidence substantially outweighed the Mitigating evidence, and if they did then they were to recommend the Death Penalty as the proper punishment.

Most court watchers were surprised that after only three and a half hours of deliberation the jury buzzed indicating that they had a reached a verdict. Within an hour, Judge Pounder's courtroom was filled to capacity. The victim's families, as well as the injured victims, milled around until they found a seat. Other judges and attorneys had migrated down the long hallway to Pounder's courtroom. The news media had to scramble quickly, since everyone thought it would be days before a verdict would be decided. Every seat was filled and there was no more standing room in the back of the courtroom.

John Monaghan took his seat with his co-prosecutor, Cathryn Brougham, at the counsel table. John had done more Death Penalty trials than anyone in the DA's Office. As a result, he had heard so many times the courtroom clerk read the words that the jury recommended the penalty of **DEATH**. There was a rumor that one of the cell blocks on Death Row was called the "MONAGHAN TIER," since so many of the defendants that John had prosecuted ended up there.

However, John was surprised by the very short deliberation by the jurors and wondered what that could mean. As the jurors filed into the courtroom, John gave them a good hard look. Was there something in their demeanor or lack of eye contact with the prosecutors that would tip him off as to their ultimate decision of these jurors? When the courtroom clerk read the words, "Life without the Possibility of Parole" John leaned slightly back in his chair and a crease of a faint smile flashed across his face.

Later, when the reporters asked him what he thought of the jurors' decision, he said, "I was not disappointed with the verdict, and I recognize the jury's tenacity. This case was particularly difficult because it wasn't clear-cut. At least they didn't find that he was simply a misguided person." It could be said that John didn't agree with the jury's result but he wasn't surprised with their decisions.

The Defense attorney told the news media, "I think they had some compassion and humanity, and they reasoned that it wouldn't be appropriate for us to kill someone who himself didn't have an intent to kill." However, it was Alvarez's wife who may have had the most telling assessment of the verdict. She said to the reporters, "I still don't believe it's justice. I think he belongs in a mental institution. Someday I will tell our children that their father had been unfairly convicted."

Immediately after the reading of the verdict, a reporter contacted several of the jurors before they left the courthouse. One juror indicated that he was leaning more for the Death Penalty for Alvarez and it was a real emotional struggle for him. That juror said, "I feel he needed to pay with death because people did die, but I felt I should follow the law and not lead with emotions." Another juror said, "There was a terrible amount of emotion during the deliberations, and we did argue a lot. I believed that Alvarez had gotten 'short changed' in life and that the man's abusive upbringing had taken a psychological toll on him."

As much as the prosecution tried to focus the jurors' attention on the victims and their relative's loss of them, the Defense won out by shifting the jurors' consideration on the hard luck story of the defendant. What was most surprising about this case was that the jury was able to reach a verdict. The outcome of this case is dependent on a person's mindset. Half the people will believe anyone who is responsible for the death of 11 individuals and injury of 180 people should pay the ultimate penalty. Another half of the population would believe that a person with mental or emotional problems can't be totally responsible for his or her actions.

This case brought together the two extremes, and the question was how were nine women and three men jurors going to react to the unique facts of this case? That is why a case like this Metrolink case had to be tried and let 12 members of the community decide what should be the appropriate punishment.

August 20, 2008, was the day that the judge was to sentence Alvarez. This was the biggest anticlimactic event, since everyone knew what was going to happen. Judge Pounder was gracious as always and permitted the victim's families and the injured to have the opportunity to voice their concerns about the appropriateness of the sentence.

About half a dozen family members of the victims who died addressed the court. One of the sisters of a crash victim looked directly at Alvarez and requested that he look at her. Surprisingly, Alvarez moved back his chair slightly so he could face her. She went on to say, "Thank you for looking at me, because I want you to know the pain you have caused me. You did a very bad and stupid thing. If you have tried to cause pain and anguish, you have definitely succeeded. If you wanted to kill yourself, why didn't you simply lie down on the tracks? Because of your selfishness, you have bestowed this terrible nightmare upon us, and it will never end."

Another speaker was a brother of one of the victims, who tried to articulate how the defendant's selfish act had touched so many lives. He recounted how his niece had broken down sobbing during a recent father-daughter dance at a bat mitzvah. She realized she would never again have a chance to dance with her dad, even at her wedding someday.

The big question is, what is the purpose of this storytelling at the time of sentencing? Is it to make sure that the judge gives the defendant the maximum sentence? Or is it to shame the defendant and make him feel guilty? Or possibly is it merely a therapeutic act to allow the victim's family member to close a dark chapter of their life?

When all the speeches were properly made part of the court record, Judge Pounders threw in his two cents. After presiding over this long trial, the judge related to the defendant that he believed that he lacked any genuine remorse for the crash. Judge Pounder leaned forward in his seat and gazed down at Juan Alvarez and in a firm, stern voice said, "I don't believe for a minute you intended to kill yourself or harm yourself in any way. I think you were setting up a scenario so you could go back to your family. If there were a sentence 'forever' I would certainly give it to you."

Judge Pounder concluded his remarks by sentencing Juan Manuel Alvarez to 11 consecutive life prison terms without the possibility of parole. The judge then left the bench and went into his chambers. Within moments, Alvarez was standing up and shuffling toward the custody door. He looked toward the audience and gave a big smile to his family members. Next, he walked through the custody door as it slammed shut behind him with a loud thud. Since Alvarez had just turned 29, he would be spending many years—possibly a half a century—behind bars.

After it was all said and done, the District Attorney's administration issued a media release stating what an admirable job **John Monaghan** and **Cathryn Brougham** had done in prosecuting the Juan Alvarez case. The public was never aware of the fact that these two prosecutors had to step into this complex case at the last minute when the assigned prosecutors got tied up in a retrial. What it showed was the incredible depth of experience and talent possessed by the members of the elite DA **Major Crimes Division.** This was emblematic of the teams that make up the infamous DELTA FORCE of the U.S. Army.

The deaths of the victims were devastating for their families. Many of the dead were the breadwinners for their families, and many of them had multiple young children who depended on them. Obviously, the primary person who is liable for these losses was Juan Manuel Alvarez. However, most of the people who are liable for committing such devastating acts have no money or assets. In other words, they cannot compensate their victims for the losses.

Every attorney learns in law school that one 'can't get blood out of a turnip,' meaning that losers don't have any money to collect from. The next thing that attorneys are taught is to look for the 'deep pocket.' That generally means finding a large corporation or government agency that may somehow be involved in the incident, and then try to sue that entity.

In the Metrolink train crash, most of the victims' families agreed to use one law firm to sue the Metrolink government entity. The first claim was that the Metrolink had been negligent in not having fences to prevent vehicles from driving onto the tracks. Since most of the commuter tracks can't completely be fenced in, this cause of action didn't get much traction.

Next, the civil attorneys claim that the 'Push-Pull' method used by Metrolink was dangerous, since cab cars are lighter than locomotives and they are prone to more passenger fatalities. A state appellate court ruled that the Metrolink could not be held negligent under FRA rules for operating a Push-Pull train during the Glendale derailment. At that point, the civil attorneys had to find another way to prove negligence by Metrolink. After several years, the attorneys learned that the engineer of Train #100 Southbound had seen the outline of the vehicle on the tracks and had 22 seconds to do something. All the engineer did was put on the regular train brake, but he failed to activate the emergency brake.

The attorneys claimed that the engineer was negligent in not pulling the emergency brake, since he had sufficient time to do so and the train would then have been able to avoid striking Alvarez's vehicle. This was the main claim of negligence against Metrolink. After years of negotiations, the Metrolink board agreed to pay $30 million to settle most of the lawsuits stemming from the 2005 train crash that killed 11 and injured 180 people.

In major calamities, the question is who should pay and who should receive. There was no question that the victims had suffered a real loss and the compensation from the lawsuit would help them pay for the family's support, such as mortgage and the usual bills. However, it is less clear whether the average users of the Metrolink should have to pay higher transportation fees to pay off the $30 million civil settlement.

Every night when Juan Manuel Alvarez goes to sleep in his tiny prison cell, does he contemplate how his action of driving his Jeep Cherokee onto the Metrolink tracks is costing everyone who uses mass transit in the Los Angeles area? The likely answer is NO. And most likely he doesn't care. The strange thing about Juan Alvarez is that he changed so many lives and he will never know how many and in what ways.

CHAPTER 33 WILLIAMS—PREPARING FOR CLEMENCY HEARING

When I, the author, was asked to work on the Tookie Williams Clemency Hearing to be heard by Governor Schwarzenegger, I thought, *What a waste of time*. With all the opponents to the Death Penalty coming out of the woodwork to try to block Tookie's execution, I honestly believed there was no way the appellate courts or even Governor Arnold Schwarzenegger would permit the execution to occur. At the time, the Governor was married to a member of the Kennedy family. For years, the Kennedy family was staunchly opposed to capital punishment. I felt the Governor's wife would put pressure on Schwarzenegger to find a way of granting Tookie clemency.

At the time, Steve Cooley was the Los Angeles District Attorney, and he had a strong belief that the LAW was the LAW. The Death Penalty was the LAW in the state of California; therefore it should be carried out. His attitude was if the voters of the state decided to do away with the Death Penalty, so be it. But until that time, the Death Penalty was the LAW, therefore it should be carried out.

I was told by Pat Dixon, the Head Deputy of Major Crimes Division, that his Division was assigned to handle the Clemency Hearing. Pat was told to assemble a team to work on the Hearing. He selected John Monaghan to head up the team. In the fall of 2005, I remember being called into a Pat Dixon's office for a meeting. Those present were John Monaghan and David Walgren, as well as

Pat and myself. I looked around the room and realized that I was the oldest—or, as I would like to say, the most senior—prosecutor in the room.

Even though I had the most years in the DA's Office, I had to admit that I had never taken part in a Clemency Hearing. Further, I had no idea where they occur, who was present at such hearings, or even how they were conducted. My understanding was that the state Attorney General's Office handled such hearings. As I sat there, I realized that at that time the Attorney General was Jerry Brown, who personally opposed Capital Punishment. Then it occurred to me that Jerry Brown's Office was literally passing off this 'Hot Potato' to the DA's Office to take the heat from the opponents of the Death Penalty. Were they doing this 'handoff' to the DA's Office with the thought we would fumble the ball since we didn't know anything about Clemency Hearings?

Since I didn't know anything, I started asking uninformed questions about the procedure involved. All of a sudden, John Monaghan turned to me and started explaining in detail how Clemency Hearings were conducted. I thought to myself, I have been in the DA's Office 15 years longer than Monaghan, so how does he know all of this. I didn't want to show any more of my ignorance, so I remained silent for the rest of the meeting.

When the meeting ended, I was instructed to work with John in preparing a PowerPoint presentation that would be shown to the Governor. Several days later, John came by my office and handed me a stack of photos and provided me with a summary of the facts of the crimes that Tookie had been convicted of. When John was finished, he asked how long it would take to prepare a draft presentation for his review. I told him, "I will tell you when it will be ready, but first tell me how the Hell do you know so much about Clemency Hearings." He stepped back into my office and in an unpretentious voice told me, "I have friends over in the AG's Office and they were the ones who gave me the heads-up regarding Clemency

Hearings." I smiled and then replied, "Thanks, I will have it ready for you at the end of the week."

With that, he walked out of my office, and I thought, *How does he do it?* This was just a further example of how John knows how to prepare himself for any situation. If he doesn't know it, he will find a way to learn about it. I realized that John was always well prepared whenever he walked into a courtroom. However, I wondered how well prepared would the DA's Office appear in this Clemency Hearing. We were entering uncharted waters that seemed to be filled with hungry sharks (the news media) ready to attack us if we made any procedural mistake.

Later in the week, I met with John to show him a draft version of the presentation. His reaction was that was a good start but much more needed to be included. I asked him how much time he had to present the prosecution's case to the Governor? He said that he had 30 minutes and that Tookie's representatives had the same amount of time. I told him that I didn't think he could do it in that limited amount of time. He looked at me and with a slight smile on his face and a no nonsense voice said, "We have to get it all in and it can't be one minute longer than 30 minutes." I asked him how he knew that there was a strict time limit? He indicated that he had contacts in the Governor's Office who informed him that the Governor had a tight schedule and never permitted anyone to go over their allotted time.

I had to think that John had anticipated every contingency and was ready for it. That was who he was. He was like a stealth submarine that the opponent never sees. It emphasizes preparation and silently waits for his opportunity to strike.

Back to the drawing board, I started inserting all the items he wanted to discuss at the Hearing. I knew he wanted the presentation to start with the first murder case. It was my job to reduce the following facts from the trial to fit on two or three slides.

On this graphic page are the slides of the 7-Eleven Market Robbery Murder and below is the Motel Robbery Murder committed by Tookie Williams will his sawed-off shotgun.

GRAPHICS 48

This was a slide showing the lay out of the market & the victim.

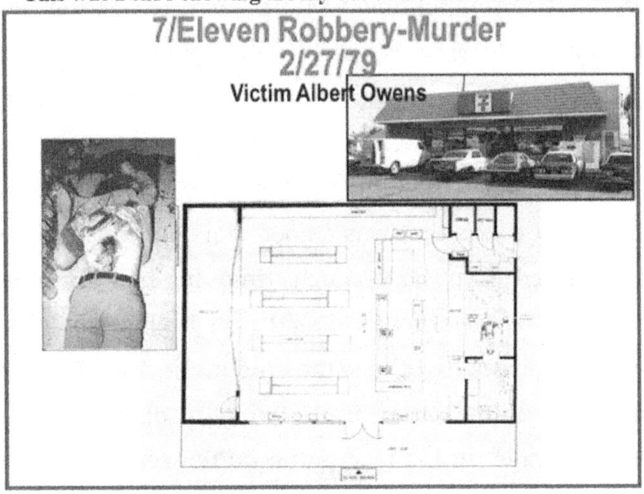

This was the diagram of the motel robbery showing the sawed off shotgun.

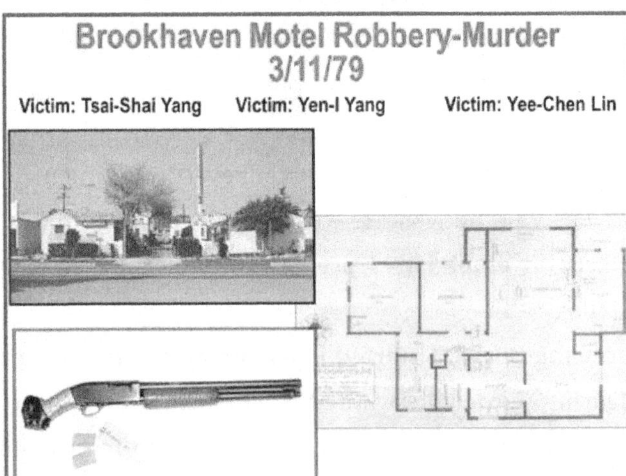

(The following are the facts of the crimes committed by Tookie Williams which came out during the original trial)

That brutal murder occurred on a chilly predawn morning on February 27, 1979. A clerk, Albert Owens, for a local 7-Eleven stepped outside the store where he worked, grabbed a push broom, and began sweeping the parking lot. A 24-year-old father of two, Owens had recently mustered out of the U. S. Air Force and applied for the temporary job until he could find something better. The location, on Whittier Boulevard about seven miles from the skyscrapers of L.A., didn't seem like a particularly dangerous area. No one told Owens that convenience store clerks suffer the highest violent death rate, along with taxi drivers, in the civilian workplace.

At about 4:00 a.m., a brown station wagon pulled into the nearly vacant parking area, followed immediately by a dark 1969 Cadillac. Four young African-American men exited the cars. Tony Sims, wearing a green jogging suit with a dark cap, and "Darryl," dressed in a brown corduroy jacket, walked immediately into the 7-Eleven. Owens, the clerk, placed his broom and dustpan on the hood of his own vehicle so he couldn't forget them, and entered just behind the pair of young men.

"Tookie" Williams, 25, and Tyrone followed Owens into the store, The clerk had no way of knowing that the fellow behind him, Williams, who sported a huge Afro and the muscular physique of a body builder, was angry at his companions. Earlier, they had bungled two planned robberies at a Stop-N-Go market and a liquor store just a few miles away. Tookie had informed them that he would demonstrate how it should be done at the next place. As he strode into the store, he carried something held low and close to his right leg.

Owens asked if he could help the men. Without warning, Williams poked a sawed-off pump-action shotgun with an improvised pistol grip into Owens' back and growled for him to shut up and keep walking. The clerk obeyed, and when he reached an office-storage room at the back of the store, he obeyed the demand to lie face down on the floor.

An explosion and the sound of breaking glass shattered the silence as Williams shot a security television monitor mounted on a table, probably thinking that it would destroy any video record of the intruders. Seconds later, another blast filled the room.

At point-blank range, the buckshot mangled Albert Owens's back. Williams calmly reloaded, chambered another round, and fired again into the prostrate body, making certain that the victim would never again draw a breath of life.

The killer had been intent on smashing the video monitor to avoid leaving evidence, but he didn't bother to pick up the ejected shotgun shells.

Hustling quickly to the cash register, the gang members scooped up the loot. They collected a grand total of one hundred and twenty dollars. One of the youths asked Williams why he had shot the clerk. Sneering, he answered, "Because I didn't want to leave any witnesses. Besides, he was white."

The next set of slides that John wanted to be added included the facts of the motel robbery/murders, which consisted of the following:

Twelve days after the 7-Eleven robbery-murder, Tookie Williams and one of his "homeboys" prowled again in search of a place to rob. Driving south of downtown L. A. on Vermont Avenue, and hour before sunrise, they stopped at the Brookhaven Motel near 104th Street and tried the front lobby door. Finding it locked, Williams slammed his muscle-bound shoulder against the entry and easily smashed it open, tearing loose a safety chain, two deadbolts, and a key lock. Behind the counter stood a trembling Asian woman clad in light blue patterned pants and a teal-colored jacket.

Tsai-Shen Yang, 63, and her husband Yen Yi Yang, 67, had emigrated from Taiwan four years earlier and purchased the motel. Their daughter, Yen Chen Lin, 43, and son Robert, 31, soon followed. The family eked out a living by working long hours and dealing with rough clientele in the dangerous South Central LA sector.

The frightened mother offered no resistance when Williams and his accomplice crashed through the door. Yet Williams leveled his pistol-grip twelve-gauge shotgun at her midsection and pulled the trigger. The blow slammed her backward and spun her around. Williams stepped forward, aimed at her back, and delivered another explosion, which blew open her stomach. She hit the floor, prone, with her right knee raised and the foot twisted near her hip.

Yen Yi, the husband, had been sleeping on a couch in the office. He started to get up, but Williams pivoted, took aim again, and fired another lethal blast. The stunned victim slumped backward with a gaping hole in his chest. Apparently averse to any chances of leaving a witness alive, Williams extended the weapon and fired yet and round, tearing off the man's left arm at the elbow.

Both intruders swiftly rifled the cash register from a dark hallway. The slain couple's daughter, Yen-Chin Lin stood in the dim light, in a state of shock. Without hesitation,

Williams chambered another round and fired at the daughter's head. The discharge blew away the left side of her face and spattered a wall with flesh, blood, and brain tissue.

This time, Williams and his pal hurriedly picked up the ejected shells but overlooked one that had rolled under a piece of furniture. The sun still lay just below the eastern horizon when Williams and his partner escaped the bloody scene in the misty morning light.

Moments later, Robert Yang emerged from his bedroom, awakened by the noise which had been muffled by three walls. Sickened and horrified by the charnel bloodbath in front of him, he managed to call 911. Emergency medical technicians arrived and found the mother, Tsai-Shen dead. Incredibly, meager signs of life still remained in the other two victims, but they expired shortly after being taken to emergency wards in two separate hospitals.

Yang sobbed to homicide detectives that his family had been slaughtered and the killers did it for a measly one hundred dollars snatched from the cash register.

It didn't take long for the bloody trail to lead detectives in the direction of Tookie Williams. He had been unable to keep his mouth shut. Boasting to one of his acquaintances, Williams mentioned knowledge that some "Buddha-heads" had been blown away on Vermont Avenue. The murders, he said, had taken place at about five in the morning. Two guys had busted into the motel, did some shooting, and got away with some money. He knew that two women and one man had died, and told exactly how many times each one was shot.

Details Williams shared were remarkable in the respect that many of them had never been released to the news media. Only the killers could have known precisely what happened.

When his confidant expressed skepticism, Williams couldn't resist stating that he knew it was all true because he was in on it. Revealing that he was planning to rob a similar place, Williams reportedly said, "I'll blow them away like I blew them away in the motel."

Fortunately for homicide detectives, the individual who listened intently to Williams' bragging cringed with revulsion at every word and made a call to the police. Other tips also came in. Investigators visited one of the "friends" and recovered the sawed-off shotgun that Tookie had purchased in 1974. Ballistics tests proved that shells recovered from both crime scenes were from that weapon. Police rounded up several of the gang members, including two who had accompanied Williams at the 7-Eleven murder (the one called "Darryl" was never found). They also arrested the Brookhaven Motel accomplice. Williams had been the shooter in each case, and none of his buddies wanted to take the rap for murder. So they agreed to talk.

Tyrone had been one of the four men present when Albert Owens was shot to death, and had later provided the police with information about it. Because Tyrone did not carry a weapon at the scene, received no money for the crime, was the least culpable of the four participants, and was willing to testify for the People if granted immunity, the District Attorney's office agreed not to prosecute him. Tyrone told the jury all of the events leading up to and including the gory shotgun killing at the 7-Eleven. He also described how Williams later boasted about the slaying and mimicked the pitiful sounds made by the victim as he died.

Three witnesses testified regarding William's involvement in the Brookhaven Motel slayings. One of them, a friend of Williams, even though not implicated in the crime, had requested and received immunity. On the witness stand, he told of meeting Williams in LA's sprawling Griffith Park twelve hours after the crime. The informants said that Tookie admitted robbing and killing three Asians for a few dollars, which he later spent to purchase drugs.

Additional testimony came from the individual who had heard Williams describe specific details of the robbery-murders and eventually confess to being the killer. The witness's wife also took the stand to corroborate his story.

After hearing all the above evidence and the Defense evidence, the Tookie William's jury started their deliberation. Within a day, the jury returned guilty verdicts on four counts of First-Degree Murder as well as finding true the Special Circumstances of Robbery-Murder and Multiple Murders. Upon hearing the verdicts, Williams growled, "Son of Bitches." His voice was loud enough for the court reporter to hear, and she included his expletive in the trial transcript.

Several days later, the Death Penalty phase of the trial began and the same jury sat and heard the prosecution present the Aggravating Evidence, which included details about an escape plan that Tookie had initiated. After both sides had presented their evidence the jury started to deliberate regarding the punishment. After a short time, the jury came back with a recommendation for Death.

While working on the Clemency Hearing, John wanted me to insert at least one slide showing the brazen escape plan that Tookie had concocted involving the bus that transported custody defendants between the jail and the courthouse. The plan involved killing a guard as well as the prisoner who was set to testify against Williams during the trial. Williams recruited a fellow inmate to help him carry out the escape. One of Williams' requests was that they needed to use dynamite so that none of the dead bodies could be identified. As a result, the authorities wouldn't know who had died and who had fled.

The information John gave me consisted of a hand-drawn map made by Tookie showing where his buddies planned to plant the dynamite to blow up the jail bus. There were several notes he wrote spelling out exactly what his friends needed to do to pull off this escape. Fortunately, the jailers discovered the map and notes and made copies of them and then forwarded them to their intended parties. Eventually, all his friends were arrested and the escape was thwarted.

As a part of the Clemency presentation, John wanted the Governor to be aware that Tookie had explored every possible appeal and each and every one of them had been denied. There was no easy way to illustrate all these appeals. I knew if John tried to discuss each and every appeal he would use up part of his precious 30 minute time on just this one point.

On the following graphic page are the copies of the escape map and notes and below is a layout of all of the appellate reviews his case went through.

GRAPHICS 49

This was part of the letters detailing the escape plan from courthouse

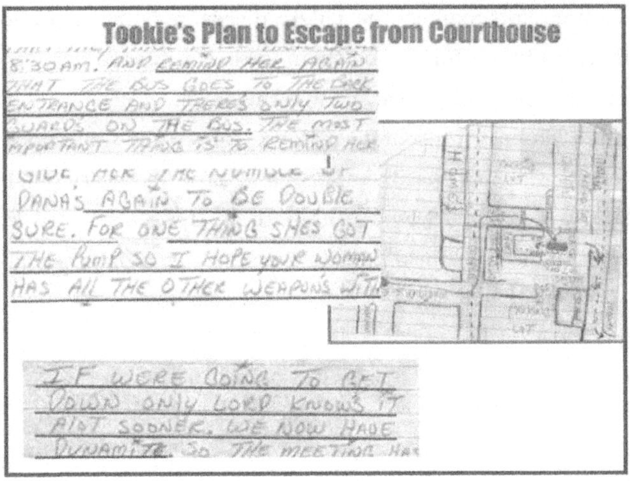

This was slide showing the various appeals the William's case had gone through.

William's Legal Appeals

4/15/81 Motion for New Trial Denied

4/11/88 State Sup. Ct affirms conviction & denied habeas petition

1/18/89 Cal. Sup. Ct. second habeas denied

1/18/89 filed first fed. Habeas in US Dist. Ct. held in abeyance

4/11/94 third Cal Habeas denied

6/21/95 Cal Sup Ct. fourth Cal habeas denied

12/21/98 US Dist. Ct. denied amended habeas

12/17/99 Motion to reopen the judgment was denied by Fed Ct.

9/10/02 US Ninth Circuit of Appeals denied direct appeal

9/9/04 US Ninth Circuit of Appeal amended opinion & denied petition for rehearing suggest rehearing en blac

2/2/05 US Ninth Circuit of Appeals denied subsequent petition for rehearing and suggest rehearing en blanc

10/11/05 US Supreme Ct denied petition for writ of certiorari

11/10/05 State Supreme Ct. denied motion for post judgment discovery

The Governor's Office set the Clemency Hearing for December 8, 2005, in his Sacramento office. Long before that date, John Monaghan worked with prosecutor David Walgren to produce a two-inch-thick response to the Petition for Executive Clemency. This document had 'chapter and verse' answers to every claim that the Tookie's supporters had conjured up. I had put the finishing touches on John's slide show presentation and condensed it into 55 slides. We had rehearsed the presentation and felt comfortable that it could be done within the 30-minute timeframe.

In order for John to be able to give this presentation to the Governor, I gave him a laptop computer loaded with his presentation and one of our DA's projectors. This was all he needed to give his presentation. I felt I had done my job and started concentrating on my other pending cases. Then I was told that I was needed to accompany the team to Sacramento for the presentation to the Governor. I was very busy and didn't have time to fly Sacramento. But the administrators told me there were last-minute changes that would have to be inserted and the crew wasn't technologically savvy enough to make the changes on their own, so that was why they needed me to go with them.

The other reason was they were seasoned veterans who were well aware of Murphy's Law. They all have had experiences where they thought everything was covered and still things went wrong. So this time they didn't want to take any chances but wanted to be 100% certain that nothing bad could happen. There was a feeling of uncertainty that something could go wrong with the computer or the projector, and they wanted me there just in case of an emergency. They assured me that there was a 1:00 p.m. flight back to LA, which meant I would only miss the morning and would be back for the afternoon cases.

The DA's Office had another concern which was for the safety of the DA delegation. Since there were so many protesters scheduled to be present at the Capitol, the DA's Office assigned DA investigators to accompany all of the delegation. I had a late afternoon flight to Sacramento, so when I arrived at the airport, I was picked up by law enforcement, who drove me to our hotel across from the Capitol. As we drove by the Capitol building, one of the investigators pointed out a large group of anti-Death Penalty protestors demonstrating. When I arrived at the hotel, I was told to make myself available, since Monaghan had some changes that he needed to have incorporated in the presentation.

I waited several hours and one of the bodyguards told me that they had lost contact with John Monaghan. He hadn't arrived on the 7:00 p.m. flight, and there was a concern regarding John's whereabouts. My main concern at that hour was that I was hungry and wanted to get something to eat. The investigators were running around trying to figure out where Monaghan was and if he was okay. So I went to the hotel restaurant and took a seat and waited to order. There out of nowhere was Monaghan walking toward me. He asked if he could join me for dinner. I quickly said, "John, did you know that the DA investigators are looking for you?" John got the biggest grin on his face and said, "I lost them at the Ontario airport."

Then I suggested that he join me for dinner so we could figure out how to incorporate these new changes into his presentation. We sat in a booth at the rear of the hotel restaurant where we couldn't be easily seen. John took delight out of the fact that he had outsmarted the bodyguard detail who had been assigned to never lose sight of him. His complaint was that it was a waste of resources to surround him with bodyguards. I thought to myself that John would never make it as the President of the USA, who has to be surrounded by Secret Service agents. I had to laugh to myself that John definitely didn't take himself too seriously.

After we ate, we got together and worked until midnight on the changes to his presentation. The next morning, I awoke early to finish up all the changes. Afterward, I went down for breakfast and there was John having breakfast with his bodyguards on both sides of him. We received word from the Governor's Office that we needed to be in the hotel lobby at 8:00 a.m. so the state police could drive us to the Capitol. I thought that was strange since we could walk across the street to the Capitol building. If we did go that way, we would have to go through the crowd of Death Penalty protesters. Then at 08:00 hours we were packed into several police cars and whisked away. I didn't understand where they were taking us, but within five minutes we were somewhere deep in an underground Capitol garage.

The Crown Vic stopped and we were instructed to get out. The state police were in full dress uniforms topped off by their Smoky-the-Bear hats, which made me think we were somewhere deep in the mountains. They placed us in a private elevator that zoomed us up several floors. When the doors opened, we were across from the entrance to the Governor's Office. We could see a massive number of photographers roped off taking our pictures as we walked in the fortified Governor's Office.

We were directed to wait in a side office until the Governor arrived in the Capitol. Then the staff escorted us and the Defense team into a sun-drenched conference room. The prosecution team had their backs to the sun, and "Tookie's" legal defense team, headed up by distinguished Defense attorney Peter Fleming Jr., was on the other side of the long antique wooden conference table.

The following graphic pages show the prosecution team entering the Governor's Office. On the next page is the room where the Clemency Hearing was held.

GRAPHICS 50

This shows the DA members arriving at the Governor's Office. The circle shows author carrying laptop and projector for presentation.

News media showing DA members entering Governor's Office.

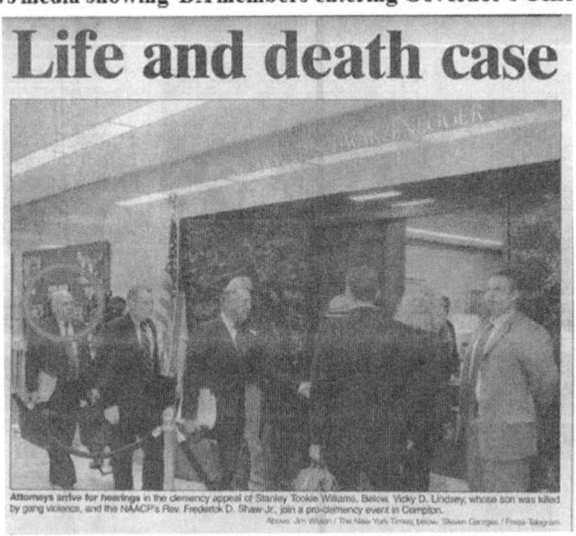

Life and death case

Attorneys arrive for hearings in the clemency appeal of Stanley Tookie Williams. Below, Vicky D. Lindsey, whose son was killed by gang violence, and the NAACP's Rev. Frederick D. Shaw Jr., join a pro-clemency event in Compton.

Above: Jim Wilson / The New York Times; below: Steven Georges / Press-Telegram

GRAPHICS 51

This photo shows DA members leaving Clemency Hearing.

This is photo of Governor's Conference room where hearing was held.

After everyone was assembled in the room, the governor's legal assistant laid out the ground rules for both sides and reminded that the 30-minute time limit was strictly adhered to. Each side could reserve five minutes for rebuttal if they so wished. Since it was the Defense who had requested the Clemency Hearing, they would go first, followed by the prosecution.

The Governor's Office had permitted us to set up the projector to make sure it would be able to be seen in the bright light of the conference room. After we were certain that the projector and the screen were in alignment, I told John, "Let's turn the projector off." We could turn it back on just before we were ready to start. John told me that he wanted the projector on all the time so there wouldn't be any delay. I was trying to explain to John that if the projector lies idle too long it will automatically shut off.

Next it was announced that the Governor was on his way, John didn't comprehend what I was trying to tell him. Then all of a sudden, the Governor entered the conference room and sat at the head of the table. I had to take a seat directly behind John. I could see that he still had the projector on and he had the controls in his hands. I thought to myself that we had 30 minutes before the projector automatically turned itself off. The Defense had assured the Governor's assistant that they would take only 20 minutes and reserve part of their time for a rebuttal. With that information, I figured we would have time to spare before the projector would automatically shut off.

CHAPTER 34 WILLIAMS—CLEMENCY HEARING BEGINS

It was time for the Clemency Hearing to begin. Governor Schwarzenegger sat in his chair ramrod straight. At that moment, a stern voice began to speak which was easily recognizable by any Terminator movie fan. One had to listen intently to this choppy Germanic accented voice. To everyone in the room they knew it was the GOVERNOR who was speaking. He announced that he took this duty very seriously regarding the issue of clemency and that he wished to hear from both sides before making a decision. He turned to the Defense team and said, "Please begin."

Fleming's Argument recited the points he had spelled out in his Clemency letter. He emphasized that Williams had redeemed himself and was a positive force in discouraging young black males from joining gangs. The Defense had numerous points they wanted to make as the clock on the wall was ticking away. One of the other attorneys read aloud a letter from victim Albert Owens' widow stating that she did not want to see Williams executed for killing her former husband. It was well past the 30-minute time limit when I noticed that our projector had automatically turned itself off. Eventually, the Williams team concluded their lengthy presentation.

The Governor turned his head and nodded to the prosecutor, John Monaghan, to begin. John pushed the control button and nothing happened. He turned around and looked directly at me like it was my fault that the projector didn't function. I stepped up to him and whispered that it would take several minutes before we could reboot the projector. John asked the obvious question, which was what was he supposed to do now. As the 'Terminator' looked daggers at the prosecution team, I thought, what the hell should I do now? I stood up and looked at Governor Schwarzenegger and explained we were having some technical problems with the projector and needed several minutes to reset it. Slowly, his grim expression turned to a radiant smile. He gave off a hardy Schwarzenegger chuckle and said, "When I was working in Hollywood, things like that happened all the time. Why don't we take a break now and resume in ten minutes?" He stood up and walked out to the room.

All of a sudden, I was surrounded by the Governor's techie crew, who brought in a large projector and set it up and in less than ten minutes we were ready to roll. The Governor reappeared and Monaghan began his slide show presentation starting out showing the viciousness of the crimes, underscoring that none of the victims had resisted or posed any threat. He noted that all of Williams' henchmen, including Sims at his own trial, had named Tookie as the shooter. Solid evidence had proved the weapon belonged to Williams.

Next, Monaghan addressed the planned escape in which Tookie intended to commit more murders. To prove this point, John flashed onto the screen Tookie's handwritten jailhouse note illustrating where and how it was planned to occur. Next, John addressed the issue of the nomination of Tookie for a Nobel Prize. John explained that such a nomination only required any professor in the world to submit a person's name to the nominating committee. Next, John discussed how simple it was to obtain the President Bush Volunteer Service Award. All a person had to do was fill out a form and pay one dollar.

The next graphic page shows the forms that anyone could fill out to receive certain awards.

As Monaghan neared the end of his thirty minutes, the Defense had a confident look as though they knew that the Governor's wife would never let Tookie be executed. At that point, the prosecutor knew he needed to address the Defense's "Redemption" issue.

Monaghan looked at the Governor and asked the question, "Has Williams really undergone redemption?" The answer, he suggested, was in a book that Williams had written. Locking eyes with the Governor, the prosecutor asked, "What redeemed person would dedicate their book to some of the most violent criminals in the 20th

Century? It resonated like a thunder clap in the room. Monaghan opened a copy of Williams' book, *Life in Prison,* published in 1998, and he read aloud four of the twelve names listed on the dedication page. He ticked off each one like a gong from a bell of doom:

Assata Ahakur—In 1973, he opened fire on a pair of State Troopers, killing one and wounding the other.

Mumia Abu-Jamal—In 1981, he shot a Philadelphia police officer in the back and then stood over him and fired four more shots in the victim's body.

Leonard Peltier—In 1975, two FBI Special Agents were wounded in a gun battle and then executed at point blank range by Peltier

George Jackson—In 1970, he and two other inmates at Soledad Prison overpowered a guard, dragged him up three flights of stairs, and threw him off the top tier to his death. During Jackson's murder trial in Marin County, his brother carried out an armed raid, commandeered the courtroom, freed the inmates, and took five hostages, including Judge Harold Haley. The escapees, led by George Jackson, taped a shotgun to the judge with the muzzle pointed under his chin. When it later fired, Haley died in the bloody violence.

Prosecutor Monaghan repeated his question, "How could anyone who has been redeemed hold up as one of his mentors the likes of George Jackson?"

On the following graphic page can be seen the book Life in Prison *that Williams claimed to have written, plus one of his so-called children's books.*

GRAPHICS 52

This was used to show how easy anyone can be nominated for Nobel Peace Prize as well as President's Service Award.

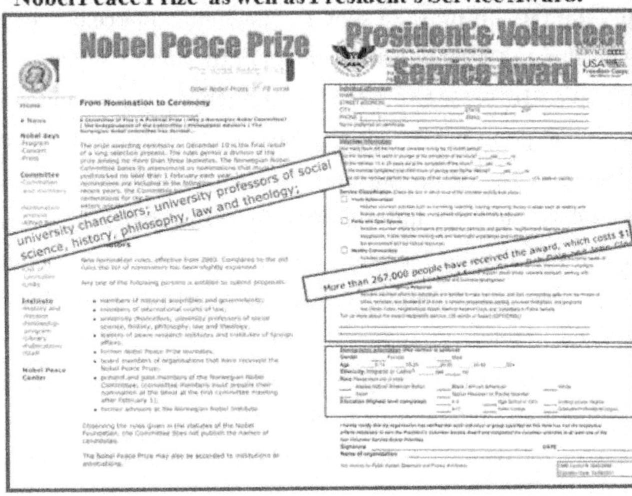

This was Tookie's book dedicated to violent killers. His children's books weren't written by him but another person.

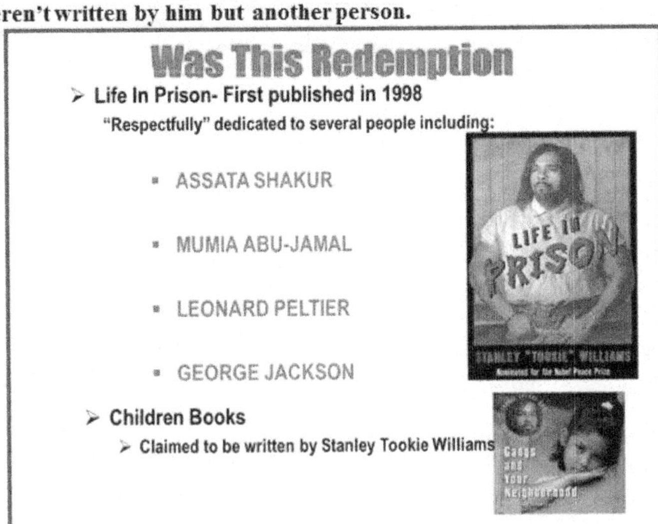

Then John sat down. While Monahan was talking about Tookie's book, the Defense team went scouring through their briefcases looking for a copy it. Someone found one and turned to the section in which he dedicated his book. There was a pained look on their face as they looked at the names.

The Governor turned to Fleming and said, "Do you have anything to add?" The Defense didn't respond to the gauntlet that had been thrown down by the prosecutor. The Defense team ended their presentation playing a tape of Tookie telling the Governor if clemency were granted he would dedicate the rest of his life to helping others. John rebutted what the Defense had argued by summarizing his earlier presentation.

The following page was prepared to easily see what all the points were.

GRAPHICS 53

This visual was a summary of the issues discussed at Hearing.

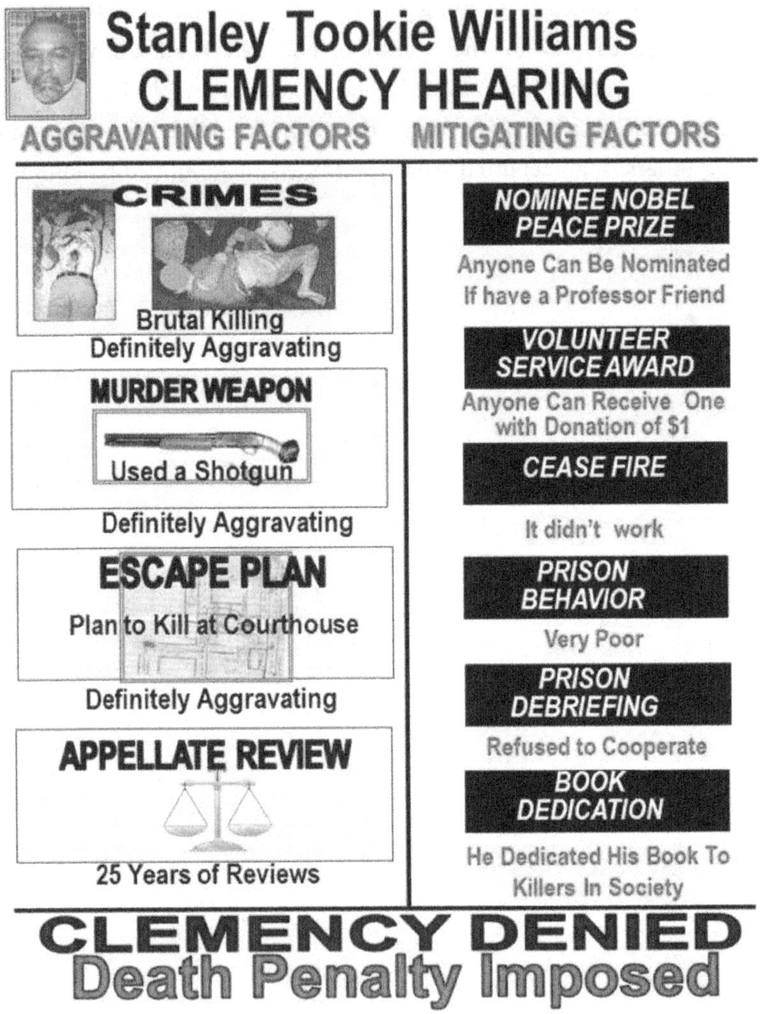

Then this solemn Clemency Hearing was over as the Governor in the same grim voice he started with uttered "Thank you." He stood up and turned and walked to his private office. There was an icy silence as he closed the door behind him. Even if one might have thought of saying in a whisper, "Hasta la vista, baby," this was not the right time or place to say it.

As the DA's team walked out, they couldn't help but notice on the wall of the conference room that there was an eye-catching framed photograph of Governor Schwarzenegger shaking hands with Nelson Mandela. This picture acknowledged the high regard the Governor had for this historical figure. Upon noticing the photo on the wall, the prosecutors gave out a sigh of relief. If only the Defense team had turned around, they would have seen this photo so well displayed on the wall. Nelson Mandela was one of the other eight people that Tookie had dedicated his book to. The Defense would have been able to deflate Monaghan's strong closing Argument by saying that Tookie and the Governor had one person they both admired, that being Nelson Mandela.

After this tense legal battle, the prosecution team was told to congregate in one of the Governor's meeting rooms. We were instructed to wait in that room for a few moments until the 'Tookie group' had finished with their press conference. While standing there waiting, I congratulated Monaghan for doing his presentation within the 30-minute time allotment. Since I was so familiar with the content, I never thought to commend John for such a moving and impressive performance.

Then the Governor's Press Secretary came into the room and said, "The news media is ready for you." I thought 'Oh my God,' Monaghan never does press conferences. He keeps his distance from the news media. Years earlier, he had issues with several reporters regarding confidentiality. Before any of us could gather our thoughts, we were ushered out of the Governor's Office into the Capitol Press Room.

When we entered the room, there was a hush that came over the crowd of reporters. There were rows of cameras mounted on tripods and strobe lights glared at the stage. Our police escort was necessary, since there were protestors all over the Capitol building. We were concerned that protestors might throw blood-red paint on us to show their contempt for prosecutors who enforced the Death Penalty law.

Looking at the massive crowd, there was no way of knowing how many protestors were implanted in the throng. Were there going to be hecklers? And how were we going to respectfully handle their questions? As we, the LA DA contingency, realized that we were not in a friendly environment, we huddled near the exit door and wondered how quickly we could get out of town.

The Governor's Press Secretary motioned to Monaghan to proceed up onto the stage. John turned to Sandi Gibbons, our DA media relations person, to see if it was safe to go on stage. She said, "Just take a few questions and we will get you off as soon as possible." John edged his way over to the step to the stage. He turned to the rest of us near the exit and motioned to us to join him on stage.

It was apparent that the news media was becoming impatient, since some had east coast deadlines and needed 40 seconds of a sound bite or two paragraphs of print. Sandi, sensing the restlessness of the 'media beast,' began directing all of us from the Los Angeles DA's Office up onto the stage. There we were: John Monaghan, his boss Pat Dixon, co-prosecutor Dave Walgren, and me. The glare of the lights blinded us. All of a sudden, we were all standing on stage as if we were in front of a firing squad. The news media was known for their scorn for the Death Penalty, and we were standing in front of them waiting for their hostile questions.

One of the reporters fired off a question: "Why do you believe Tookie Williams should be executed?" John without hesitation related to the media that Mr. Williams had committed several horrific murders, had a lengthy criminal record and was one of the founders of the violent Crips gang, which terrorized neighborhoods. For this, he had earned the Death Penalty. Then the media asked John about the fact that Mr. Williams had shown redemption. That was a question John was ready for. His tone was not apologetic but filled with confidence. He went down the list of every item that Tookie's supporters had held up as proof that he had redeemed himself, and he debunked every one of them.

I stood behind John as he answered questions laced with contempt for anyone who did not agree that Tookie should be considered for sainthood. I wondered how he did it without notes or papers in front of him. John rose to the occasion. He spoke with authority and answered all the reporters' questions. He didn't revert to name calling, such as that Tookie was nothing but a predator. At all times he was respectful of the reporters' questions and rattled off concise answers. When pressed by a reporter as to why he wouldn't permit clemency so Mr. Williams could continue to write children's books encouraging them to stay out of gangs, John directly answered by explaining the so-called children books story was a hoax in that someone else really authored those books, not Tookie Williams.

I started to look at my watch and realized I didn't have much time to catch my flight back to Los Angeles. I leaned over to our DA media secretary and whispered, "How much longer is this going to take, since we need to catch our flights?" She stepped forward and told the reporters, "We can take only one more question since we have flights to catch." With that commant, the reporters tried to get in their last questions. John took three more questions and the Media secretary grabbed the mic and said, "Thank you so much, and that concludes this news conference." We all proceeded out through the side door and were met by our police escort, which hustled us off to the airport.

While flying back to LA, I reflected on how well John had done with his presentation. Also, how well he had handled a hostile news conference without ever losing his cool. I wondered how John stayed so focused and was able to rise to the occasion. Most humans become nervous under so much pressure and lose their train of thought or have difficulty finding the right words to express themselves. John was in a league by himself.

The next day I was working on another case when I remembered that John still had the clicker for the projector. I went over to his office and he wasn't in, so I put my head in Pat Dixon's office and asked him if John had safely made it back last night from Sacramento. Pat said that John was still driving back. That comment surprised me so I said, "John flew to Sacramento; how could he be driving back?" Pat laughed and said to me, "Didn't you know that after the news conference John rented a car and drove over to Santa Cruz, where he bought a classic sports car he had seen for sale on the internet?" My response was, "You're kidding me."

I slowly headed back to my office in total dismay. I thought, How could a person do a Clemency Hearing and handle a dicey news conference while all the time thinking about buying a classic sports car on the other side of the state? John was truly a remarkable individual who knew how to do his job superbly but didn't need others to give him accolades for doing a great job.

Within a few days, the Governor's office announced its decision. In the Governor's written statement denying the clemency he stated, "The dedication of Williams' book ***'Life in Prison'*** casts significant doubt on his personal redemption....the inclusion of George Jackson on this list defies reason and is a significant indicator that Williams is not reformed and that he still sees violence and lawlessness as legitimate means to address societal problems." Twelve hours later, John Monaghan flew up to San Francisco to be the DA's representative at the execution. There at San Quentin, John as well as Tookie's family members met together in a cramped room as they watched the lethal drugs being injected into Tookie's arm. Within minutes, the convicted killer Stanley "Tookie" Williams was pronounced died in the apple-green death chamber at San Quentin. The next day, Tookie's family was preparing his funeral while John was back in his office working on his next Death Penalty case. Strangely enough, LIFE WENT ON JUST LIKE ANY OTHER DAY, except Tookie Williams was no longer part of the living.

CHAPTER 35 MONAGHAN'S CONTRIBUTION TO JUSTICE

What have we learned from this book? We have studied eight cases which have given you some insight as to the type of cases the **Major Crimes Division** handles. These cases were assigned to John Monaghan, and he left his indelible stamp on each one of them. You have seen a remarkable prosecutor in action who was involved from the investigation of these cases to ultimate sentencing. We can see what an impact this one prosecutor had on the following cases:

People vs. Aswad Pops & Byron Wilson—In this case, the victims were involved in drugs and gambling but that didn't diminish John's vehemence to prosecute this case. He was faced with a difficult task of communicating to the jurors the importance of the IROC rims and how they connected the defendant, Pops, to the killings. He fought fervently to convince the jurors to recommend the sentence of DEATH, which they did.

People vs. Chhuon Run and Samreth Pan—The victims were immigrants who were trying to make a living by selling small items from their residences. The defendants were killing innocent people throughout the state of California. Monaghan worked with the detectives and ballistic expert to connect both defendants to these vicious killings. After John got them convicted, he persuaded the jury that these killings were so brutal that both of them deserved DEATH.

People vs. Anh The Duong—John had to deal with a number of witnesses who were deathly afraid of the defendant. John spent an incredible amount of time assembling all the other crimes throughout the state in order to obtain a Death sentence for this prolific robber. This defendant and his robbery crew were like a crime wave that washed across the entire state of California. After John set his sights on Duong, this defendant's reign of terror came to an abrupt end.

People vs. David Rademaker—This was a sad cold case that had all the markings of never being solved. John worked with the detectives and eventually a pretext statement was obtained. This statement was only moderately incriminating. John worked with the two young women who had been abused by the defendant to have them tell the jury what the defendant told them about committing the murder of the victim model. Even though John was engaged in another homicide case when this case went to trial, he found time to come back to assist in the trial of this case since he didn't want to let the victim's family down.

People vs. Ivan Hill—This was a truly cold case that involved the killing of black prostitutes. The news media liked to complain that the Police and DA didn't take such cases seriously. Here John worked tirelessly and did an incredible job of convicting the defendant based on the DNA evidence as well as developing corroborating evidence. John used a strategy of proving even more diabolic murders to convince the jury that this defendant truly deserved the Death Penalty.

People vs. James Dixon—This was a brutal murder that impacted a college community. John worked with the Sheriff's detectives in hopes of finding a breakthrough. By combining the two rape cases with this homicide case, John was able to strengthen the entire case. His persuasive effort to convince the rape victims to testify gave the prosecution a formidable case. Then John negotiated an agreement to have an accomplice testify to how the kidnapping and killing occurred. All this hard work paid off in getting the Death Penalty for this 'Predator.'

People vs Juan Manuel Alvarez—John was able to pick up this high-publicity case when the assigned prosecutors became tied up on a retrial of another case. Fortunately, John was one of those remarkable people who is a 'fast learner.' In short order, he was up to speed and able to start the trial on time. Few attorneys have the ability to take on such a complex case involving the death of 11victims. On top of the factual complexities, John had to deal with the intricacies of a complete mental Defense. John, with the help of his co-prosecutor, presented an exceedingly solid case that left it up to the jurors to decide the appropriate punishment.

People vs. Stanley "Tookie" Williams—Even though many thought that the LA DA's Office couldn't handle a Clemency Hearing, John proved otherwise. As controversial as this case had become, John came up with a strategy that by using the Dedication portion of Tookie's book he was able to show that this defendant showed no remorse and hadn't given up his violent past. John did a magnificent job arguing to the governor that clemency wasn't justified. After the hearing, John handled himself well at the volatile news conference. He was able to answer hostile questions with prepared responses that caught many off guard. Within days, the Clemency was denied and the defendant was executed, much to the surprise of many.

After examining this group of cases, what have we learned? What do we know about John Monaghan? We don't know much about his personal life, since he prefers living and working below the radar. He is one of those people who doesn't need any notoriety to prove to himself his self-worth. He accomplishes incredible feats and avoids any accolades since he doesn't have to prove to anyone that he is better than someone else. To him, it isn't a contest to see who's the biggest winner. He excels in the courtroom arena as though he is playing a game of chess. He assesses all the options and prepares for every contingency. His fulfillment is the actual implementation of his plan that results in the checkmate of his opponent.

The Major Crimes Division was the perfect place for John Monaghan. There, he was given the opportunity to sharpen his skills. He didn't require constant supervision, so he could explore all the legal options and try novel approaches. He was a good mentor for the other Major Crimes deputies who looked to him for advice and trial strategies. John felt he was a member of the team and never shied away from the tough cases but happily embraced them.

John Monaghan as a seasoned veteran is well respected for his tenacious approach in presenting his case to the jury. He is thorough and doesn't leave anything to chance. By being so well prepared, he is able to exude confident in his case. He knows which battles must be won in court and which ones aren't crucial. He understands that the courtroom is an arena for advocates and not whims. He knows the legal rules and he knows how to win within the rules. On more than one occasion he has created considerable stress for his supervisors when he has aggressively attacked his adversaries.

There are times that he will go toe to toe with a judge when he believes he is right. He doesn't concede a point and doesn't like to lose. But at the end of the day he can accept reality, and by the next morning he will be ready to fight another battle. John Monaghan is a remarkable prosecutor who can do the big ones. He doesn't seek the publicity cases but enjoys the unique and complex murder cases. His reward doesn't come from his name in the newspaper or his face on TV. He loves what he does and his reward comes from within himself. He knows that he is the best of the best and no one needs to tell him that.

Fortunately for the safety of the public in Los Angeles County, he has managed to get some of the most dangerous criminals off the streets. In many of his cases, the criminal would have continued to create more victims if it weren't for John's intervention. No matter what one personally believes about the Death Penalty, everyone would agree that John was able to get so many deplorable people put away. At San Quinten, there is a prison tier on Death Row named the ***MONAGHAN TIER***. That may not have been what John wanted to be known for. Without question John Monaghan was one of the most effective and prolific members of the Major Crimes Division during so-called Golden Era (2000 to 2010). Those years were the time when everything was in perfect alignment and the **Major Crimes Division** was truly the ***DA Delta Force***.

Made in the USA
Monee, IL
13 September 2026

62981960R00184